# THE
# RULES *of the* ROAD
# AT SEA

*Comprising*

## THE INTERNATIONAL RULES
### FOR PREVENTION OF COLLISION AT SEA

## THE INLAND RULES
### APPLICABLE ON THE INLAND WATERS OF THE UNITED STATES ON THE ATLANTIC AND PACIFIC COASTS AND THE COAST OF THE GULF OF MEXICO

## THE PILOT RULES
### APPLICABLE ON THE INLAND COAST WATERS OF THE UNITED STATES

*By*

## W. H. LaBOYTEAUX

NEW YORK
BAKER, VOORHIS & CO.
1920

THE DE VINNE PRESS
NEW YORK

# CONTENTS

# TABLE OF CASES

## A

# TABLE OF CASES

# PREFACE

This work is dedicated to the American Shipmaster.

It is an effort to make available to those for whose guidance and control the "Rules of the Road" were adopted and made law, a better understanding of what these rules mean as determined by the courts of the United States and England.

As was said by the Circuit Court of Appeals in a recent decision:

> "The discretion of the navigator in the matter of speed in a fog must be exercised not wholly as a matter of individual judgment or individual views as to what is moderate speed, but also with due regard to the interpretation of the term 'moderate speed' by the maritime courts and to the general standards of good seamanship established by those courts in applying the term 'moderate speed.'"
>
> *The Sagamore,* 247 Fed. 743, 749.

The same test must be made throughout in the interpretation of the rules. The navigator must know these rules as the courts have considered them if the rules are to accomplish their purpose.

I have endeavored to make clear the spirit and meaning of the rules for their more effective use by the navigator, and if I shall have succeeded in this object to any extent, I shall be amply repaid for my labors.

W. H. LaB.

# INTRODUCTORY
## PREFATORY STATEMENT

MOST collisions result from a misunderstanding or want of understanding on the part of navigators as to the intended movements of approaching vessels. To avoid confusion, uniform rules of navigation are necessary.

The need of such rules was first formally recognized by England and France in 1862, when those countries adopted uniform rules (effective in 1863) for the prevention of collisions at sea. Those were the first international rules of this character. Historical Development of Rules.

In 1864 the United States adopted rules practically identical with those of England. In 1879 England extended the scope of her rules, and in 1884 revised them. Between 1880 and 1885 the English rules were adopted with some changes, for use on the high seas by the United States, Belgium, Germany, France, Japan, Norway and Denmark.

In October, 1889, in response to an invitation extended by the President of the United States to all the maritime nations, an international marine conference was held at Washington, D. C., to discuss and formulate uniform rules and regulations to promote the safety of lives and property at sea. The conference was the first of its kind, and the formulation of the present international rules for the prevention of collision at sea was, by far, the most important work accomplished. The delegations from the various countries were of a very representative character, being composed largely of practical seafaring men from both the naval and the merchant service, and including distinguished jurists, admiralty lawyers, shipowners and representatives of other related interests. The rules previously in force had left to the navigating officers of ves-

1

sels considerable latitude in judgment.  This was changed under the new rules adopted by the conference which were extended in scope so as to make such definite and complete provisions for practically every situation that very little is left to the discretion of the navigator.  Those rules are now incorporated in the laws of every maritime country, and are as binding upon navigators as any of the laws of the land.

In the United States, there are three general sets of rules, viz.: the International Rules, the Inland Rules and the Inspectors' Rules or Pilot Rules.

**International Rules.**

The International Rules apply to all vessels on the high seas, *i.e.,* outside of the lines dividing the high seas and coast waters as defined by governmental authority.*

**Inland Rules.**

All vessels on the inland waters of the United States, *i.e.,* inside of the lines dividing the high seas and coast waters as defined by governmental authority (except certain designated interior inland waterways which have their own prescribed rules), are subject to the Inland Rules of 1897.  The latter, in general, are similar to the International Rules, but differ in some minor respects to which attention will be directed in a later discussion of the individual rules.

**Inspectors' Rules— Pilot Rules.**

The rules prescribed by the United States Supervising Inspectors, known as the Pilot Rules (applying only to inland waters), are valid and have the force of law when they are not in conflict with the Inland Rules.  Where there is a conflict the Inland Rules control.

> *The B. B. Saunders,* 25 Fed. 727; *The John King,* 49 Fed. 469; *The Transfer No. 15,* 145 Fed. 503; *The John H. Starin,* 162 Fed. 146; *The Pawnee,* 168 Fed. 371; *The Montauk,* 180 Fed. 697; *The Aurelia,* 183 Fed. 341; *The Haida,* 191 Fed. 623, affirmed 196 Fed. 1005; *The James A. Walsh,* 194 Fed. 549.

**Object of Rules —Safety in Navigation.**

The object of the rules is to promote the safety of lives and property on the high seas and inland waters.

---

* See Appendix I for the lines dividing the high seas from the coast waters of the United States.

To accomplish this object, each rule must be known, correctly understood and implicitly obeyed by those in charge of the navigation of vessels. The failure of a navigating officer to have such knowledge and understanding is worse than negligence; it is little short of criminal. Men in other occupations have been held guilty of manslaughter where loss of life has resulted from negligence of lesser degree. It may be expected, therefore, that sooner or later negligence in not knowing and obeying the rules of the road, when resulting in loss of life, will also be held to be manslaughter, and that the offender will be punished accordingly.

The Statutes of the United States provide:

"Death through negligence, misconduct, etc.

"Every captain, engineer, pilot or other person employed on any steamboat or vessel, by whose *misconduct, negligence, or inattention to his duties on such vessel* the life of any person is destroyed, and every owner, charterer, inspector, or other public officer, through whose fraud, neglect, connivance, misconduct, or violation of law the life of any person is destroyed, shall be fined not more than ten thousand dollars or imprisoned not more than ten years, or both. . . ."

*Act March 3, 1905, Sec. 282; 35 St. at Large 1144.*

Before considering each rule separately, it is desirable that a clear understanding be had generally of their binding force, and of the effect of any deviation from their requirements. **The Binding Force of the Rules.**

*The rules are mandatory.* They are not suggestions to be followed or not, as the judgment of the individual navigator may dictate, but are laws to be obeyed implicitly. This was made clear in the following remarks of Delegate Goodrich (United States) in the Conference which framed the rules: **The Rules are Mandatory.**

"Now, I do not at all like the use of the word 'option' in the remarks of the gentleman from Germany. I do not want any option in these rules. The minute that you permit a sailor to have an option, whether he will or will not do a certain thing, you introduce confusion in the rules. I want to see these rules, as far as they can be made, as rigid as steel, so that there shall be no doubt what the Conference of Nations mean. They say, 'Obey these rules, and you will be saved from the danger of negligence; disobey them, and the courts will impose upon you the penalties of disobedience to the rules adopted by the nations of the world.' "

*Protocol of Proceedings,* page 58.

The decisions of the courts leave no doubt as to the mandatory character of the rules:

"Obedience to the rules is not a fault even if a different course would have prevented the collision, and the necessity must be clear and the emergency sudden and alarming before the act of disobedience can be excused. Masters are bound to obey the rules and entitled to rely on the assumption that they will be obeyed, and should not be encouraged to treat the exceptions as subjects of solicitude rather than the rules."

*Belden v. Chase,* 150 U.S. 674, 699.

"The obligation imposed to obey these rules is imperative, and those violating them, except under circumstances contemplated by the rules, must bear the consequences if damages ensue. . . . Citing: *The Breakwater,* 155 U.S. 252; *The Delaware,* 161 U.S. 459; *The Luckenbach,* 50 Fed. 129–134; *The Chittagong* [1901], App. Cases 597. . . . Every consideration requires that these rules should be strictly observed by those [navigators]\* for the government of whose conduct they were prescribed, and any departure therefrom should not be lightly overlooked or passed by. To do so would destroy the symmetry of the whole, and would place questions affecting the navigation of ships, now well settled and certain, in utter chaos and confusion."

*The Straits of Dover,* 120 Fed. 900, 903, 905.

"The vessels that navigate the high seas, and indeed vessels that navigate inland waters, entrusted with human lives and property of great value, must be held to the strictest standards of conduct, and when they fail to observe the requirements [Collision Rules] which the maritime law of the nations has prescribed, are to understand that they must abide the consequences."

*Yang-Tsze Insurance Ass'n et al. v. Furness, Withy & Co., Ltd.,* 215 Fed. 859, 865.

---

\* The use of italics in some of the quotations does not appear in the decisions. Also in some instances bracketed words not appearing in original decisions have been inserted to make the text clear.

In one of the leading English cases, *The Voorwarts—The Khedive,** House of Lords, 5 Appeal Cases, 876–910, Lord Blackburn said at p. 894:

> ". . . he acted with great promptitude and skill, so as greatly to alleviate the violence of that inevitable collision. But he did not stop and reverse, nor even slacken his speed; *and there he departed from the course prescribed by Regulation 16; nor was there anything in the circumstances rendering a departure from this rule necessary in order to avoid immediate danger.* Even if it would (in the absence of such a positive rule) be better seamanship to keep way on the ship in order to make her more manageable (which is not clear), the Legislature has thought it better to prescribe the course which must be followed.
>
> "I feel (though for the reasons stated before, very sorry for it) obliged to advise your Lordships to allow this appeal and restore the order of the Admiralty."

Reference is made in the rules to vessels in certain situations having the "right of way" over vessels in other situations. Vessels having such rights of way are at times referred to as "privileged vessels," and vessels required to give way are designated as "burdened vessels." The term "privileged vessel," if not a misnomer, is at least misleading. Special privileges are not granted to any vessel (sail or steam) under the rules of the road. Upon every vessel, dependent upon her character or her position in relation to an approaching vessel, are imposed positive duties. In some cases these are general in character; in others they are specific; but all are mandatory and absolute and are enforced with equal strictness and impartiality. The obligation upon the so-called privileged vessel to obey the strict letter of the rule is equally as binding as it is upon the so-called burdened vessel. The rules instruct each vessel exactly what to do, and neither is privileged to deviate from the requirements. For instance, the rules in certain situations require one vessel to

"Privileged Vessel"—Term Misleading. All Vessels Duty Bound.

---

* Although the particular rule on which this observation was made was changed when the present rules were adopted, the general principle of law herein stated as to the necessity of complying with the rules remains unchanged.

hold her course and speed and the other to keep out of
the way; but holding course and speed is, in the true sense,
no more a privilege accorded to the first vessel, as it is
certainly no less a duty enjoined upon her, than keeping
out of the way is a privilege or duty of the second vessel. Neither is really privileged. On the contrary, both
are in duty bound.

So imperative is the obligation to obey the statutory
rules that it has long since become a settled principle of
law, established by the courts of both America and England, that a breach of them constitutes such a fault as to
throw upon the offending vessel the burden of proving,
not merely that the breach might not have been one of the
causes of the collision, or that it probably was not, but
that it could not have been.

> *The Pennsylvania,* 19 Wall. 125; *The Belden v. Chase,*
> 150 U.S. 674; *The Martello,* 153 U.S. 64; *The Britannia,*
> 153 U.S. 130; *Lie, etc., v. San Francisco & Portland S.S.
> Co.,* 243 U.S. 291; *The Fanny M. Carvill,* 2 Asp. M.C.
> (N.S.) 565; *The Duke of Buccleuch,* 7 Asp. M.C. (N.S.)
> 68; *The Corinthian,* 11 Asp. M.C. (N.S.) 264; *The Beryl,*
> 9 Prob. Div. 137; *The Voorwarts—The Khedive,* L.R. 5
> App. Cases 876.

**Deviation from the Rules Not Permitted Except in Emergency.** A deviation from the rules simply to help out is not
permitted, and, should a collision result, the vessel guilty
of the breach, even though acting with the best of intentions, will be held at fault and liable for the damages.
Deviation from the rules is permitted only where the
necessity for it is clear, and where adherence to a rule will
surely result in collision.

> "Exceptions to the general rules of navigation are admitted
> with reluctance on the part of the courts, and only when an
> adherence to such rules must almost necessarily result in a
> collision . . ."
> *The Albert Dumois,* 177 U.S. 240, 249; *cited in The
> Acilia,* 120 Fed. 455 (C.C.A.).

See also *The Pocomoke,* 150 Fed. 193.

> "If you can shew that you could not adhere to the rule
> without producing danger, that is one of the specified excep-

tions. If you can shew that there was an absolute necessity for doing what you did or what you omitted to do, then again you are exempted. And it is thus left open to you to shew that you did not contribute to the mischief. . . . But in a case of immediate danger, where a collision appears to be inevitable and all depends upon the course of action immediately pursued, nothing can be more important than that those who have charge of the navigation of a vessel should know that if they depart from the rule which is laid down with sufficient distinctness, they must prove not only to their own satisfaction, but also to the satisfaction of the Court which has to decide the question, that what was done was necessary for the purpose of avoiding immediate danger. . . . If the rule is observed, every person will know precisely what he is to do, and will say, I will carry out my directions entirely with that knowledge which I possess. On the other hand, if the Court allows these rules lightly to be departed from, the result will be the very evil which the Act was intended to prevent."

*The Voorwarts—The Khedive,* 5 App. Cases 876, 908.

It is not alone sufficient that the rules be obeyed, but the compliance must be timely, and the risk of collision, as well as actual collision, avoided. This was pointed out at the International Conference, in commenting upon Article 28:

*Prompt Obedience to the Rules Necessary.*

". . . if the rules are carried out according to the spirit of them, I am sure every one will agree with me in saying that it is necessary for the keeping-out-of-the-way vessel to manœuvre so as to leave the way free for the other vessel in time, not only in time to avoid a collision, but, as far as possible, in time to avoid even the risk of a collision. Close shaving is to be avoided."

*Prot. of Proc.,* p. 524.

The courts are insistent upon the observance of the spirit of the rules and a timely compliance with the requirements thereof.

*"Precautions in such cases must be seasonable* in order to be effectual; and if they are not so, and a collision ensues in consequence of such delay, it is no defence to allege and prove that nothing could be done at the moment to prevent it, nor to allege and prove that the necessity for precautionary

measures was not perceived until it was too late to render them availing."

The America, 92 U.S. 432, 437.

"The cause for such collisions as this must generally be sought for at a time prior to the few moments immediately preceding the impact. After the vessels are in close proximity either or both, in the stress of sudden danger, may adopt an unwise and imprudent course. *The question is, who is to blame for bringing the vessels into a position where cool calculation is impossible."*

The Genevieve, 96 Fed. 859, 860.

"And the question in this case, as in all collision cases, is not what the colliding vessels do when they get down close to each other, but what was the manœuvre which they adopted, and what was the manœuvre which it was their duty to adopt, under the rules of the road *when they were still far enough apart to adopt those manœuvres deliberately and safely."*

The Transfer No. 10, 137 Fed. 666.

". . . The object of the rule is to avoid risk of collision, and we are not to be understood that a vessel is under no duty of obeying the rule . . . until the risk of collision has actually arisen. What we mean to say is that the rule applies *whenever it is or ought to be apparent that there will be risk of collision if nothing is done to prevent it."*
Lake Erie Transportation Co. v. Gilchrist Transportation
    Co., 142 Fed. 89.

". . . all that can be said is, as was said in the *Khedive* [5 Appeals Cases 876] (although the *Khedive* does not help us at all in this case), that he did not do that which the Act of Parliament declares and enacts he must do (for although he did it, he did not do it at the right time), and for this pardonable, excusable, and slight fault, I feel bound to say his owners are liable for this collision equally with the owners of the *Abeona."*
The Beryl (Court of Appeal), L.R. 9, P.D. 137, 143.

**Rules Apply to All Vessels.** The size, importance or speed of a vessel does not give her special rights over small, less important or slower vessels. All are equal under the rules and obligated to the same strict observance of them. Passenger steamers have no special rights. *The Bellingham,* 138 Fed. 619.

# THE STATUTORY RULES FOR PREVENTION OF COLLISION

## PRELIMINARY DEFINITIONS

### International Rules*

In the following rules every steam-vessel which is under sail and not under steam is to be considered a sailing-vessel, and every vessel under steam, whether under sail or not, is to be considered a steam-vessel.

The word "steam-vessel" shall include any vessel propelled by machinery.

A vessel is "under way" within the meaning of these rules when she is not at anchor, or made fast to the shore, or aground.

### Inland Rules*

Identical with International Rules.

Pilot Rules are identical except first paragraph not included.

A sailing vessel having auxiliary power is, when using such power, a steam vessel within the meaning of these rules; when not using it, she is deemed a sailing vessel. Vessels driven by motor power are to be considered steam vessels.

*Sailing and Steam Vessels.*

A vessel made fast to a buoy or other fixed object not a part of the shore is considered as at anchor. When weighing anchor, a vessel is "under way" as soon as the anchor has broken ground and she ceases to be held fast and under control of it. A vessel riding to her chains with anchors unshackled, a sailing vessel in irons or hove to, a steamer lying to or drifting, are all "under way" within the meaning of the rules. In fact, a vessel is at all times "under way" except when held fast by her anchor or moorings or when aground.

*"Under Way."*

---

*Throughout the text the International Rules and comments thereon are set forth on the left side of the pages; the Inland Rules and comments on the right side. Where differences in phraseology appear in the rules the same are shown in italics.

# THE LIGHTS, AND SO FORTH

Articles 1 to 14 inclusive contain minute directions as to the character of lights and signals to be used by the several classes of vessels in different situations, as to when such lights and signals are to be used and how they are to be placed or located on the vessel, including the screening of the side lights.

**Range of Visibility.** The white lights for steam vessels, as required by Articles 2, 3 and 4, must be visible at least five miles on a dark night in a clear atmosphere.

The colored lights (running side lights), as required by Articles 2, 3, 4 and 5, for steam and sailing vessels, must be visible and show their distinctive color at least two miles on a dark night in a clear atmosphere.

The imperative nature of the requirements of the rules as to the maintenance of proper lights has been often stated by the courts.

**Improper Lights.** "The *Royal Arch* was improperly navigated, in that she did not have her regulation side lights, and especially her green light, properly and brightly burning, and for that reason she was sole culpable cause of the collision. It was her duty to keep her course, as she did, on seeing the red light of the *Nellie Floyd.* It was the duty of the *Nellie Floyd* to avoid the *Royal Arch,* but she was relieved from such duty by the failure of the *Royal Arch* to exhibit any light which those on the *Nellie Floyd* could see before the collision; and their ignorance of the course of the *Royal Arch,* until it was too late for the *Nellie Floyd* to do anything to avoid the collision, was excusable, and was produced by such fault of the *Royal Arch.*"*

*The Royal Arch,* 22 Fed. 457, 458.

"The want of a red light was primarily the whole cause of the collision. The other vessel was deceived and misled by this failure to show that light. . . . The fault, then, being wholly on the part of the vessel libelled, there must be a decree accordingly."

*The Mary Lord,* 26 Fed. 862, 866.

---

* This quotation is taken from head note, not opinion.

"A more serious charge against the *Komuk* and the *Griggs* is, that the latter did not display lights according to Rule II of the Pilot Rules. . . . The *Griggs* concededly did not comply with this rule but only exhibited one light, which was placed on her cabin."

*The Komuk,* 120 Fed. 841, 842.

See also *Peck et al. v. Sanderson,* 17 How. 439; *The Viola,* 59 Fed. 632; *The Excelsior,* 39 Fed. 393.

Such lights must have not only the required range of visibility, but at all times must be maintained up to that standard. They must be kept in good repair, thoroughly cleaned and well supplied, and their lenses must be particularly free from smoke, grease or other foreign matter.

"The Statute (Rev. St. §4233, rules 3 and 8) requires not only that sail-vessels under way shall carry a green light on the starboard side and a red light on the port side, but that those lights shall be 'of such a character as to be visible on a dark night, with a clear atmosphere, at a distance of at least two miles.' It is very plain that the schooner's lights did not meet such requirement. They may have been burning, and visible to those on the schooner's deck, but for some cause, not at all connected with the vigilance or watchfulness of those on board of the steam-boat, the schooner's lights were not seen by them. The district judge said that without undertaking to find affirmatively why the lights were not visible, he found simply that the steam-boat was in the exercise of due diligence, and that the lights were not capable of being seen. . . . The glass of the schooner's green lantern was broken in the collision. The master of the steam-boat found a bit of it, and says that he considered it badly smoked up; that it was damp and greasy; and that if all of the lantern was in that condition it was not fit to emit light. The green light was the one which the steam-boat would have seen if the schooner was on the course claimed by the schooner. Kerosene was burned in the schooner's lights. No light from her was visible to the two persons in the pilot-house of the steam-boat, or to the bow watchman of the steam-boat, until the steam-boat was close upon the schooner; and then what appeared to be a dim, colorless light on the schooner was seen by those on the steam-boat. The light, not being seen to be green or red, was taken to be a binnacle light in the cabin of

*Unclean and Inefficient Lights.*

a vessel going the same way with the steam-boat. The bow watchman of the steam-boat says that a kerosene lamp will naturally get blurred on the top; that while a smoked green lantern would seem green near at hand, it might seem without color far off; and that to a man looking at its smoked part it might seem colorless, while to a man looking upward to it, it would seem green. All this may explain why the schooner's lights were not seen, though it is not necessary the steam-boat should do so. The libel alleges that the schooner was 'duly lighted'; that her green and red lights were 'brightly burning'; that she 'had all proper, sufficient, and lawful lights set and burning, as aforesaid.' The burden is on her to show this, and she has not done so."

*The Narragansett,* 11 Fed. 918, 920–921.

"The purpose of lights is to be seen. If they do not fulfill that office to ordinary observation, the vessel must be held in fault; . . ."

*The Amboy,* 22 Fed. 555.

"The *Pierrepont's* side lights were up and burning, but they were in bad condition, the lanterns being incrusted with smoke. . . .

"Upon these facts I am of opinion that the *Pierrepont* was in fault in not having her lights in proper condition, . . ."

*The Mary Morgan,* 28 Fed. 333, 334.

The rules prescribe only the minimum range of visibility required. An increase of power of such lights (especially of the side lights) was considered most desirable by the Committee on Lights at the International Conference, but not adopted, apparently, for the reasons stated in the report of the committee:

"It appears very difficult, if at all possible, to increase the power of a ship's side lights from the present range of 2 miles to that of 3, as proposed, without at the same time increasing the size of the lantern in a manner which would make it too cumbersome and expensive for use on board ship where the conditions are such as to make the construction of lanterns particularly difficult. . . ."

*Reports of Committees,* p. 70.

That was in 1889, over a quarter of a century ago. Had the present-day conditions then existed, a greater range of visibility would undoubtedly have been pre-scribed.

Common prudence dictates in respect to this most im-portant requirement that observance should go beyond the mere letter to the spirit of the rules, and that lights of the maximum range of visibility should be used.

The lights must be lighted at sunset, *not at darkness,* **Time of Use.** and kept burning continuously until sunrise. Periodical inspections should be made at short intervals to see that the lights are in their proper places and burning. Such inspection should always be made upon the approach of another vessel. If any light be not burning properly, or be removed for examination, repair or other reason, another similar light should be *immediately* substituted, even though the time of the removal be exceedingly brief.

All unnecessary lights, and the reflection of saloon or cabin lights, should be avoided as far as possible. The background of running lights should be kept darkened so as to make them stand out more clearly.

Special attention should be given to insure that all **Location** lights are placed in their proper locations in strict com- **of Lights.** pliance with the rules and that they are not obscured by deck houses, deck cargo, sails, smoke from the galley, or other obstruction or cause.

"But had the red light been continuously hidden by the jib, **Lights** as claimed, that would not improve the libellant's case. The **Obscured.** *Vesper* can only be charged for some fault of her own. Her duty to keep out of the way of the schooner was conditioned upon her having notice of the situation and course of the *John Jay* by proper, visible lights. The rules of navigation require that these lights shall be 'so constructed as to show a uni-form and unbroken light over an arc of the horizon of 10 points of the compass, and so fixed as to throw the light from right ahead to two points abaft the beam,' on either side. Rules 3 and 8, Rev. St. §4233. If either light is so obscured that a steamer is misled and deceived as to the course of the sailing-vessel, and a collision ensues in consequence, it is mani-festly no fault of the steamer; and if the sailing-vessel suffer damage, it must be set down to her own fault or misfortune, as the case may be."

*The Vesper*, 9 Fed. 569, 574.

"It is impossible, and it is unnecessary, to determine in what particular way, or from what cause, the red light of the *Fontenaye* was obscured. I am satisfied it was obscured. Had it been seen when it ought to have been seen, I cannot doubt that the *Johanne Auguste*, by porting earlier than she did, might have escaped the collision, and would have done so. The *Fontenaye* must be held responsible for any obscuration of her light, especially when placed in the extreme after-part of the ship, where there is such increased danger of obstruction (*The Tirzah, supra*), and it results that both vessels must be held in fault and the damages divided."

*The Johanne Auguste*, 21 Fed. 134, 140.

" . . . she was at fault, in that she was not equipped with proper side lights, that the lights were not ordinarily bright, and were not visible at as great a distance as they should have been, and that they were so placed or so obstructed by a deck load of lumber or otherwise that they were not discernible from all points ahead."

*The Virginian* (C.C.A.), 235 Fed. 98, 100.

See also *The Iberia*, 123 Fed. 865; *The Brand*, 224 Fed. 391.

**Screening.**    Great care should be exercised to see that the inboard screens of the colored running lights are placed exactly as required by the rules, and that the lights are set in their proper positions. If so placed, the rays will cross at the proper distance ahead of the ship.

Extraordinary care should always be exercised in screening and watching the running lights when placed in the rigging. In the case of lights so located, it is difficult to fix the inboard screens sufficiently rigid on a line with the keel and in perpendicular so that they will not show across the bow; but failure to have such lights conform in these and in all other respects with the regulations is a source of danger. The difficulty should, therefore, increase the caution. Side lights so located on sailing vessels are particularly apt to cause trouble, and being subject to change under sail pressure, are likely to convey to an approaching vessel the impression that the sailing vessel has changed her course.

> "This testimony from the respective vessels in regard to the course of the schooner, and the lights she displayed, apparently so contradicting, can, I think, be reconciled by reference to the fact, stated by the master of the schooner in the most positive manner, that the side lights of the schooner were placed so that when he stood at the stem he could see both the red and green light at the same time without moving his head. . . . But this explanation convicts the schooner of fault for carrying lights so arranged as to mislead an approaching vessel in regard to the course she was pursuing."
> *Clendinin v. The Steamship Alhambra*, etc., 4 Fed. 86, 88.

**Lights Improperly Placed and Screened.**

See also *The Alabama*, 10 Fed. 394.

Upon the master rests the responsibility of seeing that the proper lights are carried, correctly placed and kept burning brightly. The fact that improper lights are carried under the instructions of a compulsory pilot will not relieve the master from responsibility or the vessel from liability therefor.

It is significant that not only do the rules begin with prescribing the lights and signals to be carried, but they end with the caution in Article 29:

> "Nothing in these rules shall exonerate any vessel . . . from the consequence of any neglect to carry lights or signals. . . ."

The most rigid adherence to these rules in their minutest detail is required by the courts, and any deviation will inevitably involve the offending vessel in fault for a resulting collision.

As was said by the Circuit Court in *The Titan*, 23 Fed. 413, 416:

> "The rule requiring lights may as well be disregarded altogether as to be only partially complied with, and in a way which fails to be of any real service in indicating to another vessel the position and course of the one carrying them."

## ARTICLE I

### International Rules

The word "visible" in these rules when applied to lights, shall mean visible on a dark night with a clear atmosphere.

*Article 1.* The rules concerning lights shall be complied with in all weathers from sunset to sunrise, and during such time no other lights which may be mistaken for the prescribed lights shall be exhibited.

### Inland Rules

Identical with International Rules.

*Article 1.* Identical with International Rules.

The brightness of the evening or early morning will not excuse any departure from the rule, which is absolute in its requirement that *lights must be set from sunset to sunrise in all weathers.*

## ARTICLE II

## STEAM VESSELS—MASTHEAD LIGHT

### International Rules

*Article 2.* A steam-vessel when under way shall carry —(a) On or in front of the foremast, or if a vessel without a foremast, then in the fore part of the vessel, *at a height above the hull of not less than twenty feet, and if the breadth of the vessel exceeds twenty feet, then at a height above the hull not less than such breadth, so, however, that the light need not be carried at a greater height above the hull than forty feet,* a bright white light, so constructed as to show an unbroken light over an arc of the horizon of twenty points of the compass, so fixed as to throw the light ten points on each side of the vessel, namely, from right ahead to two points abaft the beam on either side and of such a character as to be visible at a distance of at least five miles.

### Inland Rules

*Article 2.* A steam-vessel when under way shall carry —(a) Identical with International Rules, except that portion in italics, which is omitted from Inland Rules.

## STEAM VESSELS—SIDE LIGHTS

(b) On the starboard side a green light so constructed as to show an unbroken light over an arc of the horizon of ten points of the

(b) Identical with International Rules.

compass, so fixed as to throw the light from right ahead to two points abaft the beam on the starboard side, and of such a character as to be visible at a distance of at least two miles.

(c) On the port side a red light so constructed as to show an unbroken light over an arc of the horizon of ten points of the compass, so fixed as to throw the light from right ahead to two points abaft the beam on the port side, and of such a character as to be visible at a distance of at least two miles.

(c) Identical with International Rules.

(d) The said green and red side-lights shall be fitted with inboard screens projecting at least three feet forward from the light, so as to prevent these lights from being seen across the bow.

(d) Identical with International Rules.

## STEAM VESSELS—RANGE LIGHTS

(e) A steam-vessel when under way may carry an additional white light similar in construction to the light mentioned in subdivision (a). These two lights shall be so placed in line with the keel that one shall be at least fifteen feet higher than the other, and in such a position with reference to each other that the lower light shall be forward of the upper one. The vertical dis-

(e) A *sea-going* steam-vessel . . . otherwise the same as International Rules.

tance between these lights shall be less than the horizontal distance.

(f) Not in International Rules.

(f) All steam-vessels (except sea-going vessels and ferry-boats) shall carry in addition to green and red lights required by article two (b), (c), and screens as required by article two (d), a central range of two white lights; the after-light being carried at an elevation at least fifteen feet above the light at the head of the vessel. The head-light shall be so constructed as to show an unbroken light through twenty points of the compass, namely, from right ahead to two points abaft the beam on either side of the vessel, and the after-light so as to show all around the horizon.

Notwithstanding the attitude of the International Conference, that changes should be made in the existing rules "only when considered absolutely necessary," a new rule providing for the use of range lights by steam vessels was adopted. Although range lights are much more efficient than the colored side lights, the use of range lights will not excuse an absence of the colored running lights. Some of the advantages of the range lights over the colored side lights that were pointed out in the discussions before the Conference were:

*Range Lights Most Efficient.*

The greater range of visibility (5 miles as against 2 miles) enabling the course of a steamer carrying such lights to be known much earlier and at a much greater distance than otherwise would be possible.

The use of such lights enables the course of the

steamer to be determined with a greater degree of exactness than is possible where colored side lights only are used.

Range lights indicate a change of course more quickly than do the colored side lights.

A small change of course, not ordinarily perceptible when side lights only are used, is often noticeable by reference to range lights.

In thick weather, especially in low hanging fogs, the visibility of range lights is much greater, and their location is such that they can often be seen when the side lights are not visible.

Under the Inland Rules (subdivision (f)) the use of range lights is mandatory on all steam vessels (except sea-going vessels and ferryboats). Under the International Rules and Inland Rules it is optional in respect of sea-going vessels. Having regard, however, to their greater efficiency and the now almost universal use of such lights, it would seem that the carrying of range lights should be a precautionary act of good seamanship within the fair intention of Article 29, which reasonably should be adopted.

## ARTICLE III

### STEAM VESSELS WHEN TOWING

*International Rules*

*Article 3.* A steam-vessel when towing another vessel shall, in addition to her side lights, carry two bright white lights in a vertical line one over the other, not less than *six* feet apart, and when towing more than one vessel shall carry an additional bright white light *six* feet above or below such lights, if the length of the tow measuring from the stern of the towing vessel to the stern of the last vessel towed exceeds six hundred feet. Each of these lights shall be of the same construction and character, and shall be carried in the same position as the white light mentioned in article two (a), *excepting the additional light, which may be carried at a height of not less than fourteen feet above the hull.*

Such steam-vessel may carry a small white light abaft the funnel or aftermast for the vessel towed to steer by, but such light shall not be visible forward of the beam.

*Inland Rules*

*Article 3.* A steam-vessel when towing another vessel shall, in addition to her side lights, carry two bright white lights in a vertical line one over the other, not less than *three* feet apart, and when towing more than one vessel shall carry an additional bright white light *three* feet above or below such lights, if the length of the tow measuring from the stern of the towing vessel to the stern of the last vessel towed exceeds six hundred feet. Each of these lights shall be of the same construction and character, and shall be carried in the same position as the white light mentioned in article two (a) *or the after range light mentioned in article two (f).*

Such steam-vessel may carry a small white light abaft the funnel or aftermast for the vessel towed to steer by, but such light shall not be visible forward of the beam.

The lights thus prescribed are in addition to the colored side lights. The two white lights required must be so constructed as to show an unbroken light over an arc of the horizon of twenty points, and so fixed as to throw the light ten points on each side of the vessel, viz., from right ahead to two points abaft the beam. The lights must be visible at a distance of at least five miles.

**Location of Towing Lights.**

The lights are to be carried in vertical line one over the other, not less than six feet apart, in the same relative position as the white light (mastheadlight) prescribed in Article 2, subdiv. (a). This requires the lower light to be located not less than twenty feet above the hull, and if the beam exceeds twenty feet, not less than the beam, but it need not be more than forty feet above the hull. The higher light must be located not less than six feet above this lower light.

If the length of the tow from the stern of the towing vessel to the stern of the last vessel in the tow exceeds six hundred feet, a third similar bright light *must* be carried. This third light may be located either six feet above the higher light or six feet below the lower light.

The lights are to be carried in a vertical line one over the other, not less than three feet apart, in the same relative position as the white light (mastheadlight) prescribed in Article 2, subdiv. (a). This requires the lights to be on or in front of the foremast, or if the vessel has no foremast then in the forepart of the vessel. No minimum height above the hull is prescribed, but the lights must be so located as to show an unbroken light directly ahead and over an arc of the horizon of twenty points, viz., ten points on each side of the vessel.

If the length of the tow from the stern of the towing vessel to the stern of the last vessel in the tow exceeds six hundred feet, a third similar bright light, located either three feet above the higher light or three feet below the lower light, *must* be carried.

The towing lights must be of the character and carried in the positions prescribed by the rule.

"While the tug likewise had her towing lights burning, the contention is that they were improper lights, and did not conform to Article 3 of the Inland Rules of Navigation, which provides that a steam vessel, when towing another, shall, in addition to her side lights, 'carry two bright white lights in a vertical line, one over the other, not less than three feet apart.' 30 Stat. 97 (U.S. Comp. St. 1901, p. 2877). The towing lights as carried on this tug were not in vertical line, one over the other, and could not have been by reason of their construction. Instead of being placed as required by statute, they were placed upon a prong, said by the master of the tug to be about a yard long, across the mast or flagstaff, from each end of which the lights were attached or hung by means of a cord, and let down one lower than the other, a distance supposed to be three feet. This was the condition in which the lights were at the time of this collision, and confessedly, lights so constructed were not in strict accordance with the rules of navigation, and could not be said to be in a vertical line, one over the other, having reference to the flagstaff to which they should be attached. Lights so constructed upon this prong or cross beam placed horizontally from the flagstaff would be liable to be on a horizontal rather than a vertical line, unless the greatest care was exercised in placing them by means of the cords that drew them up to the ends of the prong; and, if such should be the case, naturally one light would obstruct the view of the other to a vessel on a crossing course, and particularly to a person observing the lights from a high range, as did the ferry-boat's master. In no event would they be such as was contemplated by the statute, when it expressly provided that one should be placed vertically above the other and three feet apart. . . . The failure to properly place the lights on a ship is a serious fault, and for which liability should follow when persons or property are injured thereby. *The Conoho* (D.C.), 24 Fed. 758; *The Arthur* (D.C.), 108 Fed. 557; *The Komuk* (D.C.), 120 Fed. 841."

*Foster v. Merchants' & Miners' Transp. Company,* 134 Fed. 946, 967.

See also *The Robert Robinson,* 55 Fed. 123.

The vessel in charge of the towing operation is under a duty to see that all the vessels comprising the tow (including towing vessel) exhibit the proper lights. Failure in this duty involves fault. The other vessels in the tow also are liable for their own failure or neglect in this or other respects.

It appears to be the more common practice in America for the control of the towing operation to be exercised by those in command of the towing vessel, while in England the rule is to the contrary. Responsibility does not depend, however, on custom or practice, but on the facts as to who is actually in control in the particular case. The law on this point has been clearly defined by the courts of the United States, as shown by the following excerpts from the cases:

"As the *Echo* was not responsible for the proper navigation of the fleet, and in all respects complied with the laws and regulations applicable to her handling and management in the premises, and in no way by her fault contributed to the collision, she ought not to be held responsible for faults, if there were any, in the navigation of the *Pendleton*. In *Sturgis v. Boyer*, 24 How. 110–121, 16 L. Ed. 591, after full argument, the Supreme Court said: 'Cases arise, undoubtedly, when both the tow and the tug are jointly liable for the consequences of a collision; as when those in charge of the respective vessels jointly participate in their control and management, and the master or crew of both vessels are either deficient in skill, omit to take due care, or are guilty of negligence in their navigation. Other cases may well be imagined when the tow alone would be responsible; as when the tug is employed by the master or owners of the tow as the mere motive power to propel their vessels from one point to another, and both vessels are exclusively under the control, direction, and management of the master and crew of the tow. Fault in that state of the case cannot be imputed to the tug, provided she was properly equipped and seaworthy for the business in which she was engaged; and if she was the property of third persons, her owners cannot be held responsible for the want of skill, negligence, or mismanagement of the master and crew of the other vessel, for the reason that they are not the agents of the owners of the tug, and her owners in the case supposed do not sustain towards those intrusted with the navigation of the vessel the relation of the principal.' . . . The opinion in the *Edgar Baxter,* 8 Ben. 162, Fed. Cas. No. 4278, by a distinguished admiralty judge, afterwards an ornament to the Supreme Court of the United States, is so clear and pointed, and so applicable here, that we quote in full: '*Blatchford, District Judge.* The evidence shows that the movements of the propeller were under the direction of a pilot who was on board of, and belonged to, and was in the employ of, the schooner. The tug furnished only the motive power, while the guidance of the two vessels, considered as one in their relations to other vessels, the schooner being lashed alongside of the tug, was under the direction of the schooner, through such pilot. Under those circumstances the tug is not liable for the damage complained of in this case, and the libel must be dismissed, with costs.' On principle, and after full consideration of the subject in the light of the text-books and adjudged cases, we concur with Parsons, *supra:* 'The question has arisen when a vessel is in tow of a steam tug, and collision occurs with another vessel, which is responsible, the steam tug or the vessel in tow? It is obvious that two perfectly distinct views may be taken of the relation between them. According to one, the vessel towing is but the servant of that which is towed; this latter is the master, and is responsible for the acts of the former as his servant. According to the other, the vessel towed is for the time under the absolute control of the vessel towing, and this latter is therefore responsible for any mischief done. We apprehend it to be an error to assume that either of these relations must exist in any particular case. The inquiry should always be, which party is the principal, and which the servant? And, wherever the relation of principal and agent exists, the case should be decided on the principles of agency. Generally, we should say that the tug was probably the servant, and the vessel which employed her the principal, and responsible as such. But it will be seen that the cases are in irreconcilable conflict.' In this case, we think the *Echo* was the servant, and without fault, and the *Pendleton* was the principal, and responsible as such."

*In re Walsh et al.,* 136 Fed. 557, 559.

In another case, the court said:

"On the evidence actually submitted, we cannot agree with the conclusion of the district judge as to the irresponsibility of the ship on account of her being in tow of, or being handled by a tug. In moving large steamers around in ports, tugs are frequently employed to aid in the movement without any control of the navigation or responsibilty therefor. In this case the capacity of the tug, the contract of employment in and about the moving of the ship, and whether the tug in fact or under contract controlled the navigation of the ship is left to conjecture, with the presumption of fault against the ship."

*The Degama,* 150 Fed. 323, 324.

The views above set forth were approved by the Supreme Court of the United States in *The Eugene F. Moran,* 212 U.S. 466, 53 L. Ed. 600.

In England, the same rule was laid down in *The American* and *The Syria,* 2 Asp. M.C. (N.S.) 350.

When in command the towing vessel is responsible.

**When Towing Vessel Responsible.**

"The *Titan* was in fault for so locating her starboard light that it was not visible, as required by the rules. No doubt is entertained that it was obscured by the umbrella of the float and by the cars on the float forward of the place on the tug where it was located, so that it was not visible to the pilot of the *Hills.* The rule requiring lights may as well be disregarded altogether as to be only partially complied with, and in any way which fails to be of any real service in indicating to another vessel the position and course of the one carrying them."

*The Titan,* 23 Fed. 413, 416.

"I conclude, therefore, that neither pilot saw the colored light of the other until after the ferryboat had passed, because the colored lights were not visible, through the obscuration caused by the pilot house of the barge on the port side of *No. 13.*

"For this obscuration *No. 13* was responsible, and she must take the risk of navigating in that condition of her lights, and of her tow; because it was in violation of the rule of navigation that requires lights to be *visible* for 10 points around the horizon. *The Seacaucus,* 34 Fed. 68, 70."

*The Buffalo,* 50 Fed. 628, 630.

"But it is urged by the master of the *Tice* that he ordered the master of the canal boat to put the light out, and it is claimed that his duty began and ended upon doing this. He was in charge of the boat, and, if the command that the rule be observed was not sufficient, that command should have been enforced. This accords with the holding in *The Lyndhurst* (D.C.) 92 Fed. 681."

*The Nettie L. Tice,* 110 Fed. 461, 462.

"The *Cheney's* [towing vessel] side lights were set and burning. The *Hart* had a white light in her rigging while at anchor, which she took down when picked up by the *Cheney*. Her side lights were not lit at any time before collision. The District Judge held her in fault for not exhibiting them, and held the *Cheney* in fault for not seeing to it that she did so. From this decision the claimants of these two vessels appeal.

"Article 5 of the rules enacted by Congress provides that: 'Sailing vessels under way or being towed shall carry the same lights as are prescribed by article 2 for a steam vessel under way, with the exception of the white lights mentioned therein, which they shall never carry.'

"Article 2 provides for the regulation colored lights. Manifestly the *Hart* failed to comply with this rule. This failure is sought to be excused by reference to the following rule of the board of supervising inspectors, approved by the Secretary of Commerce and Labor: 'Barges or canal boats towed alongside a steam vessel, if on the starboard side of said steam vessel, shall display a white light on her own starboard bow; and if on the port side of said steam vessel, shall display a white light on her own port bow.'

"(2) Since the *Hart* was neither a barge nor a canal boat, she was not covered by the provisions of this rule. . . . We concur, therefore, with the District Judge in the conclusion that the *Hart* was in fault for not displaying her colored lights, and that the *Cheney* was in fault for not directing her to do so. It was the master of the *Cheney* who ordered the *Hart* to take the white anchor light out of the rigging and put it on the starboard bow."

*The Merrill C. Hart,* 188 Fed. 49, 50.

See also *North American Dredging Co. v. Cutler et al.,* 162 Fed. 457; *The Eugene F. Moran,* 154 Fed. 41; *The Lizzie Crawford,* 170 Fed. 837.

The fact, however, that the vessel *in command* is responsible does not relieve the vessel *not in command* from liability for her own fault or failure to observe the rules. *The Nettie L. Tice,* 110 Fed. 461.

In the English case of *The Mary Hounsell,* 4 Asp. M.C. (N.S.) 101, a sailing vessel (being in command) having a pilot cutter towing astern was held at fault for a collision through the pilot cutter's exhibiting an improper light; while in the cases of *The Romance,* 9 Asp. M.C. (N.S.) 149 [1900]; *The Devonian,* 9 Asp. M.C. (N.S.) 179 [1901], the vessels being towed (being in command) were held at fault.

In the last mentioned case, the ship was held liable because the tug had anchor lights exhibited when she should have had towing lights set.

## ARTICLE IV
## SPECIAL LIGHTS

*International Rules*

*Inland Rules*

*Article 4.* (a) A vessel which from any accident is not under command shall carry at the same height as the white light mentioned in article two (a), where they can best be seen, and if a steam-vessel in lieu of that light, two red lights, in a vertical line one over the other, not less than six feet apart, and of such a character as to be visible all around the horizon at a distance of at least two miles; and shall by day carry in a vertical line one over the other, not less than six feet apart, where they can best be seen, two black balls or shapes, each two feet in diameter.

(b) A vessel employed in laying or in picking up a telegraph cable shall carry in the same position as the white light mentioned in article two (a), and if a steam-vessel in lieu of that light, three lights in a vertical line one over the other, not less than six feet apart. The highest and lowest of these lights shall be red, and the middle light shall be white, and they shall be of such a character as to be visible all around the ho-

Not in Inland Rules.

rizon, at a distance of at least two miles. By day she shall carry in a vertical line, one over the other, not less than six feet apart, where they can best be seen, three shapes not less than two feet in diameter, of which the highest and lowest shall be globular in shape and red in color, and the middle one diamond in shape and white.

(c) The vessels referred to in this article, when not making way through the water, shall not carry the side-lights, but when making way shall carry them.

(d) The lights and shapes required to be shown by this article are to be taken by other vessels as signals that the vessel showing them is not under command and can not therefore get out of the way.

These signals are not signals of vessels in distress and requiring assistance. Such signals are contained in article thirty-one.

**Location of Lights.** The two red lights provided in (a) for a vessel, which from any accident is not under command, and the three lights (two red and one white) required by (b) for a vessel engaged in laying or picking up a telegraph cable, must be carried where they can best be seen. They must be at a height of not less than 20 feet above the hull, and, if the beam of the vessel exceeds 20 feet, not less than the beam, but need not be carried at a greater height above the hull than 40 feet.

Rule (a) is applicable only to a vessel *"which from any accident is not under command."* It does not apply to a vessel deliberately kept in an unmanageable condition. It is not applicable to a sailing vessel in irons or becalmed or hove to and unable to maneuver, as such condition has not arisen *"from any accident"* as prescribed by the rule.

In *The Cheruskia,* 92 Fed. 683, the court said at p. 685:

> "I do not think the brigantine, however, was 'not under command,' in the sense of Article 4. I understand that article to refer to vessels in some way disabled, so as to be no longer under control. That was not the situation of the brigantine. She was in perfect condition. She was simply moving very slowly in a light wind. She had not complete steerageway for all maneuvers. She could not change her tack by luffing; but she could do so by wearing around. She was substantially keeping her course and had sufficient steerageway for that purpose, whether making only ¾ of a knot or from 2 to 3 knots, as the mate testifies. I think Article 4 is not applicable to such a case."

*Lights for a Vessel Aground.* A vessel aground in or near a fairway is required under the International Rules, article 11, to carry anchor lights and the two red lights prescribed by Rule (a) above. *Signals by Day for a Vessel Aground.* The rules do not specifically provide what signals, if any, shall be exhibited in the daytime by a vessel in that situation, but, in the case of *The Carlotta,* 8 Asp. (N.S.) 544, the court expressed the opinion that the two black balls or shapes as prescribed in this article would not be required. At the International Conference it was suggested that a vessel so aground, when the fact of her being aground was not clearly apparent to approaching vessels, could properly hoist the International Code Signals if there was any danger to be apprehended.

Mr. Hall (Great Britain) said:

> "I will only say to the delegate from China that as regards the proposal in his amendment that a vessel shall by day exhibit the international code signals—there is nothing what-

ever to prevent her from doing that now if she wishes, and if approaching mariners cannot see that a vessel is aground by daylight, the vessel should hoist the code signals showing that she was aground if there was any danger to be apprehended."

*Prot. of Proc.,* p. 395.

Rule (c) provides that a vessel not under command, which is under way, but not making way through the water, shall not carry any side lights; but where such a vessel is making way through the water, she must carry the proper side lights.

**A Vessel "Not Under Command."** The question as to whether a vessel is or is not under command is one to be decided by practical seamen. In the case of *The P. Caland,* 7 Asp. M.C. (N.S.) 317 (House of Lords), the court, without definitely committing itself to any general rule, seemed to indicate that a vessel may be properly said to be within the operation of the rule if, owing to some disablement, she cannot execute the proper maneuvers to keep out of the way of a vessel coming near her; or, if, because of a disablement, she answers her helm very slowly so that she cannot get out of the way of another vessel in the manner reasonably to be anticipated by the other vessel; or, though she may be able to stop and reverse, if she can do so only after great or unusual delay; or, if, because of damage, such a breakdown of the machinery is imminent as will render her incapable of performing necessary maneuvers.

The foregoing is the only decision in which the question appears to have been discussed, but the reasonable view would seem to be that where a vessel, through an accident, has sustained damage, by reason of which she is rendered incapable of executing necessary maneuvers in the prompt and efficient manner which another approaching vessel would have reason to expect of her, such vessel is within the meaning of the rule "not under command," and should indicate the fact by the proper signals.

In commenting on the duty of a vessel "not under command" the court said in the case of *The P. Caland, supra:*

> "I do not think  .  .  .  that a vessel not under command  .  .  .  is always justified in continuing so to make way [through the water].  This must depend upon the circumstances, and in my opinion a vessel which cannot show that they were such as to justify her in taking this course, must be held to blame for not acting in a reasonable and seamanlike manner,  .  .  .  It never was intended that under all circumstances a vessel [not under command] should be entitled to proceed at a considerable speed through the water, throwing upon other vessels, out of whose way she would ordinarily have to get, the obligation to get out of her way.  .  .  ."

## ARTICLE V

## LIGHTS FOR SAILING VESSELS
## AND VESSELS IN TOW

| *International Rules* | *Inland Rules* |
|---|---|
| *Article 5.* A sailing vessel under way *and any vessel being towed* shall carry the same lights as are prescribed by article two for a steam-vessel under way, with the exception of the white lights mentioned therein, which they shall never carry. | *Article 5.* A sailing-vessel under way *or being towed* shall carry the same lights as are prescribed by article two for a steam-vessel under way, with the exception of the white lights mentioned therein, which they shall never carry. |

The lights prescribed by this article are the red and green side lights described in Article 2, subdivisions (b) and (c). The white lights never to be carried are the masthead light and the range lights.

Particular attention is called to the difference in the text of the International Rules and the Inland Rules. The International Rules prescribe that the colored side lights are to be carried by "a sailing vessel under way *and any vessel being towed,*" and that such vessel shall *not* carry the white masthead light or the range lights. Under the International Rules, therefore, a vessel being towed must carry only the colored side lights. In the text of the Inland Rules, however, mention is made only of "a sailing vessel under way or being towed," which inferentially would seem to exclude from the operation of the article any vessels in tow except sailing vessels. Such interpretation has been put on the Inland Rule in the recently decided case of *The Scandinavia* (not yet reported). In that case the United States District Court for the Southern District of New York held that an ocean-going steamer (with steam up but not using her own power) when proceeding in tow in the harbor of New York should have exhibited the lights prescribed by Article 2, viz., the colored side lights and the white masthead light.*

---

* It is difficult to find any controlling reason why this distinction should be made in the Inland Rules between a steamer in tow and not using her own power, and a sailing vessel in tow.

The discussions on the subject of lights at the International Conference make clear that the different lights provided to be carried by the several classes of vessels in different situations are for the purpose of conveying valuable information to other vessels in respect to her ability or lack or impairment of ability to maneuver. The rules on lights, taken as a whole, clearly indicate this spirit and intention. In so far as approaching vessels are concerned, with respect to the risks of collision, the knowledge as to whether a vessel in tow is a steamer (if she is not using her own power) or a sailing vessel, would seem to be of little, if any value. Article 15, subdiv. (e) (Inland Rules) in prescribing for "a vessel towed" (either sail or steam) the identical fog-signal on a fog-horn, seems to recognize this principle. It is possible the words "any vessel," which appear in the International Rules and are absent in the Inland Rules (in which particular only do the rules differ), may have been unintentionally omitted, or again that the preliminary definition of the Inland Rules, "every steam vessel which is under sail but not under steam is to be considered a sailing vessel," was considered by Congress as being sufficiently broad to include within its terms a steamer in tow. This seems to be the interpretation put upon this article of the Inland Rules by the Bureau of Navigation in its publication of the "Navigation Laws of the United States," in which this article is given the heading "Lights for sailing vessels and vessels in tow."

In the case of the *Scandinavia, supra,* the court, applying the literal text of the article, held that it did not apply to a steamer in tow, and, in the absence of any other provision in the Inland Rules as to the lights to be carried by a steamer being towed, decided that such vessel must carry the lights prescribed in Article 2, including the white masthead light.

This decision, until either confirmed or reversed, makes it necessary that a steamer in tow, when under the Inland Rules, should carry the colored side lights and the masthead light.

## ARTICLE VI
## LIGHTS FOR SMALL VESSELS

*International Rules*

*Inland Rules*

*Article 6.* Whenever, as in the case of small vessels under way during bad weather, the green and red side-lights can not be fixed, these lights shall be kept at hand, lighted and ready for use; and shall, on the approach of or to other vessels, be exhibited on their respective sides in sufficient time to prevent collision, in such manner as to make them most visible, and so that the green light shall not be seen on the port side nor the red light on the starboard side, nor, if practicable, more than two points abaft the beam on their respective sides. To make the use of these portable lights more certain and easy the lanterns containing them shall each be painted outside with the color of the light they respectively contain, and shall be provided with proper screens.

*Article 6.* Same as International Rules, except the Inland Rule says instead of *small vessels:*
*Vessels of less than ten gross tons.*

## ARTICLE VII
## LIGHTS FOR SMALL STEAM AND SAIL VESSELS AND OPEN BOATS

*International Rules*

*Inland Rules*

*Article 7.* Steam-vessels of less than forty, and vessels under oars or sails of

Not in Inland Rules.

less than twenty tons gross
tonnage, respectively, and
rowing boats, when under
way, shall not be required to
carry the lights mentioned
in article two (a), (b), and
(c), but if they do not carry
them they shall be provided
with the following lights:

*First.* Steam-vessels of
less than forty tons shall
carry—

    Not in Inland Rules.

(a) In the fore part of
the vessel or on or in front
of the funnel, where it can
best be seen, and at a height
above the gunwale of not
less than nine feet, a bright
white light constructed and
fixed as prescribed in article two (a), and of such a
character as to be visible at
a distance of at least two
miles.

(b) Green and red side-
lights constructed and fixed
as prescribed in article two
(b) and (c), and of such a
character as to be visible at
a distance of at least one
mile, or a combined lantern
showing a green light and
a red light from right ahead
to two points abaft the
beam on their respective
sides. Such lanterns shall
be carried not less than
three feet below the white
light.

*Second.* Small steam-
boats, such as are carried by
seagoing vessels, may carry
the white light at a less
height than nine feet above

    Not in Inland Rules.

the gunwale, but it shall be
carried above the combined
lantern mentioned in sub-
division one (b).

*Third.* Vessels under          Not in Inland Rules.
oars or sails of less than
twenty tons shall have
ready at hand a lantern
with a green glass on one
side and a red glass on the
other, which, on the ap-
proach of or to other vessels, shall be exhibited in
sufficient time to prevent
collision, so that the green
light shall not be seen on
the port side nor the red
light on the starboard side.

*Fourth.* Rowing boats,         Same as International
whether under oars or sail,      Rule (but numbered Article
shall have ready at hand a       seven).
lantern showing a white
light which shall be tem-
porarily exhibited in sufficient time to prevent collision.

The vessels referred to in       Not in Inland Rules.
this article shall not be
obliged to carry the lights
prescribed by article four
(a) and article eleven, last
paragraph.

## ARTICLE VIII

## LIGHTS FOR PILOT VESSELS

*International Rules*              *Inland Rules*

*Article 8.* Pilot-vessels       *Article 8.* Same as Inter-
when engaged on their sta-       national Rules.
tion on pilotage duty shall
not show the lights re-
quired for other vessels,
but shall carry a white light

at the masthead, visible all around the horizon, and shall also exhibit a flare-up light or flare-up lights at short intervals, which shall never exceed fifteen minutes.

On the near approach of or to other vessels they shall have their side-lights lighted, ready for use, and shall flash or show them at short intervals, to indicate the direction in which they are heading, but the green light shall not be shown on the port side, nor the red light on the starboard side.

A pilot-vessel of such a class as to be obliged to go alongside of a vessel to put a pilot on board may show the white light instead of carrying it at the masthead, and may, instead of the colored lights above mentioned, have at hand, ready for use, a lantern with green glass on the one side and red glass on the other, to be used as prescribed above.

In the Inland Rules it is expressed "with a green glass on the one side and a red glass on the other," etc.

Pilot-vessels when not engaged on their station on pilotage duty shall carry lights similar to those of other vessels of their tonnage.

A steam-pilot vessel, when engaged on her station on pilotage duty and in waters of the United States, and not at anchor, shall, in addition to the

Not in Inland Rules.

lights required for all pilot
boats, carry at a distance of
eight feet below her white
masthead light a red light,
visible all around the horizon and of such a character as to be visible on a dark
night with a clear atmos-
phere at a distance of at
least two miles, and also the
colored side lights required
to be carried by vessels
when under way.

When engaged on her
station on pilotage duty
and in waters of the United
States, and at anchor, she
shall carry in addition to
the lights required for all
pilot boats the red light
above mentioned, but not
the colored side lights.

When not engaged on
her station on pilotage
duty, she shall carry the
same lights as other steam
vessels.

Not in Inland Rules.

## ARTICLE IX
### LIGHTS, ETC., OF FISHING VESSELS

*International Rules*

*Inland Rules*

*Article 9.* Fishing ves-
sels and fishing boats, when
under way and when not required by this article to
carry or show the lights
hereinafter specified, shall
carry or show the lights
prescribed for vessels of
their tonnage under way.

(a) Open boats, by which
is to be understood boats
not protected from the en-

*Article 9.* (a) Fishing-
vessels of less than ten
gross tons, when under way
and when not having their
nets, trawls, dredges, or
lines in the water, shall not
be obliged to carry the colored side-lights; but every
such vessel shall, in lieu
thereof, have ready at hand
a lantern with a green glass
on one side and a red glass

try of sea water by means of a continuous deck, when engaged in any fishing at night, with outlying tackle extending not more than one hundred and fifty feet horizontally from the boat into the seaway, shall carry one all-around white light.

Open boats, when fishing at night, with outlying tackle extending more than one hundred and fifty feet horizontally from the boat into the seaway, shall carry one all-round white light, and in addition, on approaching or being approached by other vessels, shall show a second white light at least three feet below the first light and at a horizontal distance of at least five feet away from it in the direction in which the outlying tackle is attached.

(b) Vessels and boats, except open boats as defined in subdivision (a), when fishing with drift nets, shall, so long as the nets are wholly or partly in the water, carry two white lights where they can best be seen. Such lights shall be placed so that the vertical distance between them shall be not less than six feet and not more than fifteen feet, and so that the horizontal distance between them measured in a line with the keel, shall be not

on the other side, and on approaching to or being approached by another vessel such lantern shall be exhibited in sufficient time to prevent collision, so that the green light shall not be seen on the port side nor the red light on the starboard side.

(b) All fishing-vessels and fishing-boats of ten gross tons or upward, when under way and when not having their nets, trawls, dredges, or lines in the water, shall carry and show the same lights as other vessels under way.

(c) All vessels, when trawling, dredging, or fishing with any kind of dragnets or lines, shall exhibit, from some part of the vessel where they can be best seen, two lights. One of these lights shall be red and the other shall be white. The red light shall be above the white light, and shall be at a vertical distance from it of not less than six feet and not more than twelve feet; and the horizontal distance between them, if any, shall not be more than ten feet. These two lights shall be of such a character and contained in lanterns of such construction as to be visible all round the horizon, the white light a distance of not less than three miles

less than five feet and not more than ten feet. The lower of these two lights shall be in the direction of the nets, and both of them shall be of such a character as to show all around the horizon, and to be visible at a distance of not less than three miles.

Within the Mediterranean Sea and in the seas bordering the coasts of Japan and Korea sailing fishing vessels of less than twenty tons gross tonnage shall not be obliged to carry the lower of these two lights. Should they, however, not carry it, they shall show in the same position (in the direction of the net or gear) a white light, visible at a distance of not less than one sea mile, on the approach of or to other vessels.

(c) Vessels and boats, except open boats as defined in subdivision (a), when line fishing with their lines out and attached to or hauling their lines, and when not at anchor or stationary within the meaning of subdivision (h), shall carry the same lights as vessels fishing with drift nets. When shooting lines, or fishing with towing lines, they shall carry the lights prescribed for a steam or sailing vessel under way, respectively.

and the red light of not less than two miles.

### Lights for Rafts, or Other Craft, Not Provided for

(d) Rafts, or other water craft not herein provided for, navigating by hand power, horse power, or by the current of the river, shall carry one or more good white lights, which shall be placed in such manner as shall be prescribed by the Board of Supervising Inspectors of Steam Vessels.

Within the Mediterranean Sea and in the seas bordering the coasts of Japan and Korea sailing fishing vessels of less than twenty tons gross tonnage shall not be obliged to carry the lower of these two lights. Should they, however, not carry it, they shall show in the same position (in the direction of the lines) a white light, visible at a distance of not less than one sea mile on the approach of or to other vessels.

(d) Vessels when engaged in trawling, by which is meant the dragging of an apparatus along the bottom of the sea—

*First.* If steam vessels, shall carry in the same position as the white light mentioned in article two (a) a tri-colored lantern so constructed and fixed as to show a white light from right ahead to two points on each bow, and a green light and a red light over an arc of the horizon from two points on each bow to two points abaft the beam on the starboard and port sides, respectively; and not less than six nor more than twelve feet below the tri-colored lantern a white light in a lantern, so constructed as to show a clear, uniform, and unbroken light all around the horizon.

*Second.* If sailing vessels,

Not in Inland Rules.

Not in Inland Rules.

Not in Inland Rules.

Not in Inland Rules.

shall carry a white light in a lantern, so constructed as to show a clear, uniform, and unbroken light all around the horizon, and shall also, on the approach of or to other vessels, show where it can best be seen a white flare-up light or torch in sufficient time to prevent collision.

All lights mentioned in subdivision (d) first and second shall be visible at a distance of at least two miles.

(e) Oyster dredgers and other vessels fishing with dredge nets shall carry and show the same lights as trawlers.

Not in Inland Rules.

(f) Fishing vessels and fishing boats may at any time use a flare-up light in addition to the lights which they are by this article required to carry and show, and they may also use working lights.

Not in Inland Rules.

(g) Every fishing vessel and every fishing boat under one hundred and fifty feet in length, when at anchor, shall exhibit a white light visible all around the horizon at a distance of at least one mile.

Not in Inland Rules.

Every fishing vessel of one hundred and fifty feet in length or upward, when at anchor, shall exhibit a white light visible all around the horizon at a distance of at least one mile, and shall exhibit a second light as provided for vessels of such lengths by article eleven.

Should any such vessel, whether under one hundred and fifty feet in length or of one hundred and fifty feet in length or upward, be attached to a net or other fishing gear, she shall on the approach of other vessels show an additional white light at least three feet below the anchor light, and at a horizontal distance of at least five feet away from it in the direction of the net or gear.

(h) If a vessel or boat when fishing becomes stationary in consequence of her gear getting fast to a rock or other obstruction, she shall in daytime haul down the day signal required by subdivision (k); at night show the light or lights prescribed for a vessel at anchor; and during fog, mist, falling snow, or heavy rain storms make the signal prescribed for a vessel at anchor. (See subdivision (d) and the last paragraph of article fifteen.)

Not in Inland Rules.

(i) In fog, mist, falling snow, or heavy rain storms drift-net vessels attached to their nets, and vessels when trawling, dredging, or fishing with any kind of drag net, and vessels line fishing with their lines out,

Not in Inland Rules.

shall, if of twenty tons gross tonnage or upward, respectively, at intervals of not more than one minute make a blast; if steam vessels, with the whistle or siren, and if sailing vessels, with the fog horn, each blast to be followed by ringing the bell. Fishing vessels and boats of less than twenty tons gross tonnage shall not be obliged to give the above-mentioned signals; but if they do not, they shall make some other efficient sound signal at intervals of not more than one minute.

(k) All vessels or boats fishing with nets or lines or trawls, when under way, shall in daytime indicate their occupation to an approaching vessel by displaying a basket or other efficient signal where it can best be seen. If vessels or boats at anchor have their gear out, they shall, on the approach of other vessels, show the same signal on the side on which those vessels can pass.

Not in Inland Rules.

The vessels required by this article to carry or show the lights hereinbefore specified shall not be obliged to carry the lights prescribed by article four (a) and the last paragraph of article eleven.

Not in Inland Rules.

## ARTICLE X
## LIGHTS FOR AN OVERTAKEN VESSEL

| *International Rules* | *Inland Rules* |
|---|---|
| *Article 10.* A vessel which is being overtaken by another shall show from her stern to such last-mentioned vessel a white light or a flare-up light. | *Article 10.* A vessel which is being overtaken by another, *except a steam-vessel with an after range-light showing all around the horizon,* shall show from her stern to such last-mentioned vessel a white light or a flare-up light. |
| The white light required to be shown by this article may be fixed and carried in a lantern, but in such case the lantern shall be so constructed, fitted, and screened that it shall throw an unbroken light over an arc of the horizon of twelve points of the compass, namely, for six points from right aft on each side of the vessel, so as to be visible at a distance of at least one mile. Such light shall be carried as nearly as practicable on the same level as the side lights. | Second paragraph not in Inland Rules. |

All steam vessels (except sea-going vessels and ferryboats) are required under Article 2, subdivision (f) of the Inland Rules to carry range lights, the after light to be so constructed and placed as to show all around the horizon. This after range light is accepted under this article of the Inland Rules in lieu of the white light or flare-up required to be shown from the stern. With this **The Rule is Mandatory.** one exception, which is operative only under the Inland Rules, this article is mandatory in requiring that a vessel being overtaken shall show from her stern to the overtaking vessel either a white light or a flare-up light.

It is optional as to whether the light shall be a fixed white light of the character described in the rule, or a flare-up. The option was provided by the International Conference because, as pointed out by the Committee on Lights, it would not be practical to require small vessels to carry a fixed stern light.

Whilst the light to be exhibited may be either a white light or a flare-up, the use of a flare-up or any light of such temporary character will throw upon the vessel using it the burden of exhibiting the light at the proper time and as often as may be necessary to afford warning to the approaching vessel.

The fixed white light as described in the second paragraph is the safer light and should be used by vessels large enough to carry it.

An overtaking vessel is defined in Article 24 as follows:

". . . Every vessel coming up with another vessel from any direction more than two points abaft her beam, that is, in such a position, with reference to the vessel which she is overtaking that at night she would be unable to see either of that vessel's side-lights, shall be deemed to be an overtaking vessel; and no subsequent alteration of the bearing between the two vessels shall make the overtaking vessel a crossing vessel within the meaning of these rules, or relieve her of the duty of keeping clear of the overtaken vessel until she is finally past and clear.

"As by day the overtaking vessel can not always know with certainty whether she is forward of or abaft this direction from the other vessel she should, if in doubt, assume that she is an overtaking vessel, and keep out of the way."

This article does not apply to vessels approaching from a direction less than two points abaft the beam, as such vessels are not overtaking, but "crossing." A flare-up may, however, be used for such crossing vessel under Article 12.

These overtaking lights are *not* to be used when a vessel is at anchor, but a vessel at anchor may show a flare-up light under the conditions prescribed in Article 12.

Vessels hove to, or lying to, either under sail or steam, being "under way" must show these lights when required to any vessel approaching from astern.

The flare-up when used must be an efficient light and such as will give fair warning to an approaching vessel. A lookout astern is necessary where a flare-up light, instead of a fixed stern light, is used. The courts have rigidly upheld the requirements of the rule.

*Use of Flare-up Requires a Lookout Astern.*

"The schooner had no set stern light, but carried a flare-up light, which was in the cabin, ready to be lighted that night. The schooner showed no stern light that night at any time, and was not more than from 150 to 300 feet from the steamer when first seen on the steamer. Both vessels had the proper green and red lights burning forward, and the steamer had the proper masthead light burning, also.

"On these facts I think that the schooner was in fault for not exhibiting a stern light to the steamer, and for not keeping a good lookout astern. The tenth rule of navigation is as follows (Proc. Dec. 31, 1896; 29 Stat. 887):

" 'A vessel which is being overtaken by another shall show from her stern to such last mentioned vessel a white light, or a flare-up light.

" 'The white light required to be shown by this article may be fixed and carried in a lantern, but in such case the lantern shall be so constructed, fitted and screened that it shall throw an unbroken light over an arc of the horizon of twelve points of the compass, viz., for six points from right aft on each side of the vessel, so as to be visible at a distance of at least one mile. Such light shall be carried as near as practicable on the same level as the side lights.' The libelant's counsel claims that under this rule an overtaken vessel has an option to use at the stern either a white light or a flare-up light, or a fixed and screened white light, and that, if she chooses to use a flare-up light, all that is required of the overtaken vessel is that, as soon as she sees or can reasonably be expected to see the overtaking vessel, she shall show a flare-up light, if there is time to do so. It is true that under this rule the master of a vessel has an option to use either kind of light, but I think, if he chooses to use a flare-up light, instead of a screened light set at the stern, there are strong grounds for holding that he is bound to make it as efficient as the set light, and that it is no defense that he had not time to get it, light it, and show it after the overtaking vessel was seen or might have been seen. *If he uses a flare-up light, of course, a lookout astern is necessary.* If he uses a set screened light, no lookout astern is necessary. The set light looks out itself. . . . But it seems to me that, under the present rule, if an overtaken vessel chooses to use a flare-up light, instead of a set screened light, she is bound to use it in such a manner as to make it equally effective. Without definitely deciding this question, however, *it is clear, that if a flare-up light is to be used, an efficient lookout astern must be maintained, and the flare-up light displayed as soon as an overtaking vessel can be seen on the overtaken vessel, in order to have the overtaken vessel comply with the rule."*

*The Bernicia,* 122 Fed. 886, 887, 888.

"The term 'flare-up light' is not defined in the articles, but since it is provided as the alternative for a fixed white light at the level of the side lights, it certainly must be one kept where it will be at hand and in proper condition when wanted, and which will not blow out in a high wind, but will burn with such continuity, as to give fair warning to the approaching vessel . . ."

*The Kaiserin Maria Theresa,* 149 Fed. 97, 98.

**Timely Use of Flare Required.**

The warning light must be given in sufficient time to afford the overtaking vessel ample opportunity to keep out of the way. The burden rests upon the vessel being overtaken to judge when she is so nearly approached that the time has arrived for the exhibition of the stern light.

*The Columbia,* 27 Fed. 238; *The Bernicia,* 122 Fed. 886; *The Main,* 6 Asp. M.C. (N.S.) 37.

One exhibition of a flare is not to be depended upon, but the light should be exhibited from time to time so long as the vessel continues to be an overtaken vessel.

*The Essequibo,* 6 Asp. M.C. (N.S.) 276; *The Bassett Hound,* 7 Asp. M.C. (N.S.) 467.

The positive character of the rule is further shown in the following cases:

"The fault of the schooner is clear. The steamer was plainly an overtaking vessel. She was more than two points abaft the schooner's beam; being nearly astern on her starboard quarter. The schooner could not know, and had no right to act upon the guess or assumption, that the steamer was moving off more to leeward. The contrary was the fact; and she was bound to show, even to the red light, a white light or a flare-up light, under rule 2. The libelant's evidence shows, however, that the steamer's two colored lights were seen some three or four minutes before collision. It was manifest negligence in the schooner not to have at least a lantern ready to be exhibited at once, and not to show it in much less time than three or four minutes."

*The City of Savannah,* 41 Fed. 891, 892.

"Upon the whole case, I find that the schooner was in fault, in that she was heading in such a direction that the steamer was coming up more than two points abaft her beam and unable to see her side lights, and that the schooner did not make known her presence by exhibiting a white light or flare-up light from her stern."

*The Baltimore,* 155 Fed. 405, 407.

## ARTICLE XI

## ANCHOR LIGHTS

*International Rules*

*Article 11.* A vessel under one hundred and fifty feet in length when at anchor shall carry forward, where it can best be seen, but at a height not exceeding twenty feet above the hull, a white light, in a lantern so constructed as to show a clear, uniform, and unbroken light visible all around the horizon at a distance of at least one mile.

A vessel of one hundred and fifty feet or upwards in length, when at anchor, shall carry in the forward part, at a height of not less than twenty and not exceeding forty feet above the hull, one such light, and at or near the stern of the vessel, and at such a height that it shall be not less than fifteen feet lower than the forward light, another such light.

The length of a vessel shall be deemed to be the length appearing in her certificate of registry.

A vessel aground in or near a fair-way shall carry the above light or lights and the two red lights prescribed by article four (a).

*Inland Rules*

*Article 11.* Identical with International Rules.

Not in Inland Rules.

A vessel is "at anchor" when held by an anchor or made fast to a buoy.

When weighing anchor a vessel remains "at anchor" until her anchor has left the ground, or until she is no longer held fast, after which she is "under way."

A vessel being towed up to her anchor is "at anchor," and should exhibit anchor light or lights, but the tug towing her is "under way" and should exhibit "under way" lights. *The Romance,* 9 Asp. M.C. (N.S.) 149.

A vessel riding to her chains in a gale with her anchors unshackled is not at anchor, but is "under way." *The Faedrelandet,* 8 Asp. M.C. (N.S.) 1.

Anchor lights should be placed strictly in accordance with the rule. They should not be placed in too close proximity to the masts, nor where they will be obscured in any direction by the masts, spars, sails or rigging.

Sails and all gear should be so stowed that they will not obstruct the anchor lights in any way.

The forward light for vessels of 150 feet or upwards* in length must be located in the forward part of the vessel. The forestay is the usual and probably the best place. The light must be between twenty feet and forty

---

*Excerpts from remarks made by delegates at the International Conference: Mr. Hall (Great Britain): " . . . We have found now that vessels are built of such an extreme length that it is frequently misleading to vessels approaching one of them at anchor, if they only see one riding-light on her. . . . We think, perhaps, that we should not put this duty upon small vessels upon which one light is amply sufficient, but that in all vessels, beyond a certain length, they should be bound not only to carry the riding-light, which is carried forward as at present, but that they should carry a second light aft at a different altitude, and at such a marked difference in altitude that any sailor approaching could see that it was two lights on board of one vessel and not one light on board of two different vessels."

*Prot. of Proc.,* p. 47.

Captain Shackford (United States): " . . . Now, it is a very serious matter to know which one of these lights is on the stern and which one is on the bow."

*Prot. of Proc.,* p. 297.

Mr. Hall (Great Britain): "In answer to that I would point out that we have endeavored to provide for that by making the altitude of the after light different from the forward light, so that when a sailor sees a high light and a low light he will be put on his guard and will at once be led to suppose that it is a long vessel."

*Prot. of Proc.,* p. 297.

feet above the hull.    The word "hull" includes the fore-castle deck.    *The Europe,* 190 Fed. 475.    The after light must be *at or near the stern* and not less than fifteen feet lower than the forward light.    A light in the main shrouds, 100 to 120 feet from the stern of a ship 455 feet long, was held not to be "at or near the stern" as required by the rule.    *The Gannet,* 9 Asp. M.C. (N.S.) 43.    In a more recent case an after light placed 80 feet from the stern was held to be improperly located. *The Red Jacket,* Shipping Gazette, Mar. 21, 1908.

The rule is more specific as to the required location of the after light than it is as to that of the forward light. The after light must be placed at or as near the stern as practicable, in strict compliance with the provision of the rule.

**Character of Lights.**

The lights must strictly comply with the requirements of the rule, and must be visible all around the horizon. They must be maintained in good order, thoroughly clean, well supplied and free from smoke, grease or other foreign matter that might impair their range of visibility, which must be not less than one mile.

**Set at Sunset and Kept Burning Brightly.**

They must be set at sunset, irrespective of the brightness of the day, and must be kept burning brightly until sunrise.

In an early decision, the court said:

"But the law of navigation which requires vessels lying at anchor *in a fair-way* to have a light up is imperative.    It must be obeyed.    It must be effectively obeyed.    It will not do for the master to hang up a light after nightfall, and then go to bed, trusting to the moon to serve as a light, in the event that the winds or other cause shall put out the light.    Obedience to this important requirement of law must be certain and unremitted.    The master must know that the light is continually up.    Conjecture will not do.    When lying in a fair-way the anchor light must be known to be all the time up, and this cannot be with certainty unless a watch be kept on deck to keep it burning, and to be able to say positively that the light was up, in the event of a collision.

"I do not know that there is any rule of navigation which

requires a vessel at anchor to keep a watch on deck; but, rule or no rule, it is very careless for a vessel lying in deep water, in the course pursued by sailing vessels, not to have a watch on deck. . . ."

*The Oliver,* 22 Fed. 848, 851.

All vessels at anchor are now required to carry anchor lights irrespective of where they may be anchored.

*Anchor Lights Rule Rigidly Enforced.*

In the case of *The Santiago,* 160 Fed. 742, the barge was lying at anchor inside the Delaware Breakwater. A vigilant anchor watch had been maintained and two riding lights, one forward, the other aft, were set and were burning up to within five minutes of the collision, when the after light was blown out and the watchman took it into the after house to relight it.

The court said at p. 745:

"These rules require that where a vessel is of 150 feet or upward in length two lights must be displayed when at anchor, the stern light lower than the one forward to indicate they are both upon the same vessel and the direction she is pointing. The importance of this is indicated by the occurrence of this accident, and the omission on the part of the barge to observe this rule as to the stern light for the short space of five minutes shows the danger in permitting this regulation to be violated for a moment, and if it be violated, the loss caused by an accident that may occur as a result must fall upon those who are guilty of a failure in this regard. Obedience to this important requirement of the law must be certain and unremitted. The master must know that the lights are continually up. *The Oliver* (D.C.), 22 Fed. 851. When this light went out there should have been another at hand to put up at once so that the stern of the vessel would not be left in darkness, unguarded by a watch, while a seaman with no special knowledge for the work was attempting to repair a defective lamp."

The following extracts will further illustrate the courts' insistence on strict obedience to this rule.

"The weight of evidence is clearly to the effect that at the time of the collision no light was visible . . . It is not necessary to inquire by what mistake of the captain of the schooner, or by what accident, the light failed at the time of the collision; . . ."

*The Erastus Corning,* 25 Fed. 572, 573.

"The fact, therefore, to which the master testifies, that when he took the light down shortly after the collision the wick was afire, is a pretty strong indication that the light had gone out gradually through want of oil, and not by the sudden blow of the collision. *Chamberlain v. Ward,* 21 How. 548, 564. I feel constrained, therefore, to hold, upon the testimony of so many witnesses, that the light was not properly burning at the time when the *Drew* approached, whatever may have been the cause of its failure. . . ."

*The Drew,* 35 Fed. 789, 791.

"The necessity for the *Lillie* to show a light was therefore imperative. This is not denied. The evidence indicates that a lantern had been previously hung up, but the light must have gone out before the *Westfield* came along. . . . In not maintaining a light the risk rested wholly upon the *Lillie,* and she must accordingly bear the blame."

*The Westfield,* 38 Fed. 366, 367.

"The lantern in use on the *Fristad* has been brought into court, and made an exhibit in the case. The globe and frame of it are of the best material, and the proper size. I find no fault with it, except that the burner is not reliable. In experimenting with it, a sudden jarring of the stand on which it was placed, caused only smoke instead of flame to issue. Two or three repetitions of a similar jarring caused it to burn again, and give a strong light. From the testimony it appears to me to be quite probable that during part of the night before the collision this burner was smoking instead of giving light. . . . After considering and weighing the evidence upon the point, I find that there is a fair preponderance of it to sustain my conclusion that this lantern did not, on the night of the collision, give a uniform or steady light."

*Fristad v. The Premier,* 51 Fed. 766, 767, 768.

**Dredges Must Carry Anchor Lights.**

Dredges are considered vessels, and where moored in navigable waters must carry the anchor lights prescribed for vessels of their size.

"A dredge lawfully fixed in a channel for improving it is to be considered as a vessel at anchor, and is under obligation to use the same precautions to guard against collisions that a vessel at anchor is in respect to the exhibition of lights, maintaining a watch, and measures calculated to make its situation known."

*The Bailey Gatzert,* 179 Fed. 44, 48.

"This dredge was not authorized to carry two white lights while at anchor. She was but 75 feet long, and had therefore by Articles 1 and 11 of the act of June 7, 1897, no right to carry more than one white light while at anchor. . . . I think the dredge must be held in fault for carrying an unauthorized and misleading light. . . ."

*The Arthur,* 108 Fed. 557, 558.

The International Rules require that in addition to the usual anchor light or lights a vessel aground in or near a fair-way is required to carry the two red lights as prescribed in Art. 4, subdiv. (a). Such red lights must be of a character to be visible all around the horizon at a distance of two miles. They must be placed in a vertical line one over the other not less than six feet apart and carried at a height above the hull of not less than 20 feet, or if the vessel's beam be greater than 20 feet then at a height above the hull not less than the breadth of the vessel, except that they need not be carried more than 40 feet above the hull.

*Anchor Lights Required of Vessels Aground in or near a Fair-way.*

See Article 4, p. 31, for signals to be exhibited by day when a vessel is aground.

## ARTICLE XII
## SPECIAL SIGNALS

*International Rules*

*Article 12.* **Every vessel may, if necessary in order to attract attention, in addition to the lights which she is by these rules required to carry, show a flare-up light or use any detonating signal that cannot be mistaken for a distress signal.**

*Inland Rules*

*Article 12.* Same as International Rule.

**Detonating Signal to Attract Attention to Presence.**

The object * of this rule is to permit a vessel, when uncertain as to whether her presence is known to an approaching vessel, to use a flare-up light or a detonating signal to attract the attention of the latter.

The detonating signal is the only sound signal prescribed by the International Rules by which a holding-on vessel can make its presence known to an approaching vessel. All the whistle signals under the International Rules indicate a change either of course or of speed. As the holding-on vessel is required to maintain her course and speed, manifestly she cannot use signals devised to indicate a change thereof. This article authorizes a sound signal by which a vessel may attract attention to her presence.

Prior to the adoption of the present rules, Section 4234

---

* Excerpts from the discussion of Article 12 at the International Conference:

Mr. Hall (Great Britain): " . . . What we propose is that every ship may at any time, in addition to the lights which she is by these regulations required to carry, show a flare-up light, or use a detonating signal to attract attention. I think this will be of great use to sailing vessels. But we propose it as of assistance to both sailing vessels and steamers. It may be of advantage to steam-vessels, because, if by any chance the side lights should be obscured, as has been pointed out by the delegate from France has occurred in many instances, then the steamer will have the additional assistance of the flare-up light or the detonating signal to make her aware of the presence in the vicinity of a vessel out of the way of which she has to keep."

*Prot. of Proc.,* p. 323.

of the United States Revised Statutes required sailing vessels, upon the approach of a steam vessel at night, to show a lighted torch from that point or quarter toward which the steamer was approaching. That statute, however, was repealed in respect to its application to vessels on the high seas upon the enactment of the present rules.

Although the statute was mandatory in character, whereas the present rule is by its terms permissive, the following decisions under the statute when it was effective show the desirability of using the signals whenever occasion makes such use prudent:

"The law, as expressed by the statute implies that the display of such a light will assist approaching steam-ships in ascertaining the position and course of sail-vessels, and thus aid them in keeping away. The failure to display this light must therefore in all instances be regarded as a contributory fault, at least, where collision occurs under such circumstances, except only where it is clearly shown that owing to extraordinary facts it could have no influence upon the result. Here no such extraordinary facts appear. On the contrary, the circumstances— (the condition of the atmosphere and sea) —rendered the display of a torch in this instance especially important. The schooner's approach being undiscoverable in time for deliberate examination and judgment, it was essential to reasonable chance of escape that the steam-ship should have instant information of the former's exact position and course —such as the torch was calculated to afford."

*The Pennsylvania,* 12 Fed. 914, 916.

See also, *The Roman,* 12 Fed. 219; *The Excelsior,* 12 Fed. 195.

"In this case no torch-light was shown by the schooner, nor was one ever shown to be aboard, and therefore the schooner was clearly in fault. The libelants contend that showing a torch-light in this case would have done no good, and that such failure did not contribute to the collision. This contention is not well founded."

*The I. C. Harris,* 29 Fed. 926, 928.

A schooner, whose side lights were set in the curve of her bow and were not visible abaft the beam, and whose lights, although burning brightly, were not seen by a vigilant watch on a steamer on a converging course, was held in fault for failure to exhibit a flare-up light, the court saying in dismissing the libel:

> "But the schooner was in positive fault. She saw the steamer an hour before the collision, and knew that she was approaching her; and was where it was evident that the courses of the vessels crossed each other, and the danger of collision was threatening. She failed to light and exhibit the torch which she kept on board for the very purpose of giving warning under such circumstances. If she had exhibited the torch, it is reasonably certain that a collision could only have occurred by the willful act of the steamer; and her fault is not condoned or mitigated by the fact that her side lights were burning brightly, and the assumption that they could have been and ought to have been seen by the steamer. The law gives her no such discretion, but required her to inform the steamer, in this mode, of her proximity and course; and, if she consciously omitted to do it, the unfortunate consequences of her failure are imputable to her alone."

*The Algiers,* 28 Fed. 240, 242.

See also, *The Stranger,* 44 Fed. 815.

## ARTICLE XIII
## NAVAL LIGHTS AND RECOGNITION SIGNALS

| *International Rules* | *Inland Rules* |
|---|---|
| *Article 13.* Nothing in these rules shall interfere with the operation of any special rules made by the Government of any nation with respect to additional station and signal-lights for two or more ships of war or for vessels sailing under convoy, or with the exhibition of recognition signals adopted by ship-owners, which have been authorized by their respective Governments and duly registered and published. | Identical with International Rule. |

## ARTICLE XIV
## STEAM VESSEL UNDER SAIL BY DAY

| *International Rules* | *Inland Rules* |
|---|---|
| *Article 14.* A steam-vessel proceeding under sail only but having her funnel up, *shall* carry in day-time, forward, where it can best be seen, one black ball or shape two feet in diameter. | *Article 14.* Same as International Rules, except *may* instead of *shall.* |

This article is applicable to steam vessels proceeding under sail and not using the engines, but manageable, a very rare occurrence at the present time. It does not apply to a steam vessel "not under command." The signals for such vessel are prescribed by Article 4, subdiv. (a).

## ARTICLE XV
### SOUND SIGNALS FOR FOG, AND SO FORTH
### PRELIMINARY

*International Rules*

*Article 15.* All signals prescribed by this article for vessels under way shall be given:

*First.* By "steam vessels" on the whistle or siren.

*Second.* By "sailing vessels" and "vessels towed" on the fog horn.

The words "prolonged blast" used in this article shall mean a blast of from four to six seconds duration.

A steam-vessel shall be provided with an efficient whistle or siren, sounded by steam or by some substitute for steam, so placed that the sound may not be intercepted by any obstruction, and with an efficient fog horn, *to be sounded by mechanical means,* and also with an efficient bell. (*In all cases where the rules require a bell to be used a drum may be substituted on board Turkish vessels, or a gong where such articles are used on board small sea-going vessels.*) A sailing-vessel of twenty tons gross tonnage or upwards shall be provided with a similar fog horn and bell.

*Inland Rules*

Identical with International Rules.

A steam-vessel shall be provided with an efficient whistle or siren, sounded by steam or by some substitute for steam, so placed that the sound may not be intercepted by any obstruction, and with an efficient fog horn; also with an efficient bell. A sailing-vessel of twenty tons gross tonnage or upward shall be provided with a similar fog horn and bell.

In fog, mist, falling snow, or heavy rain storms, whether by day or night, the signals described in this article shall be used as follows, namely:

Identical with International Rules.

### PILOT RULE XII
In fog, mist, falling snow, or heavy rainstorms, whether by day or night, signals shall be given as follows:

## STEAM VESSEL UNDER WAY

(a) A steam-vessel *having way upon her shall* sound, at intervals of not more than *two* minutes, a prolonged blast.

(a) A steam-vessel under way shall sound, at intervals of not more than *one* minute, a prolonged blast.

### PILOT RULE XII
A steam vessel under way, *except when towing other vessels or being towed,* shall sound, at intervals of not more than one minute, on the whistle or siren, a prolonged blast.

(b) A steam vessel under way, but stopped, and having no way upon her, shall sound, at intervals of not more than two minutes, two prolonged blasts, with an interval of about one second between.

(b) Not in Inland Rules.

## SAIL VESSEL UNDER WAY

(c) A sailing vessel under way shall sound, at intervals of not more than one minute, when on the starboard tack, one blast; when on the port tack, two blasts in succession, and when

(c) Identical with International Rule.

with the wind abaft the beam, three blasts in succession.

## VESSELS AT ANCHOR OR NOT UNDER WAY

(d) A vessel when at anchor shall, at intervals of not more than one minute, ring the bell rapidly for about five seconds.

(d) Identical with International Rule.
Identical with Pilot Rule.

## VESSELS TOWING OR TOWED

(e) A vessel when towing, *a vessel employed in laying or in picking up a telegraph cable, and a vessel under way, which is unable to get out of the way of an approaching vessel through being not under command, or unable to maneuver as required by the rules,* shall, instead of the signals prescribed in subdivisions (a) and *(c)* of this article, at intervals of not more than *two* minutes, sound three blasts in succession, namely: One prolonged blast followed by two short blasts. A vessel towed may give this signal and she shall not give any other.

(e) A *steam*-vessel when towing, shall, instead of the signals prescribed in subdivision (a) of this article, at intervals of not more than *one* minute, sound three blasts in succession, namely, one prolonged blast followed by two short blasts. A vessel towed may give this signal and she shall not give any other.

### PILOT RULE XII

A steam-vessel when towing other vessels shall sound, at intervals of not more than one minute, on the whistle or siren, three blasts in succession, namely, one prolonged blast followed by two short blasts.

A vessel towed may give, at intervals of not more than one minute, on the fog horn, a signal of three blasts in succession, namely, one prolonged blast followed by two short blasts, and she shall not give any other.

## SMALL SAILING VESSELS AND BOATS

Sailing vessels and boats of less than twenty tons gross tonnage shall not be obliged to give the above-mentioned signals, but, if they do not, they shall make some other efficient sound signal at intervals of not more than one minute.

Not in Inland Rules.

## RAFTS, OR OTHER CRAFT NOT PROVIDED FOR

Not in International Rules.

(f) All rafts or other water craft, not herein provided for, navigating by hand power, horse power, or by the current of the river, shall sound a blast of the fog-horn, or equivalent signal, at intervals of not more than one minute.

This Article requires every steam vessel to be fitted with an efficient whistle or siren, sounded by steam or some substitute for steam, and so placed that the sound may not be intercepted by any obstruction. Equipment.

As to what constitutes an efficient whistle or siren, the rules are silent. At the International Conference it was proposed that instruments (whistles or fog-horns) should be required having a sound-carrying capacity of not less than a minimum fixed standard. This was rejected as impracticable at that time.*

---

* Extract from Protocol of Proceedings at the International Marine Conference:

Mr. Hall (Great Britain): " . . . I would point out that the word 'efficient' is put in to require the vessel to have a proper instrument. It is used because it was thought impossible at that time to decide the actual distance to which the sound would penetrate. I do not know whether or not, having regard to the absence of any experiments, the better course would not be, as we are unable to deal with this for

Manifestly, it is contemplated that the whistle or siren shall be such that the sound produced by blasts therefrom as required under this article will be of the greatest carrying quality. The fact that the whistles or sirens with which many steam vessels are equipped have not an efficient sound-carrying quality was commented upon in the Report of the Committee on Sound Signals at the Conference, as follows:

> "(1) We are of the opinion that many of the steam-whistles, and the fog-horns and bells now in general use cannot be heard a sufficient distance; we therefore recommend the use of instruments giving a louder sound; and we consider it desirable that the sounds given by steam-whistles and fog-horns should be regulated so that the tones of the steamer's fog-whistle should be as distinct as possible from the sound of the sailing vessel's fog-horn."
>
> *Reports of Committees, p. 85.*

That this condition still exists is common knowledge amongst practical navigators, and is evidenced by the many collisions in which the fog signals are not heard on the other vessel until a moment before the collision, notwithstanding that such signals were being regularly sounded.

---

want of data, that we should suggest in a note as one of the results of the deliberation in the Conference, to the various powers, that it is desirable that experiments should be made in order to arrive at the distance at which signals are capable of being heard. . . .

"Then, sir, in order to get the discussion in order, I will move a resolution that it is desirable that the minimum distance should be fixed at which these signals can be heard, and call the attention of the various powers to that resolution in a note. That will invite them to make experiments. I think we are all agreed that at present we are not in a position to prescribe a minimum distance. Therefore I will move that it is desirable that there should be a common standard as to the minimum distance at which whistles, fog-horns, and bells should be heard in ordinary weather." (pp. 359, 360.)

The following resolutions were approved by the Conference and recommended to the attention of the powers represented thereat:

"All steam whistles, sirens, fog-horns, and bells should be thoroughly tested as to their efficiency, and should be capable of being heard at a stated minimum distance, and should be so regulated that the tones of whistles and sirens should be as distinct as possible from the sound of fog-horns."

*Reports of Committees, p. 67.*

Location of
Whistle or
Siren.

The rule also requires that the whistle or siren be so placed that the sound may not be intercepted by any obstruction. Usually the whistle or siren is located immediately in front of and up against the smokestack. It is suggested that if located not so close to the smokestack the requirement of the rule would be more nearly met.

Owners should use special care to see that vessels employed in waters where during certain seasons fog is prevalent are properly, and even exceptionally, equipped in this respect; and the United States Inspectors of Hulls and Boilers ought to exercise their authority for the strict enforcement of this requirement.

Sailing vessels, of twenty tons and upwards, must be provided with an efficient fog-horn to be sounded by mechanical means, and an efficient bell. Steam vessels under the rule, must be similarly equipped in addition to their whistles or sirens.

A sailing vessel not having a mechanical fog horn as required by the rules is guilty of fault unless it can be shown "that by no possibility could the presence of a fog horn (such as required by the rules) have prevented the collision."

*The Martello*, 153 U.S. 64; *The Love Bird*, 6 Prob. Div. 80; *The Trave*, 55 Fed. 117; *The Catalonia*, 43 Fed. 396; *The Bolivia*, 49 Fed. 169; *The Wyanoke*, 40 Fed. 702; *The Energy*, 42 Fed. 301.

As to Density
of Fog, Mist,
Falling Snow or
Heavy Rain
Storms
Requiring
Fog Signals.

The rules do not prescribe, nor have the courts decided, what density of fog, mist, falling snow or heavy rain storms requires the use of fog signals. As under the rules the side lights are required to show a minimum distance of two miles, it is suggested that the required fog signals should always be given whenever on account of the weather conditions the side lights of a vessel, if lighted, could not be clearly seen at a distance of two miles.

The use of passing signals (as provided in Art. 28 of the International Rules and Art. 18 of the Inland Rules for vessels in sight of one another) is not permitted in fog, mist, falling snow or heavy rain storms, unless and until the vessels are in sight of each other. Indeed, in the Inland Rules, Article 18, subdiv. 9, passing signals are specifically prohibited in fog, etc., when vessels cannot see one another.

The question of passing signals for vessels in fog, mist, falling snow or heavy rain storms was carefully considered at the International Conference when the present rules were discussed and agreed upon. The conclusion reached was that any passing signals under such conditions would be unwise, and the rules were so worded as only to permit such signals when vessels are in sight of each other.

The use of the three short blasts signal to indicate "my engines are going full speed astern" is not permitted by the rules unless and until the vessels are in sight of each other. This question was also discussed at length and so decided in the Conference. (See Art. 28.)

While such passing signals are at times interchanged between vessels in a fog and before they are in sight of each other, such practice is a positive breach of the regulations and extremely dangerous and should be discontinued. Vessels using passing signals under such conditions will surely be held in fault should collision occur through dependence upon them, or through the other ship being misled by them.

"... the *North Point* sounded two blasts of her whistle, a signal which ordinarily would indicate her purpose of passing the *Pennsylvania* starboard to starboard, but *which signal had no place during the existence of fog, as the rules of navigation in terms prescribe that during such weather passing signals shall not be given,* and that fog signals only must be given. ...

"The duty imposed upon navigators of complying strictly with the rules prescribed for their guidance is imperative, and in cases of fog a strict adherence to the requirements is the only method whereby vessels can safely move at all; . . ."

*The North Point,* 205 Fed. 958, 962, 963.

"We think that the evidence shows that the *Syracuse* did not sound the regulation fog signals. She did blow a series of short toots, but the law does not provide for such signals and the absence of the regulation long blast signals may well have confused and misled the master of the *Flemington.* Certainly the burden was on the *Syracuse* to show that the failure to blow the long blasts, as required by law, did not contribute to the injury. We do not see how we can say that this clear violation of the rules might not have caused or contributed to the collision."

*The Flemington* (C.C.A.), 234 Fed. 864, 865.

"The *Woodmere* heard the *Rosalia* and the *Spero* exchanging two-blast signals. What should the *Woodmere* have done? She should at once have obeyed the rule and stopped her engines. She did not do so. She did not blow a long blast for fog, but repeated the two-blast signals which she had heard the other vessels blow. *That was wrong according to the rules.*"

*The Rosalia* [1912], P. D. 109, 111.

See also, *The San Rafael,* 141 Fed. 270; *The City of Lowell,* 152 Fed. 593.

As between steam vessels in a fog and not in sight of each other, there is no right of way. The fog signals are intended solely for the purpose of indicating the presence of one to the other. All rights of way and crossing rules applicable in clear weather are, in thick weather, qualified and suspended by Article 16. If steam vessels come in sight of each other under such conditions, both are required, under the note to Article 21, and Articles 27 and 29, to take action to avert a collision. *[No Right of Way Exists Between Steamers in a Fog.]*

## STEAM VESSEL UNDER WAY

| *International Rules* | *Inland Rules* |
| --- | --- |
| (a) A steam-vessel having way upon her *shall* sound, at intervals of not more than *two* minutes, a prolonged blast. | (a) A steam-vessel under way *shall* sound, at intervals of not more than *one* minute, a prolonged blast. |

(b) A steam vessel under way, but stopped, and having no way upon her, shall sound, at intervals of not more than two minutes, two prolonged blasts, with an interval of about one second between.

(b) Not in Inland Rules.

This rule does not apply to a steam vessel being towed; such vessels are covered by subdiv. (e).

When in waters subject to the International Rules, steam* vessels under way are required to sound the fog signals at intervals of not more than *two* minutes, but, when in waters subject to the Inland Rules, fog signals must be sounded at intervals of not more than *one* minute.

Under the *International* Rules when a steam vessel under way is making way

No distinction is made in the Inland Rules between the signal from a vessel un-

---

*An extract from Lloyd's Calendar, 1915, p. 325, on the subject of sound in a fog is interesting and instructive:

"Fog Signals. Sound is conveyed in a very capricious way through the atmosphere. Apart from the wind, large areas of silence have been found in different directions and at different distances from the fog signal station, in some instances even in close proximity to it. . . . When sound has to travel against the wind, it may be thrown upwards; in such a case a man aloft might hear it when it is inaudible on deck. . . . The mariner should not assume: 1. That he is out of hearing distance, because he fails to hear the sound. 2. That because he hears a fog signal faintly, he is at a great distance from it. 3. That he is near it, because he hears the sound plainly. 4. That the distance from and the intensity of the sound on any one occasion, is a guide to him for any future occasion. 5. That the fog signal has ceased sounding, because he does not hear it even when in close proximity."

A warning against answering too quickly a fog signal from an approaching vessel follows. It is suggested that immediately following the blowing of a fog signal the ears of those on board the vessel giving the signal are deafened by the noise and they are therefore unable to immediately hear signals from other vessels.

All officers should be warned that if they blow their horn immediately after hearing another one they will not be heard. They should wait at least half a minute before they answer a distant call in order to allow those on board the other vessel to regain the full use of their ears.

Attention is further directed to a danger which also exists, that the fog signals of two approaching vessels may be blown simultaneously, in which event neither vessel would hear the signal of the other. This danger is greatest when signals are being given too often or where the vessels are using automatic signals. It can best be minimized by some irregularity in the periods between the signals.

through the water, one prolonged blast is required, but when lying dead in the water, two prolonged blasts with an interval of a second between must be given.

The mere stopping of the engines does not justify the giving of the two blast signal. Such signals should not be given until all way is off the vessel.

der way having way upon her and one lying dead in the water. One prolonged blast every minute is required in both cases.

## SAIL VESSEL UNDER WAY

### International Rules

(c) A sailing vessel under way shall sound, at intervals of not more than one minute, when on the starboard tack, one blast; when on the port tack, two blasts in succession, and when with the wind abaft the beam, three blasts in succession.

### Inland Rules

Identical with International Rules.

Under the old regulations sailing vessels were required to sound their signals at intervals of not more than two minutes, whereas, under the present rules, the signals must be sounded at intervals of not more than *one* minute.

Shortly after the new rules became effective, a schooner sounding the fog signal at intervals of two minutes, instead of one minute, was held liable for the collision. *The Frank S. Hall,* 116 Fed. 559.

A sailing vessel lying to in a fog, but having some of her sails up, is under way, and, where the wind is on her starboard side, is on the starboard tack and should give the required fog signal.  *Burrows et al. v. Gower,* 119 Fed. 616.

A sailing vessel "going about" should sound signals for the tack she is lifting, and not change the signal until she gets the wind on the other side.  *Burrows et al. v. Gower, supra.*

A sailing vessel becalmed or in irons is under way but being unable to maneuver is, when under the International Rules, in a situation covered by subdiv. (e) and should sound one prolonged blast followed by two short blasts. If, however, the vessel is in waters where the Inland Rules are operative, the signal to be given is prescribed in subdiv. (c), viz., one blast when on the starboard tack; two blasts in succession when on the port tack; or three blasts in succession with the wind abaft the beam.

As the signals prescribed for sailing vessels indicate which vessel has the right of way, the giving-way vessel should immediately give as wide a berth as possible. It should be remembered, however, that in a fog too much reliance cannot be placed either upon the direction or distance of the sound signals (see foot-note, p. 70).  If the vessels come into sight of each other, both may have to act promptly and intelligently to avoid collision.

## VESSELS AT ANCHOR OR NOT UNDER WAY

| *International Rules* | *Inland Rules* |
| --- | --- |
| (d) A vessel when at anchor shall, at intervals of not more than one minute, ring the bell rapidly for about five seconds. | Identical with International Rules.<br>Identical with Pilot Rule XII. |

Vessels at anchor or not under way (and this includes a vessel aground or made fast to the shore) must sound the fog-signal (ring the bell) as prescribed by this rule at intervals of not more than *one* minute.

A steamer at anchor was held at fault for ringing the

bell every two minutes, instead of every minute as required. *The Georgia*, 208 Fed. 635.

A vessel moored at a wharf and out of the way of traffic is not required to sound fog-signals. If, however, the position of the vessel is such as to be a possible obstruction to vessels moving in the fairway, she is required (under Art. 29) to give fog signals as a precaution required by the special circumstances of the case.

A vessel aground in a fairway or narrow channel in the usual path of traffic where other vessels are frequently moving may also (under Art. 29) be required to take additional precautions to apprise approaching vessels of her position.

The signals provided by this section do not apply to vessels "under way" such as a sailing vessel becalmed and unable to maneuver. The signals for such vessel are prescribed in Inland Rules in subdiv. (c) and in International Rules in subdiv. (e) below.

## VESSELS TOWING OR TOWED

### International Rules

(e) A vessel when towing, a vessel employed in laying or in picking up a telegraph cable, and a vessel under way, which is unable to get out of the way of an approaching vessel through being not under command, or unable to maneuver as required by the rules, shall, instead of the signals prescribed in subdivisions (a) and (c) of this article, at intervals of not more than two minutes, sound three blasts in succession, namely: One prolonged blast followed by two short blasts.

### Inland Rules

(e) A *steam*-vessel when towing, shall, instead of the signals prescribed in subdivision (a) of this article, at intervals of not more than one minute, sound three blasts in succession, namely, one prolonged blast followed by two short blasts. A vessel towed may give this signal and she shall not give any other.

**A vessel towed may give this signal and she shall not give any other.**

This International Rule requires the signal to be given every *two* minutes by vessels (sail or steam) in any of the following situations:

A vessel when towing;

A vessel being towed may give the signal on the foghorn, but is not required to do so unless the conditions are such as to make it a precaution required by good seamanship or the special circumstances of the case;

A vessel when employed in laying or picking up a telegraph cable;

A vessel when under way but unable to get out of the way of an approaching vessel because of an inability to maneuver. This applies not only to steamers disabled and not under command, but also to sailing vessels becalmed or in irons, or to vessels in any situation in which they are physically unable to maneuver as required by the Rules;

A vessel hearing the above signal is required to act upon the knowledge that

This Inland Rule requires the signal to be given every (*one*) minute by a steam vessel when towing.

The vessel being towed may give the signal, but is not required to do so unless the conditions are such as to make it a precaution required by good seamanship or the special circumstances of the case.

it may mean any one of the above conditions, and to take all necessary precautions in their navigation as will avoid danger of collision.

While Rule 15 does not in itself require a vessel not actually in a fog, etc., to use the signals prescribed therein, all vessels are required, under Article 29, not to neglect "any precaution which may be required by the ordinary practice of seamen or by the special circumstances of the case." The courts have decided in several cases that a vessel approaching a fog bank should, as a matter of precaution, reduce her speed and sound fog signals so as to give notice of her position to any vessel which may be concealed in the fog. If there be a thick snowstorm, fog or heavy rain ahead, so that nothing can be seen in the area affected, good seamanship requires that the approach thereto be at a moderate speed, with the vessel under proper control and fog signals blowing.

The St. Paul (Ct. of App.), 11 Asp. M.C. (N.S.) 169;<br>The N. Strong (Admiralty), 7 Asp. M.C. (N.S.) 194.

Vessels running outside and alongside a fog bank, but not entering it, are not required to slacken their speed or to give fog signals unless a signal is heard from the fog, but in the event of such a signal being heard, Article 29 clearly requires that fog signals be sounded and Article 16, that the engines be stopped. *The Bernard Hall,* 9 Asp. M.C. (N.S.) 300.

*General Considerations.*

*A Vessel Approaching a Fog Bank.*

*A Vessel Running Outside and Alongside a Fog Bank.*

## ARTICLE XVI

### SPEED IN FOG

*International Rules*

*Article 16.* Every vessel shall, in a fog, mist, falling snow, or heavy rain-storms, go at a moderate speed, having careful regard for the existing circumstances and conditions.

A steam vessel hearing, apparently forward of her beam, the fog-signal of a vessel the position of which is not ascertained shall, so far as the circumstances of the case admit, stop her engines, and then navigate with caution until danger of collision is over.

*Inland Rules*

*Article 16.* Both paragraphs same as International Rule, except "regard *to*," instead of "regard *for.*"

Rule XIII of Pilot Rules identical with Inland Rules except that it mentions only steam vessels.

This rule was most thoroughly considered and discussed at the International Conference, by which it was regarded as one of the most important rules of the road.

**"Moderate Speed"— Steamers.**

Many of the delegates held the view that the words "moderate speed" which were in the then existing rule should be more precisely defined. Some delegates were strongly in favor of fixing a maximum speed beyond which no vessel in a fog should be permitted to proceed. It was, however, the general sense of the Conference that, whilst a more accurate description was desirable, it was impracticable to frame a rule which would precisely define "moderate speed" as applicable under all the varying circumstances and conditions of navigation.

As was stated by a number of the delegates, the words "moderate speed," as used in this rule, constitute a relative term which cannot be so defined as to apply in all cases. What would be a moderate speed under some

circumstances, as, for instance, the speed of a steamer
in an unfrequented part of the ocean, would be an excessive speed under different conditions, as, *e. g.,* in approaching port where other vessels are apt to be met.*

The views of the Conference are most clearly expressed
by the wording of the present rule:

> "Every vessel shall, in a fog, mist, falling snow, or heavy
> rain-storms, go at a moderate speed, having careful regard
> for the existing circumstances and conditions."

It was said by the delegate from the United States:

> ". . . in the flexibility of this rule is its safety. Its
> flexibility permits a man to adapt his speed according to cir-
> cumstances; and the duty which is put upon him by this rule
> is that he shall comply with it according to the circumstances
> under which he finds himself placed."
>
> *Protocol of Proceedings,* p. 433.

Amongst the circumstances and conditions for which
careful regard must be had in determining what shall
constitute moderate speed, the following were mentioned
in the discussion before the conference:

**Circumstances Affecting Speed.**

The density of the fog and the condition of the
weather for hearing fog signals;

Whether the vessel is in narrow waters or on the
broad ocean;

Whether on fishing grounds or in frequented or
unfrequented waters;

The possibility or probability of meeting other
vessels;

The readiness with which a vessel (if laden or
in ballast) is able to maneuver;

The quickness with which she can be brought to a

---

* Steamers equipped with wireless apparatus and also those equipped
with submarine signalling apparatus should make full use of these systems
to safeguard to the utmost navigation in a fog. Navigators whose vessels
are so equipped must not, however, rely upon information secured
through the use of such apparatus to disregard the positive requirements
of the rule in respect to moderate speed or the stopping of the engines
upon hearing a fog signal forward of the beam.

standstill with the reserve of steam available for that purpose;

Her position with respect to heavy tideways, strong currents or other dangers.

The rate of speed constituting "moderate speed" under the requirement of this rule, therefore, will depend entirely upon the location of the vessel, the probability of meeting other vessels, the density of the fog, her ability to maneuver or bring herself to a standstill quickly, and any and all other surrounding circumstances and conditions affecting her own safety or the safety of others.

This rule permits only such speed in a fog as a vessel may maintain without danger to herself or without endangering others.

**Moderate Speed, as Defined by the Courts.** "Moderate speed," as required under this rule, has been defined by the American and English courts in almost identical terms.

The United States Supreme Court has said:

> "She was bound, therefore, to observe unusual caution, and to maintain only such a rate of speed as would enable her to come to a standstill, by reversing her engines at full speed, before she should collide with a vessel which she should see through the fog. This is the rule laid down by this court in the case of *The Colorado,* 91 U.S. 692, 702, citing *The Europa,* 2 Eng. Law & Eq. 557, 564, 14 Jurist pt. 1, 627, and *The Batavier,* 40 Eng. Law & Eq. 19, 25, and 9 Moore, P.C. 286. The rule laid down in the last-named case is that, at whatever rate a steamer was going, if she was going at such a rate as made it dangerous to any craft which she ought to have seen, and might have seen, she had no right to go at that rate. See also *The Pennsylvania,* 19 Wall. 125, 134."
>
> *The Nacoochee,* 137 U.S. 330, 339.

And again:

> "While it is possible that a speed of six miles an hour, even in a dense fog, may not be excessive upon the open ocean and off the frequented paths of commerce, a different rule applies to a steamer just emerging from the harbor of the largest port on the Atlantic coast, and in a neighborhood where she is likely to meet vessels approaching the harbor from at least

a dozen points of the compass. Under such circumstances, and in such a fog that vessels could not be seen more than a quarter of a mile away, it is not unreasonable to require that she reduce her speed to the lowest point consistent with a good steerage way, which the court finds in this case to be three miles an hour. *The Southern Belle (Culbertson v. Shaw),* 18 How. 584; *The Bay-State (McCready v. Goldsmith),* 18 How. 89."

*The Martello,* 153 U.S. 64, 70.

In the case of *The Umbria,* 166 U. S. 404, 417, the collision occurred about 12 miles outside New York Harbor, in the track of vessels bound into and out of the harbor, during an intermittent or variable fog which was sometimes so dense that vessels could not see each other more than one or two lengths off. The *Umbria* was running at a speed of from 16 to 19 knots and the *Iberia* at a speed of from 3½ to 4 knots. The *Umbria* was held at fault for excessive speed whilst the *Iberia* was exonerated. The Supreme Court of the United States said:

"The general consensus of opinion in this country is to the effect that a steamer is bound to use only such precautions as will enable her to stop in time to avoid a collision, after the approaching vessel comes in sight, provided such approaching vessel is herself going at the moderate speed required by law."

In the case of *The Chattahoochee,* 173 U. S. 540, 548, in which a collision took place with the schooner *Golden Rule,* south of Nantucket Shoals, not in the most frequented path of coastwise traffic, but in waters where other vessels were frequently met and not far from the usual track of trans-Atlantic steamers, the Supreme Court said:

"It has been said by this court, in respect to steamers, that they are bound to reduce their speed to such a rate as will enable them to stop in time to avoid a collision after an approaching vessel comes in sight, provided such approaching vessel is herself going at the moderate speed required by law."

The schooner, which was going at a rate of seven knots, was also held at fault for excessive speed.

The most recent discussion in the American courts of

the meaning of the words "at a moderate speed having due regard to the existing circumstances and conditions," appears in the case of *The Sagamore,* 247 Fed. 743, decided by the Circuit Court of Appeals for the First Circuit.

The steamer *Sagamore,* a large vessel, length 430 feet, beam 47 feet, normal speed 12 to 13 knots, on a voyage from Liverpool to Boston, when in the vicinity of the Grand Banks ran into a dense fog. Upon entering the fog her speed was reduced to 5½ knots. The court found:

> "She was then in a part of the ocean where her officers well knew that fishing vessels were usually found, and where special precautions for discovering and avoiding them were necessary. . . . The night was so dark and the fog so dense that, while going at this rate [5½ knots] the discovery of the lights of other ships could not be relied upon to enable the *Sagamore* to avoid collision by stopping and reversing. . . . 'Sight, as both sides agree, was of little use in avoiding collision.' "

Under these conditions the steamer collided with and sunk the fishing schooner *Olympia.* A single blast from the schooner's fog horn was heard a few moments before the collision.

The court said:

> "The primary question is whether the *Sagamore,* before the collision, was going, as required by Art. 16 of the International Rules, 'at a moderate speed having due regard to the existing circumstances and conditions.' "

and, after a review of the authorities, found the circumstances and conditions demanded a slackening of speed to the lowest point consistent with good steerageway, which requirement had not been met.

**Limitations on Discretion of Navigator as to what is "Moderate Speed."** An interesting feature of the decision is in the reference of the court, on page 749, to the limitations on the discretion of the navigator.

> "The discretion of the navigator in the matter of speed in a fog must be exercised not wholly as a matter of individual

judgment or of individual views as to what is moderate speed, but also with due regard to the interpretation of the term 'moderate speed' by the maritime courts and to the general standards of good seamanship established by those courts in applying the term 'moderate speed.' "

Reference is made in the discussion to what was termed by the court as the "rule of sight" or "seeing distance" prescribed in several of the leading cases, as a test of proper speed, and the omissions in such cases of any reference to the presence or absence of sound signals as an element for consideration upon the question of whether a general rate of speed was moderate or excessive. *"Rule of Sight" or "Seeing Distance."*

The decision apparently concedes the impracticability of adhering to the strict letter of the "rule of sight" or "seeing distance" in the navigation of a vessel in a dense fog, and recognizing that the immediate presence of danger in a dense fog will ordinarily be made known by fog signals somewhat earlier than the time of sighting, inferentially suggests that vessels are entitled to proceed with some reliance upon that expectation.

The discussion of this feature is, however, closed by the court as follows:

"While it is apparent that the discretion of the navigator as to speed will be affected by reliance upon the performance of other vessels of their statutory duty to signal in a fog, thus giving him time to act, it seems doubtful, upon the authorities, whether it is practical to attempt to modify the rule stated in *The Umbria, Chattahoochee, Nacoochee,* and *Counsellor* (even though theoretically it is justly subject to criticism, as is pointed out in Hughes on Admiralty), except by reading it in conjunction with the requirements stated in *The Colorado,* 91 U.S. 692, 23 L. Ed. 379, 'Very slow speed, just sufficient to subject the vessel to the command of her helm,' and in *The Martello,* 153 U.S. 64, 14 Sup. Ct. 733, 38 L. Ed. 637, 'Reduce her speed to the lowest point consistent with good steerageway.'

"In a fog so dense as existed in this case the right to maintain steerageway and the obligation to go so slow as to be able to avoid a vessel which can be sighted approach inconsistency; but both rules are to be applied so far as is possible."

The English courts, in the case of *The Great Eastern*, Browning and Lushington, 287, cited with approval in *The Umbria*, said of the rule:

> ". . . their Lordships are of the opinion that it is the duty of the steamer to proceed only at such a rate of speed as will enable her, after discovering a vessel meeting her, to stop and reverse her engines in sufficient time to prevent any collision from taking place."

In the case of *The Kincora v. The Oceanic*, a collision occurred in the Irish Channel during a dense fog. The *Oceanic* (at that time the largest ship afloat), a twin-screw steamship of 17,274 tons gross, with triple expansion engines of 2,800 I.H.P., loaded with general cargo, mails and 1,070 passengers, was proceeding at a speed of 6⅓ knots, at which speed she could be brought to a standstill in 400 feet. The *Oceanic* was held at fault for going at an excessive speed. The House of Lords said:

> "She was going at a speed which rendered it impossible to stop within the limit of observation."
>
> *The Oceanic*, 9 Asp. M.C. (N.S.) 378, 380.

While the foregoing interpretations of the requirement of "moderate speed" may be considered very drastic, they are now the accepted law as established by the courts of both countries, and must be observed.

In a number of collision cases it has been argued that moderate speed, as defined by the decisions, is not practical for the modern fast steamers. Claim has been made that such steamers cannot reduce their engines sufficiently to produce such speed, and cannot with safety to their own navigation proceed at such speed, and that what would be an entirely safe speed for a slower steamer would be unsafe for these fast and more powerful vessels. The courts, however, have refused to accept this view, stating in positive terms that the avoidance of delay and inconvenience, or the necessity for taking additional precautions for a vessel's own safety, even if it involves stopping the engines from time to time, to attain a moderate speed, or perhaps stopping and anchoring altogether, will not be accepted as an excuse for non-compliance with the regulations.

This is apparent from the following comments of the courts:

> "It was suggested upon the argument that it was customary for large passenger steamers carrying the mails to run at full speed in a fog, and that this was really the safer course for them, as the greater the speed the sooner they pass the foggy belt. However this may be, the custom is not one to which the courts can lend their sanction as it implies a flagrant disregard of the safety of other vessels."
>
> *The Umbria,* 166 U.S. 404, 409.

> ". . . if a steam vessel in a fog cannot be continuously navigated at such a slow speed as will comply with the requirement of Article 16, she must, in the absence of exceptional dangers of navigation, such as may arise from narrow waters or current, be stopped from time to time to take off her way."
>
> *The Eagle Point* (C.C.A.), 120 Fed. 449, 454.

> "But if a vessel cannot reduce her speed sufficiently with the continuous action of her engines, and therefore cannot go at what would be a reasonable speed in a fog without occasionally stopping her engines, it is her duty to occasionally stop them. Masters can always carry out the manœuvre in that way, and I will not yield to what I know is the strong disinclination of the masters of these large vessels to stop their engines. They hate and abhor the very idea, but it is, to my mind, their duty to do so, if they cannot otherwise reduce their speed sufficiently."
>
> *The Resolution,* 6 Asp. M.C. (N.S.) 363, 364.

Also see *The Campania,* 9 Asp. M.C. (N.S.) 151, 154 (Ct. of App.), 9 Asp. M.C. (N.S.) 177, 179.

The rule that "every vessel shall (in a fog, etc.) go at a moderate speed" does not give permission to a vessel to proceed when the conditions are such that she should stop and, if necessary, come to anchor. Vessels have been held to blame for not stopping or anchoring, where this is practicable, when the fog was so dense that they

**Dense Fog May Require Stopping and Anchoring.**

should have done so.   *The Otter,* 2 Asp. M.C. (N.S.) 208.

The question was discussed by the delegate from Great Britain (Mr. Hall) at the International Conference, as follows:

> ".   .   . When a vessel is in a fog so dense that it is not safe for her to proceed, I apprehend that common caution requires her to bring up or to anchor, and that is in accordance with the decisions in our law courts; as I apprehend, it is with the decisions of the courts of the United States,   .   .   . You cannot say that a man in fog, mist or falling snow is to lie to or come to anchor, because it must depend upon whether the fog is so dense as to make it unsafe for him to proceed at all.   That must be a question of degree.   .   .   .   I think that every seaman will say that if he is in a place where he is liable to meet other vessels, in a dense fog, and it is dangerous for him to proceed, he ought to lie to.   We can only frame general rules; and we cannot make rules to apply to all circumstances."
>
> *Prot. of Proc.,* p. 496.

When vessels are stopped, however, care should be taken that the proper fog signals as required by Article 15, subdiv. (b) or (d) are sounded.

**Moderate Speed—Sailing Vessels.** The requirement of a moderate speed applies to sailing vessels as well as to steamers.

A speed of about seven knots an hour under nearly full canvas was held an excessive speed for a schooner in a fog so thick that the hull of a vessel could only be seen at a distance of a few hundred feet.   Of it, the Supreme Court said:

> ".   .   . So much depends upon the density of fog and the chance of meeting other vessels in the neighborhood, that it is impossible to say what ought to be considered moderate speed under all circumstances.   It has been said by this court, in respect to steamers, that they are bound to reduce their speed to such a rate as will enable them to stop in time to avoid a collision after an approaching vessel comes in sight, provided such approaching vessel is herself going at the moderate speed required by law.   It is not perceived why the

considerations which demand a slackening of speed on the part of steamers in foggy weather are not equally persuasive in the case of sailing vessels. The principal reason for such reduction of speed is that it will give vessels time to avoid a collision after coming in sight of each other. . . . The very fact that a sailing vessel can do so little by maneuvering is a strong reason for so moderating her speed as to furnish effective aid to an approaching steamer charged with the duty of avoiding her."

*The Chattahoochee,* 173 U.S. 540, 548.

Also in the more recent case of *The Oceania Vance* (C.C.A.), 233 Fed. 77, it was said by the Circuit Court of Appeals:

". . . The place where the collision occurred was one much frequented by vessels, and there was a thick fog prevailing. . . .

"We think the evidence in the case justified the conclusion that the speed of the schooner was from 6½ to 7 knots an hour, and we are also of the opinion that that speed, under the circumstances then prevailing, was immoderate, and therefore that the schooner was in that respect rightly held in fault. *The Chattahoochee,* 173 U.S. 540 . . .; *The Umbria,* 166 U.S. 404 . . .; *The Belgian King,* 125 Fed. 869 . . .; *The Eagle Point,* 120 Fed. 449 . . . Speeds much less than 6 knots have frequently been condemned. *The Geo. W. Roby,* 111 Fed. 601 . . .; *The Michigan,* 63 Fed. 280 . . . The same rule in respect to the necessity of slackening speed in foggy weather that applies to steamers is equally applicable to sailing vessels. . . ."

A moderate speed for a sailing vessel is such speed as will enable her to be kept properly under command, but no more.

The provision "having careful regard for the existing circumstances and conditions" is intended as a warning that strict attention and consideration must be given by mariners to all conditions, *the density of the fog,* etc., the state of the weather, the proximity of the land or rocks, *the position of the vessel in respect to the possibility or probability of other vessels being in the vicinity;* and, in fact, to any and all circumstances which could in any man-

Having Careful Regard for the Existing Circumstances and Conditions.

ner make the navigation of the ship a source of danger either to herself or to others.

**Running with the Fog, etc., Abeam.**

A vessel is not required to go at a moderate speed when she is running on the outside of a fog bank, but under Article 29 it is necessary that extreme care be exercised in such navigation, and especially in the maintenance of lookout, etc. Although the rules do not directly prescribe it, it would seem the part of good seamanship under such conditions to sound the fog signal as a warning to any vessels which may be enveloped in the fog. *The Milanese,* 4 Asp. M.C. (N.S.) 318.

The sounding of the fog signal is necessary when a fog signal has been heard from the fog bank; and, in the event such fog signal is heard from forward of the beam, the engines must be immediately stopped and the ship navigated with caution until the danger of collision is over. *The Bernard Hall,* 9 Asp. M.C. (N.S.) 300.

**Running into the Fog.**

A vessel must reduce her speed before she enters the fog, so that at the time of actually entering the fog bank she will be going at the moderate speed required by the rule. It is not sufficient to reduce her speed after she is actually in the fog.

In the case of *The Bernard Hall,* 9 Asp. M.C. (N.S.) 300, 302, the English court said:

> "If a vessel is running into a fog ahead, I have held— and I think I may say rightly held, because I think the Court of Appeal took the same view—that there is an obligation upon her, although she is not actually in it at the moment, not only under the first part of art. 16, but under the general rules of seamanship, to go at a moderate speed. It seems to me only common sense, and according to the advice which competent sailors could not fail to give to this court."

And again in *The St. Paul and The Gladiator,* 11 Asp. M.C. (N.S.) 153, at 157:

> " 'Over and over again we have had cases in this court where a vessel not herself in a fog has been blamed because,

seeing fog ahead, [although herself not in the fog at all]
she has not taken precautions, so that her speed shall be off
when she enters the fog.' . . . If there is a thick snowstorm [this equally applies to fogs, mists or rain-storms]
ahead, so that nothing can be seen in it, good seamanship
requires there should be a moderate rate of speed, so as to
approach that place under proper control."

The rule of law as above stated was approved by Court
of Appeal, 11 Asp. M.C. (N.S.) 169.

Knowledge of the course of an approaching vessel,
seen before the fog set in, will not excuse a failure of a
vessel when entering a fog to go at a moderate speed.

In the case of *The Julia Luckenbach*, 219 Fed. 600,
605, the steamer *Indrakuala* saw the *Julia Luckenbach*
before the fog shut in between them. At that time the
vessels were on courses by which they would pass clear.
The *Indrakuala,* relying on what she had seen before the
fog shut in, did not slow down until she entered the fog.
The court said, at p. 605:

"The *Indrakuala* insists that she should not be held in
fault because until within a few minutes prior to the collision, the weather was clear; that her navigators could see
the course they were on, and that the same was not obstructed; and that it was not necessary for their vessel to
slow down until she had actually entered the fog bank, after
which time they did all that was necessary to be done.

"The court cannot agree with these contentions under
the circumstances attending this collision. It is true the
fog came on quickly, and did not last long, not over half
an hour, perhaps; but the *Indrakuala* was in full view of
its approach, saw that her course took her directly into it,
and, while at first it was naturally thinner on its outer edges,
that in a very short time it must envelop her, as it did, and
she should not have continued at full speed, certainly 10
knots an hour, until she ran into a dense fog, which was being rapidly driven by the wind across her pathway, but
should have checked her speed in anticipation thereof, and this
duty became the more apparent by the known presence of
a vessel ahead of her in the fog, which might cross her
course, and the fog signals of which vessel she had twice
heard."

The Engines
Must be
Stopped on
Hearing the
First Fog
Signal Forward
of the Beam.

The second paragraph of Article 16 provides:

"A steam-vessel hearing, apparently forward of her beam, the fog-signal of a vessel the position of which is not ascertained shall, so far as the circumstances of the case admit, *stop her engines, and then navigate with caution until danger of collision is over.*"

This part of Article 16 applies to steam vessels only.

Under the regulations in force prior to the adoption of the present rules, the necessity of stopping the engines was left to the discretion of those in charge of the navigation of the ships.

Under the present rules no latitude of judgment is allowed the navigator either as to the necessity or the time for stopping them. *The rule is imperative that the engines be stopped immediately the first fog signal is heard apparently forward of the beam.*

In the case of *The El Monte,* 114 Fed. 796, the *Rappahannock,* on hearing the first fog signal, immediately put her engines at slow and *before* hearing the second signal, stopped them. The collision took place within three minutes after the first signal was heard; three other signals being heard from the approaching vessel. The *Rappahannock* was held at fault for not stopping her engines immediately upon first hearing the fog signal forward of her beam. The court referred, at p. 800, to the proceedings of the International Conference * at the time the rule was framed, saying:

---

* Extract from the remarks by delegates at the International Marine Conference, 1889. *Protocol of Proceedings,* pp. 453-461:

The President: The Secretary will please read the amendment as an addition to present Article 13.

"The amendment is as follows:

"Art. 13. Every ship, whether a sailing-ship or a steam-ship, shall in a fog, mist, or falling snow, go at a moderate speed.

"(a) A steam-vessel hearing, apparently, before her beam, the fog signal of a vessel the position of which is not ascertained, shall, so far as the circumstances of the case admit, stop and then proceed with caution until all danger of collision is over.

"Captain Richard (France), at pp. 453-454: 'Mr. President, I have an objection to make to the amendment proposed by our honorable colleague, Mr. Goodrich. It provides for the case where a vessel on hearing the whistle of another must stop and go ahead with caution. I should like to

"An instructive discussion of the reasons for this amendment occurred when it was being considered in the International Maritime Conference of 1889, showing that the duty of stopping should be made imperative in order to avoid the danger of leaving too much to the navigator's judgment."

Again, in the case of *The Seneca,* 159 Fed. 578, 580 (affd. 170 Fed. 937), it was said:

"  .  .  .  She also violated rule 16, because, hearing, apparently forward of her beam, the fog signal of a vessel, the position of which was not ascertained, she did not stop her engines and navigate with caution until danger of collision was over."

Also in the case of the *Georgic,* 180 Fed. 863, the court said, at p. 870:

"*In re Clyde S. S. Co.,* 134 Fed., at p. 97, it was held that a failure to observe the precaution imposed by this article 'creates a presumption of fault'; and the same rule was applied in *El Monte,* 114 Fed. 796. In the case last cited at page 800, is a reference to the proceedings of the Maritime Conference which adopted this rule, and I entirely agree with Judge Adams that it was put on the statute book on the recommendation of that conference *in order that stopping at the first whistle should be imperative* and because the Conference and the Legislature did not wish 'to leave too much to the navigator's judgment.' Any violation thereof should in my opinion create a very strong presumption of fault, and cast upon the offender the burden of showing by clear testimony that his error did not contribute to collision and subsequent damage."

---

be informed whether stopping is a good manœuvre. When you stop a vessel you take away from her the power to obey her helm. I understand that she should go with caution. But if you stop a vessel it generally deprives her of the means of manœuvring under proper conditions. Consequently I would prefer the language which has been submitted to us by the honorable delegates from Great Britain: "stop if necessary"; but does not say in clear and emphatic terms that the vessel must first stop. If she stops she can no longer manœuvre. Consequently you simply expose her to a collision.'

"Captain Sampson (United States), at p. 454: 'Mr. President, *I cannot agree with the gallant delegate from France as to the danger of making the rule to stop imperative.* On the contrary, I think that if it is optional to stop, when necessary, great danger will arise. For example, an officer of one ship might deem it necessary to stop and the other might think it unnecessary. This would be the condition most likely to result in a col-

See also,

> *The Admiral Schley,* 142 Fed. 64; *The John A. Hughes,*
> 156 Fed. 879; *The Easton,* 239 Fed. 859; *The Britannia,*
> 10 Asp. M.C. (N.S.) 65; *The Koning Willem I,* 9 Asp.
> M.C. (N.S.) 425; *The Bernard Hall,* 9 Asp. M.C. (N.S.)
> 300; *The Chinkiang* [1908], App. Cas., 251.

The English courts have placed the same interpretation upon this rule and have said in respect to the necessity (upon hearing a fog signal apparently forward of
her beam) of immediately stopping the engines:

> "The reason given by her master for not stopping his en-
> gines when he first heard the whistle of the *Bittern* or at
> the second or third whistle, was this—that his ship was going
> so slow and the signal seemed to be so far off that he thought
> it better to wait until he heard it again; and that so soon
> as he heard it more ahead, that is finer on the bow, he stopped
> his engines immediately. Not having ascertained the position
> of the *Bittern* when her signals were first heard, in my opinion
> the engines should have been stopped, apart altogether from
> Article 16, but certainly in accordance with that article."
>
> *The Koning Willem I* [1903], P. D. 114, 121.

Also,

> "The *Rosalia* admits that, hearing, in a fog, a whistle on
> her starboard bow forward of her beam, she did not obey the
> rule and stop her engines. That is the initial fault of the
> whole case."
>
> *The Rosalia* [1912], P. D. 109, 111.

The latest and most authoritative American interpreta-

---

lision, for he has correctly stated that a ship lying at rest on the water
has not the power to manœuvre as well as a vessel under way. It must
be evident that if two ships are approaching, and in danger of collision,
if it is made an absolute rule that when they hear the fog-signals of each
other they shall both stop, the conditions are the most favorable possible
for avoiding a collision. A vessel, as I pointed out this morning, in some
cases at least, will stop in a shorter distance than she can manœuvre in.
*I think that it would not be wise to leave this discretionary, and that it
should be made obligatory on both vessels to stop.* They thus move from
the position at which they heard the signals the shortest possible distance.
They make the chances of collision least possible. To be sure both vessels lose their power to manœuvre, but if they both stop, I think the danger
will be the least possible.
" 'The question is asked whether by stopping it is meant to stop the

tion of the rule stated in the second paragraph of Article
16 is the recent decision of the United States Supreme
Court in *Lie, etc., v. San Francisco & Portland S. S. Co.,
etc.,* 243 U. S. 291.

The Norwegian steamer *Selja,* in-bound to the port
of San Francisco from China, first heard the fog whistle
of the steamer *Beaver,* out-bound from San Francisco to
the port of Astoria, Oregon, at 3 P. M., at which time
she was proceeding at half speed of about six knots.
Thereafter she continued to hear the *Beaver's* fog whistle
every minute.   At 3:05 the *Selja's* engines were put at
slow and her speed reduced to three knots, at which
speed she continued to run until 3:10, when, for the first
time, her engines were stopped.   She continued to forge
slowly ahead until 3:15, when, as the *Beaver* came into
view, she was reversed.   The collision occurred at 3:16,
at which time the *Selja* was practically, if not entirely, at a standstill.   The *Beaver* had been proceeding
in the fog at a high rate of speed and was held culpably
negligent.   The United States District Court, the United
States Circuit Court of Appeals, and, finally, the United
States Supreme Court held the *Selja* in fault for not having obeyed Rule 16 by stopping her engines at 3:00
o'clock on first hearing the fog signal of the *Beaver.*   The
Supreme Court in giving judgment remarked that from
the time the first whistle was heard the ships must be con-

---

engines or stop the ship.  I understand that this means to stop the ship in
the water.  When the signal is heard, of course the two vessels will be in
proximity to each other, and the engines should be reversed and continued
in motion until the ship is at rest in the water.'

"Mr. Hall (Great Britain), at pp. 454-455: 'Mr. President, I am very
glad to hear the remarks which have fallen from the gallant delegate
from the United States with reference to making this stop mandatory.  The
gallant delegate from France will see that words have been inserted to
meet exceptional cases, "so far as the circumstances of the case require."
It may be possible that a sailor might have a steamer astern of him when
it would be dangerous for him to stop.  Then he would be covered by
that exception; *but he has to stop, under this rule, unless there is some
circumstance that makes it dangerous for him to do so.*  I think it is
better that we should have this amendment to read that she shall stop, so

sidered as within the danger zone, and, of the rule, it said at p. 296:

> "The most cursory reader of this rule must see that while the first paragraph of it gives to the navigator discretion as to what shall be 'moderate speed' in a fog, the command of the second paragraph is imperative that he shall stop his engines when the conditions described confront him. The difficulty of locating the direction or source from which sounds proceed in a fog, renders it not necessary to dwell upon the purpose and obvious wisdom of this second paragraph of the rule."

And at p. 298:

> "Such a state of fact makes sharply applicable the conclusion of this court in *The Pennsylvania,* 19 Wall. 125: 'But when, as in this case, a ship at the time of a collision is in actual violation of a statutory rule intended to prevent collisions, it is no more than a reasonable presumption that the fault, if not the sole cause, was at least a contributory cause of the disaster. In such a case the burden rests upon the ship of showing, not merely that her fault might not have been one of the causes, or that it probably was not, but that it could not have been.' "

**Fog-Signals Faintly Heard Apparently Far Distant.** That the fog-signal is faint or may sound a long way off will not excuse a failure to stop the engines immediately upon hearing such signal. From the moment a fog-signal is first heard apparently forward of the beam, no matter how faint or far distant it may seem, the vessels are considered within the danger zone and the duty is

---

far as the circumstances of the case admit. I think that this amendment includes the wise provisions which appear in both of the amendments of the delegate from The Netherlands. It complies, to a certain extent, with the wishes of the delegate from Japan. I think it meets what has been laid down as the proper course for a sailor to adopt when he hears a whistle in a fog. If the delegates will read the report of the Committee on Sound-Signals, they will see that it is pointed out there that prudent seamen would do this if they heard a sound-signal in a fog; and this is only making the law that which practical seamen have believed and acted upon as the most prudent course under the circumstances.

" 'I will point out that it is necessary to have the word "apparently" in the amendment, so that it will read: "A steam-vessel hearing, apparently before her beam, the fog-signal of a vessel, the position of which is not ascertained," etc.; for two reasons. Of course, if the whistle is aft and you only hear it once, that is a vessel passing; that

imposed by the rule to stop the engines immediately. This has been definitely decided by the United States Supreme Court in the case of *Lie, etc., v. San Francisco & Portland S. S. Co.,* supra, in which it was said at p. 293:

> "The master of the *Selja* admits that he heard, what ultimately proved to be the warning fog whistle of the *Beaver,* at three o'clock, and therefore the ships must be considered as within the danger zone from that time forward, and the decision of the case turns upon what was done by the two vessels during the sixteen minutes which elapsed between three o'clock and the moment of collision."

This same principle has also been laid down by the English courts in the case of the *Britannia,* 10 Asp. M.C. (N.S.) 65, in which it was said at pp. 67 and 68:

> "It is said that there was no reason for stopping at first, because the whistle was a long way off, and other ships were of assistance in judging the situation and distance, and that there was, therefore, no breach of art. 16 by the *Britannia.* *That is a view of this case with which I cannot agree.* It appears to me that it was the positive duty of those on board the *Britannia* to stop their engines as soon as they heard that whistle for the first time. It is not true to say that because a whistle sounds distant those on the ship hearing it are entitled to treat it as distant. Many cases in this court have shown that an apparently distantly sounding whistle is really close to. . . . If one was to hold that, upon hearing a whistle which sounded to be distant, a vessel was justified in not stopping, although its position was not ascertained, except that it sounded a long way off, every case in this court

---

is, not a vessel overtaking. But so long as the whistle appears to be before the beam, then of course it is necessary to find out the position of the vessel which is not ascertained. These vessels often travel in company. A steamer may have a steam-vessel bound in the same direction as herself, and she may be using her signal whistle continuously exchanging signals, and the officer would know practically the position of that vessel. It would then not be necessary for her to stop. Therefore I think it is necessary to have these words.

"'I have one further remark to make, and that is with reference to the word "stop." I apprehend that it may be very necessary sometimes for a vessel to stop her engines and even stop her way in the water; but I do not think it would be desirable to lay down that as a rule. I think that ought to be left to the officer in charge of the vessel, as a prudent seaman. He can stop his engines, and then if he finds the other vessel is so near to him that he ought to stop his way, he will do so

would be that the whistle sounded such a long way off that those who heard it were justified in not stopping their engines."

See also, *The Koning Willem I,* 9 Asp. M.C. (N.S.) 425.

The rule does not require the ship to stop. Its prescription is to *"stop her engines."* The stopping of the engines does not immediately take the way off the ship, but it does put her in better control.

The imperative character of the requirement "to stop the engines" admits of no latitude of discretion. Its disobedience means liability for a resulting collision.

**Duty to Reverse the Engines.**

Although Article 16 does not in terms require the engines to be reversed, the circumstances may make this necessary under the requirement of cautious navigation and also as a precaution of good seamanship under Article 29.

If the fog-signal, either the first or any subsequent signal, be heard on either bow and approaching apparently in close proximity, and the location of the approaching vessel be not definitely known as to position and course, the engines should be immediately reversed.

"The doctrine laid down by the Privy Council in *The Frankland* has been recognized by the Court of Appeal in *The John McIntyre,* 9 P. D. 135, *The Dordogne,* 10 P. D. 6, and *The Ebor,* 11 P. D. 25, all of which were cases of

as a prudent seaman. I think it would not be wise to put that into the rules, because, as has been often said with regard to this rule, what we ought to avoid is the taking of the command of the vessel out of the seaman's hands. Give him general rules and then let him be responsible for his conduct. I support this proposal, because it carries into effect the idea of the delegate from The Netherlands and of the delegate from Japan, and of the learned delegate from Germany . . .'
"Mr. Goodrich (United States) at p. 457: ' . . . There is more in this amendment—if the gentleman will pardon me for saying so—than seems to have been discovered. . . . In the first place, as the rule stands, it provides that a vessel in a fog shall go at a moderate speed. That is the condition of things when the sound of the whistle is heard. Now an additional duty is imposed upon a vessel in a fog; she is to do something more; she is to stop; which means that the speed at which she is going is not sufficiently slow or sufficiently moderate for

collision in dense fog.   In the first of these cases, the present
Master of the Rolls said (9 P. D. 136):

" 'It may be laid down as a general rule of conduct that it
is necessary to stop and reverse, not indeed every time that
a steamer hears a whistle or fog-horn in a dense fog, but
when in such a fog it is heard on either bow and approaching, and is in the vicinity, because there must then be a risk
of collision.'

"To the proposition so stated I entirely assent.   When
the approaching vessel is nearly ahead, the duty to stop and
reverse is obvious; but it appears to me to be equally imperative when the other vessel is drawing near upon either bow.
It matters not whether the bearings of the approaching ship
be one point or four; either position is fraught with danger
of collision if it continues to advance without change of
bearing."

*The Ceto* (House of Lords), 14 Appeal Cases, 670, 687.

"In the dense fog which is proved to have prevailed in
this case, those on board the *Kirby Hall* were bound not to
speculate, but to bring their vessel to a standstill on the
water at once."

*The Kirby Hall* [1883], P. D. 71.

In the case of *The Koning Willem I,* 9 Asp. M.C.
(N.S.) 425, 428, the court held that when the whistle of
an approaching vessel is found to be narrowing on the
bow, the engines should be immediately reversed.

"   .   .   .   he ought to have stopped his engines; and when
he found shortly after, as he did find and as he admitted he
found, that the other vessel was porting and that her whistle

---

the circumstances.  She must proceed slower; she must go with caution.
What is the caution?  Take away her speed and add to her lookouts;
make her methods of observation keener and closer.  It means more than
going at moderate speed. . . . '

"Mr. Hall (Great Britain), at pp. 458-459: 'Mr. President, I will
move, in order to get over the difficulty that was pointed out by the
gallant delegate from the United States, to insert the words "her engines"
after the word "stop." It is clear from what has fallen from the gallant delegate that it would be argued that she must stop her way, which
would be dangerous to some vessels under certain circumstances. I
should have proposed to put in these words originally, if the matter
had been called to my attention.'

"The President, at p. 459: 'If there be no objection, those words will
be inserted.'

"Captain Sampson (United States), at p. 459: . . . 'Mr. President,

signals were narrowing on his bow, indicating to him a position of extreme danger—the position being then that a vessel which could only be seen at about 150 yards was porting across his course—he ought not only to have stopped his engines, but to have reversed them. That is not only required by the rules, but is necessary for proper navigation."

Navigators in control of a steamer should also remember that a sailing vessel whose fog-signal is heard forward of the beam is not required under the rules to stop; whereas the steamer is required not only to stop her engines, but if necessary to avoid collision to reverse them immediately upon first hearing such signal.

Similarly, it may be necessary, upon hearing the fog signal of a vessel at anchor, not only to stop the engines, but also to reverse them. This is especially so where the tide or current is setting in the apparent direction of the sound. Under Article 23 the active responsibility to keep clear is upon the steamer.

It cannot be too strongly emphasized that the command to "stop her engines" is a command to steamers observing the previous requirement of the rule, namely, "going at a moderate speed," under which conditions the stopping of the engines results in the steamer losing headway much more rapidly than if she were going at a higher rate of speed.

Without in any way extenuating or lending countenance to those vessels which in spite of the rule, may be

---

I assume that the words added by the learned delegate from Great Britain to this amendment by inserting the words "her engines" after the word "stop" would not exclude stopping the ship if the necessity arose. I think it is entirely proper; but I am not sure that all the delegates are quite in favor of the change.'

"Mr. Hall (Great Britain), at p. 459: 'Mr. President, the reason why I proposed to insert these words was that it might not be thought necessary to stop the way of the ship. Of course a master has the right to do so; but if we put it in as it is now, he might consider that he was bound to stop her under all circumstances.'

"The President, at p. 459: 'Does the delegate from the United States accept that?'

"Mr. Goodrich (United States), at p. 460: 'Yes, sir; I accept this suggestion. . . .'

"The President, at p. 461: 'The question is upon extra amendment

proceeding at an immoderate speed in a fog, it may be said that a greater obligation to reverse exists in such cases. Such vessels should, by reversing the engines, more quickly take the way off, in order to comply, so far as possible, with the spirit and purpose of the rule prescribed by the second paragraph of Article 16.

For all practical purposes the provision "the position of which is not ascertained" means that a vessel which fails to stop her engines, on hearing a whistle forward of the beam, must be able to prove that the position of the approaching vessel was definitely and exactly known. It is not sufficient that the general direction, or even the exact direction of the approaching vessel is known. The distance must also be known, and while the rule does not explicitly so state, it implies that knowledge of the course of such vessel, involving, as it does, changes in her location, is essential to the proper ascertainment of her position, as required by the rule.

"The Position of Which Is Not Ascertained."

Many cases have been before the courts of England and the United States where, after collision, it has been claimed that the position of the approaching vessel had been ascertained within the requirement of this rule, through an approximation of her location formed from hearing a fog-signal. That the courts will not accept any such "approximation" as the "ascertainment" required by the rule is shown from the following excerpts from the decisions:

> "There is no such certainty of the exact position of a horn blown in a fog as will justify a steamer in speculating upon the probability of avoiding it by a change of the helm, with-

No. 39. The Secretary will please read it as it now stands, after alteration.'
"The amendment is as follows:
"Article 13. Every ship, whether a sailing ship or a steam-ship, shall in a fog, mist, or falling snow go at a moderate speed; and a steam-vessel hearing, apparently, before her beam, the fog-signal of a vessel the position of which is not ascertained, shall, so far as the circumstances of the case admit, stop her engines, and then proceed with caution until all danger of collision is over."
"The question upon the addition to Article 13 was put to the conference and carried." p. 461.

out taking the additional precaution of stopping until its location is definitely ascertained."

*The City of New York,* 147 U. S. 72, 84.

See also, *The Martello,* 153 U. S. 64; *The Hypodame,* 6 Wall. 216; *The Sea Gull,* 23 Wall. 165; *The Kirby Hall,* 8 P. D. 71; *The Ceto,* 6 Asp. M.C. (N.S.) 479.

In the case of *The Celtic Monarch,* 175 Fed. 1006, it was held unlawful to assume that an approaching steamer, which cannot be seen because of prevailing fog, is on any particular course, and to continue ahead without reducing speed.

Similarly, it was said in *The Britannia,* 10 Asp. M.C. (N.S.) 65, 68:

"Again, it is not correct to say that a whistle having been heard can be located so as to be certain it is at a precise bearing on the bow. Case after case in this court shows that it is not so."

In the case of *The Bernard Hall,* 9 Asp. M.C. (N.S.) 300, the steamer *Holyrood,* not herself in a fog, heard a fog-signal apparently forward of her beam from a fog bank lying on her port bow. It was claimed that the position of the vessel giving the signal was ascertained under the rules. The court said at p. 301:

"It is said in this case that there was a certain ascertainment. There was this. The vessel was not on the starboard side, and was not right ahead, but was in a bank of fog on the port bow, and that fog was a certain distance. It cannot be disputed there was that amount of ascertainment. But the Elder Brethren point out that there would be extreme difficulty in knowing how far off the vessel would be in a fog, and therefore they do not think there was any such ascertainment as to justify the *Holyrood* in not complying with the clear terms of art. 16, by stopping her engines when she first heard the whistle of the *Bernard Hall,* . . ."

From these decisions it is clear that ascertainment of the position of the approaching vessel within the meaning of this rule signifies that she has either been seen, or her position so accurately determined by repeated hearing of her signals, that there is no possibility of error. The decisions further show that pending such accurate ascertainment, the engines are to be stopped and the vessel navigated with caution until all danger of collision is over.

The rule does not require a vessel to stop and never move again, nor, *per contra,* is it a compliance with the rule that after stopping the engines they be immediately started ahead again. The engines must remain stopped until by hearing repeated signals from the other vessel the position of such vessel is so ascertained that by cautiously feeling her way as required by the rule, all danger of collision will be averted.

It was said by the United States Supreme Court in *The Umbria,* 166 U. S. 404, at p. 409:

> "As was said by Sir Robert Phillimore, in the case of *The Kirby Hall,* 8 P. D. 71: 'We wish to state with as much emphasis as possible, that those in charge of a ship, in such a dense fog as was described in this case, should never conjecture anything when they hear a whistle in such close proximity, as was the case here, whether the sound appears to them to come from a vessel approaching them or not.' Of course there is a point depending upon the number, distinctness and apparent position of the approaching signals, beyond which precautions are unnecessary and the master has the right to assume that he has shaken off the other vessel, but it is entirely clear that that point had not been reached in this case, and that the immediate cause of the collision was the order to go ahead at full speed before the course and position of the *Iberia* had been definitely ascertained."

In the more recent case of *The Tillicum,* 230 Fed. 415, the court said at p. 416:

> " . . . when the *Rosalie* first heard a whistle ahead, her engine was stopped for about a minute, during which time she drifted, and, hearing no response to the whistle she gave, was started forward; but her engine was almost immediately reversed—she having heard another whistle, followed by a danger signal from the *Tillicum.* In the dense fog then prevailing, the *Rosalie,* in our opinion, cannot be

regarded as having been navigated with caution in being started ahead so quickly without ascertaining anything in regard to the location of the vessel whose whistle she had heard, and therefore violated the express provision of the statute above quoted, and was clearly in fault. . . . "

In England the same rule is enforced:

"It [Rule 16] does not say that a vessel is to stop and never move again in the fog. On the contrary all she has to do is to stop her engines and then navigate with caution, and she is to do that because she hears forward of her beam a fog-signal of a vessel, the position of which is not ascertained. *She is to keep them stopped until she can, by hearing further signals from the other vessel, ascertain the position of that other vessel.* The rule does not say that in terms, but that appears to me to be the meaning."

*The Rondane,* 9 Asp. M.C. (N.S.) 106.

See also, *The Aras,* 10 Asp. M.C. (N.S.) 358; *The Britannia,* 10 Asp. M.C. (N.S.) 65.

**"So Far as the Circumstances of the Case Admit."**

The words, "so far as the circumstances of the case admit," are inserted to meet exceptional cases where the stopping of the engines would place the vessel in danger from some peril other than the approaching vessel, as, for instance, a vessel in an exceptionally strong current in the vicinity of dangerous shoals or rocks where she might be carried ashore if her engines were stopped.

Such cases are, however, rare, and it would have to be very clearly proved before a court that immediate danger existed before a failure to stop the engines would be excused.

That another vessel is following astern will not excuse a failure to stop the engines unless it can be clearly shown that to have done so would have created imminent danger of collision with the vessel following.

**"And Then Navigate With Caution Until All Danger of Collision is Over."**

"And then," namely, after the engines are stopped, the vessel must "navigate with caution." It is clear that the intent of this provision is to require something more than ordinary care, something more than the maintenance of a good lookout and a moderate speed, as prescribed in the first paragraph of Rule 16. It requires the highest degree of vigilance and caution in the navigation of the vessel. If headway is lost, and the position of the other vessel has not been ascertained, the two-blast "stopped" signal must be sounded; or, if it is unsafe to have the vessel falling off her course, the engines may be given a turn ahead from time to time just sufficient to keep her on her course, and the regulation single blast sounded.

There is no specified direction in Rule 16 not to alter the course in a fog. It is entirely a question of good seamanship as required by Article 29, or of cautious navigation, as required by the closing provision of Article 16. *Changing Course in Fog.*

As the rules do not provide any signals to indicate changes of course where vessels are not in sight of each other, as in a fog, etc., any change in course at least has this disadvantage and sometimes leads to trouble, as shown by the decisions:

"The steamship, however, had no right to speculate upon this contingency. Hearing the horn as she did, and being thus apprised of the bearing and course of the approaching vessel, being, as she must necessarily have been, in doubt as to her distance from the steamship, it was the duty of the latter at once to stop, until, by repeated blasts of the horn, she could assure herself of the exact bearing, speed, and course of the approaching vessel. . . . ' . . . There is no such certainty of the exact position of a horn blown in a fog as will justify a steamer in speculating upon the probability of avoiding it by a change of the helm, without taking the additional precaution of stopping until its location is definitely ascertained. *The Hypodame,* 6 Wall. 216; *The Sea Gull,* 23 Wall. 165, 177; *The Kirby Hall,* 8 P. D. 71; *The Ceto,* 6 Asp. Mar. Law. Cas. 479; S. C. 14 App. Cas. 670.' "

*The Martello,* 153 U. S. 64, 71.

"Under such circumstances, and in view of the fact that the exact position and course of the *Umbria* could not be determined, we think it would have been more prudent on the part of the *Iberia* not to have changed her course until the position and course of the approaching steamer had been definitely ascertained, although we should be reluctant to hold that such change of course was a fault on her part, which should condemn her in a moiety of the damages. There are undoubtedly authorities and some expressions of this court to the effect that a change of the helm, in ignorance of the exact position and course of an approaching vessel, is a fault, although we have never held that it would be a fault in every case presenting these conditions. *The Sea Gull,* 23 Wall. 165, 175, 177; *The City of New York,* 147 U. S. 72, 85; *The James Watt,* 2 W. Rob. 270; *The Alberta,* 23 Fed. Rep. 807, 811; *The Bougainville,* L.R. 5 P. C. 316; *The Franconia,* 4 Ben. 181,185; *The Shakespeare,* 4 Ben. 128; *The Lorne,* 2 Stu. Vice Adm. 177; *Western Metropolis,* 2 Ben. 399, 402; *The Hammonia,* 4 Ben. 515, 522; *The Northern Indiana,* 3 Blatch. 92, 110; *The North Star,* 43 Fed. Rep. 807, S.C. 22 U. S. App. 242, 252; *The Fountain City,* 22 U. S. App. 301; *The Arthur Orr,* 69 Fed. Rep. 350; *The Resolution,* 6 Asp. Mar. Cas. 363.

"We think, however, that a more reasonable position in this connection was taken by the House of Lords in the case of *The Vindomora,* (1891) App. Cas. 1, in which it was held that there was no rigid rule that where two steamships were approaching each other in a fog so as to involve risk of collision, neither ship ought to alter her helm until the signals of the other gave clear indication of her direction; and that each case must depend upon its own circumstances, which might afford reasonable ground for believing what the direction must be."

*The Umbria,* 166 U. S. 404, 410, 411.

In the case of *The Counsellor* [1913], P.D. 70, 72, 73, the steamer *Camdale,* which had been carefully navigated up to the time she heard the whistle of *The Counsellor* in the fog, immediately ported her helm and stopped her engines. The court said at page 73, 74:

"He said: '9.33, heard whistle ahead, ported helm and stopped engines.' It struck me at once that that is not obedience to the rule. The rule says that when a vessel in a fog hears the whistle of another vessel forward of her beam she shall stop her engines at once and then proceed to navigate with caution. How can you navigate with caution if, before doing anything at all to ascertain where the other vessel is whose whistling is heard, you port your helm? . . .

"In my opinion both vessels are to blame; one vessel for going too fast in fog, and the other for not shewing proper seamanlike regard to the rule which says that, hearing another vessel's whistle, you must proceed with caution. In my opinion there was no caution shewn at all by the *Camdale*. She took upon herself to port her helm without any inquiry and without waiting to hear another blast and to ascertain where the other vessel was, and in my opinion that porting contributed to the collision."

In the case of *The Resolution,* 6 Asp. M.C. (N.S.) 363, altering of the helm was condemned as acting in the dark, and both vessels were held in fault on that ground.

In the case of *The Vindomora,* 6 Asp. M.C. (N.S.) 569, the House of Lords held substantially that until there is sufficient evidence to indicate the position of the other vessel, namely, until her position is "ascertained," as that term has been hereinbefore defined, neither vessel is justified in altering her course.

It will be observed from the foregoing decisions that any change of course based upon a guess as to the direction, distance, or course of the approaching vessel is perilous. If collision ensue, the vessel so changing her course will have the burden of proving that her act did not contribute to the collision.

Vessels sounding the signals prescribed by Article 15, subdiv. (e) should not alter their course in a fog, as other vessels should give them as wide a berth as possible.

## STEERING AND SAILING RULES
## PRELIMINARY

| *International Rules* | *Inland Rules* |
|---|---|
| Risk of collision can, when circumstances permit, be ascertained by carefully watching the compass bearing of an approaching vessel. If the bearing does not appreciably change, such risk should be deemed to exist. | Same as International Rules. |

In introducing this preliminary article, the British delegate to the International Conference (Mr. Hall) said:

"  .  .  . The members of the Conference will have observed that in the steering rules, of which there are a considerable number, the words 'risk of collision' is the motive point; these rules only applying when 'risk of collision' exists. Although we know it is impossible to frame a definition which will include every case in which there is 'risk of collision,' yet we have thought, upon advice which has been given to us from a very powerful committee which met to discuss this point, that it would be most desirable, if we could, to do something or to pass something which would call the attention of sailors to the all-important point of watching the bearings of vessels, and of pointing out, especially at night, the only accurate way in which a seaman can judge of the actions of another vessel of which he only has a light in sight. The only really accurate way is by watching carefully the compass-bearings of that vessel; therefore, it is that we propose to put in a preliminary paragraph, which will not be an article under the rules of the road, but which will be simply a paragraph for the guidance of seamen, especially in following the subsequent steering and sailing rules, in which the words 'risk of collision' exist.

"I want to make it clear that we do not endeavor to give an exhaustive definition of the words 'risk of collision,' because, as has been pointed out by eminent judges, it is impossible to do anything of the kind, as it must depend upon the circumstances in each particular case. But we apprehend that certainly we may, at any rate, be doing something to lessen the large number of collisions which undoubtedly do occur, if we can impress upon the minds of officers the all-important point of watching the compass bearings of vessels which they see at night, or by day. . . .

"I think there will be a consensus of opinion amongst nautical men upon this fact, that watching the compass-bearings is the best method by which you can tell what the action of another vessel is. If we can once instill this into the minds of officers in charge of vessels, then I think we should be taking a very long step towards lessening, at any rate, the very great dangers which exist at the present time from risk of collision."

*Prot. of Proc.,* pp. 99–100.

"I will point out that we are not attempting such an absurd labor as to define the words 'risk of collision.' That, of course, we are all agreed it is absolutely impossible to do. But we wish very much, and I will say that this opinion is strongly entertained by all of our sailors, and, I believe, by every skilled sailor of the seas, that it is a very important thing for a sailor, when he is in charge of a vessel and sees another vessel anywhere near him and wants to know what that vessel is going to do, to take the compass-bearing of that vessel. We wish to call the attention of sailors to the fact that the best thing for them to do is to take the compass-bearing so as to be able to ascertain what the vessel is doing. We think that this caution, for that is what it is, should be put at the commencement of the steering and sailing rules. . . . *It is not a rule. It is only a suggestion to mariners.*"

*Prot. of Proc.,* pp. 509–510.

The same thought was expressed by the court in the case of *Wilder's S. S. Co. et al. v. Low et al.,* 112 Fed. 161, at p. 166, in the following words:

". . . the preliminary note is not a rule of navigation, but merely a suggestion of one method of determining a risk of collision from a particular compass bearing of an approaching vessel. It does not determine or assume to suggest that all other compass bearings involve no risk of collision, nor does it suggest the only method of determining a risk of collision under the conditions mentioned. Manifestly, vessels approaching each other at about the same time on crossing courses, with compass bearings gradually changing, involve the risk of collision in the highest degree. It is only when the bearings alter quickly, and the vessels are a considerable distance apart, that there is no risk of collision."

**"Risk of Collision"**

The following articles, 17 to 24, inclusive, all deal with the duties of vessels "approaching one another so as to involve risk of collision," in which situations the articles mentioned become operative.

As pointed out in the above quoted comments of the British delegate, it is not possible to give an exhaustive definition of "risk of collision" which will cover all cases. It can be said, however, that the risk of collision, as used in these articles, is always involved when two vessels are approaching in a situation where, if both maintain their course and speed, the slightest possibility of collision between them exists. To involve risk of collision, it is not necessary that collision be inevitable or even probable, nor even that there be danger of collision. All that is necessary to bring these rules into operation is the possibility of collision.

In situations where any doubt exists as to whether there is risk of collision, these articles become operative. Any slight change of course by the giving-way vessel, even though not clearly necessary and by way of caution merely, is sufficient to show that the risk of collision existed. The United States Supreme Court so held in *The Carroll*, 8 Wall. 302; where the court said at p. 305:

> "The fact that the vessels did collide explodes the theory that there was no risk of collision, and besides, why did the mate port his helm if in his judgment there was no risk of it? He says this was done as soon as he saw the schooner. If so, he believed at the time the relations of the vessels to each other were such that they might collide, *and the possibility of it* [colliding] is all that is required to charge the steamer, unless she can establish that she was without fault."

See also, *The Ashton*, 10 Asp. M.C. (N.S.) 88.

With collision resulting, it will manifestly be extremely difficult to prove that risk of collision did not exist.

## ARTICLE XVII
## SAILING VESSELS

*International Rules*

*Article 17.* When two sailing vessels are approaching one another, so as to involve risk of collision, one of them shall keep out of the way of the other, as follows, namely:

(a) A vessel which is running free shall keep out of the way of a vessel which is close-hauled.

(b) A vessel which is close-hauled on the port tack shall keep out of the way of a vessel which is close-hauled on the starboard tack.

(c) When both are running free, with the wind on different sides, the vessel which has the wind on the port side shall keep out of the way of the other.

(d) When both are running free, with the wind on the same side, the vessel which is to the windward shall keep out of the way of the vessel which is to the leeward.

(e) A vessel which has the wind aft shall keep out of the way of the other vessel.

*Inland Rules*

*Article 17.* Identical with International Rules.

This article prescribes a sailing rule for every possible situation in which two sailing vessels (approaching so as to involve risk of collision) may find themselves. In all of them one of the two vessels is to keep out of the way of the other; the other vessel, under Article 21, is required to hold her course and speed.

As the principles of law in relation to burdened and privileged vessels are identical in respect to all vessels (sail or steam) in "giving way" and "holding on" positions, reference is made to Articles 21, 22 and 23, under which are discussed the duties of each.

It will, however, be noted that as between sailing vessels, the relation of "burdened" and "privileged" vessel is determined, not by the position of the vessels in respect to each other (as with steamers), but by the course of **Apparent Wind** the vessels in respect to the prevailing wind.  The direc- **—True Wind.** tion of the wind being the controlling factor in determining which vessel is "burdened" and which is "privileged," it is essential that the true direction of the wind be positively known.  In this connection it should be borne in mind that on a moving vessel the apparent is not always the true direction of the wind, and that it is the latter which fixes the respective obligations of the vessels.

It will also be noted that the relation of "burdened" and "privileged" vessel is not confined as between sailing vessels to a time when they are on crossing courses, but is also applicable to a time when they are meeting end on, or nearly so.

This rule is not necessarily operative as soon as two sailing vessels are in sight of each other, but begins at the moment the vessels approach each other so as to involve risk of collision.  *The Mary Buhne*, 95 Fed. 1002.

A vessel hove to and making both headway and leeway is deemed close-hauled within the meaning of the rule. *The Ada A. Kennedy*, 33 Fed. 623.

A ship close-hauled and sailing within 6½ points of the wind is not running free and is the privileged vessel where the crossing vessel is admittedly running free.  *The Queen Elizabeth*, 100 Fed. 874.

A vessel has the "wind aft" when it is not more than 2½ points from directly aft.  *The Gov. Ames*, 187 Fed. 40.

## ARTICLE XVIII

## STEAM VESSELS

*International Rules*

*Article 18.* When two steam-vessels are meeting end on, or nearly end on, so as to involve risk of collision, each shall alter her course to starboard, so that each may pass on the port side of the other.

This article only applies to cases where vessels are meeting end on, or nearly end on, in such a manner as to involve risk of collision, and does not apply to two vessels which must, if both keep on the respective courses, pass clear of each other.

The only cases to which it does apply are when each of the two vessels is end on, or nearly end on, to the other; in other words, to cases in which, by day, each vessel sees the masts of the other in a line, or nearly in a line, with her own; and by night, to cases in which each vessel is in such a position as to see both the side-lights of the other.

It does not apply by day to cases in which a vessel sees another ahead crossing her own course; or by night, to cases where the red light of one vessel is opposed to the red light of the other,

*Inland Rules*

*Article 18.* Rule 1. When steam-vessels are approaching each other head and head, that is, end on, or nearly so, it shall be the duty of each to pass on the port side of the other; and either vessel shall give, as a signal of her intention, one short and distinct blast of her whistle, which the other vessel shall answer promptly by a similar blast of her whistle, and thereupon such vessels shall pass on the port side of each other. But if the courses of such vessels are so far on the starboard of each other as not to be considered as meeting head and head, either vessel shall immediately give two short and distinct blasts of her whistle, which the other vessel shall answer promptly by two similar blasts of her whistle, and they shall pass on the starboard side of each other.

The foregoing only applies to cases where vessels are meeting end on or nearly end on, in such a manner as to involve risk of collision; in other words, to cases in which, by day, each vessel sees the masts of the other in a line, or nearly in

or where the green light of one vessel is opposed to the green light of the other, or where a red light without a green light, or a green light without a red light, is seen ahead, or where both green and red lights are seen anywhere but ahead.

a line, with her own, and by night to cases in which each vessel is in such a position as to see both the side-lights of the other.

It does not apply by day to cases in which a vessel sees another ahead crossing her own course, or by night to cases where the red light of one vessel is opposed to the red light of the other, or where the green light of one vessel is opposed to the green light of the other, or where a red light without a green light or a green light without a red light, is seen ahead, or where both green and red lights are seen anywhere but ahead.

Identical with Pilot Rule IV.

This article of the International Rules directs the manner of passing of steamers meeting end on, or nearly end on, so as to involve risk of collision, whilst the Inland Rules not only prescribe the manner of passing of such meeting steamers but also include the sound signals to be exchanged in this and several other designated situations.

To permit of a closer comparison of the requirements of the International and Inland Rules reference will be made under the present article only to the passing rule. All sound signals indicating a change of helm or course, for vessels in sight of each other, will be considered under Article 28.

**The Passing Rule.** Manifestly this rule is applicable only to steamers in sight of each other. Although expressed somewhat differently, the requirements of the International and Inland Rules are the same for steamers meeting on opposite courses.

The effort to make the rule so plain that it could not be misunderstood has resulted in perhaps undue length, and some repetition. Its requirements are, however, very simple. When two steamers are approaching on opposite courses, end on, or nearly so, and in such a situation that if both maintain their courses they may collide, each vessel shall change her course to starboard, so that the passing shall be port to port.

The rule does not mean, as some navigators seem to think, that steamers proceeding in opposite directions must in all cases pass port to port. On the contrary, the rule is applicable only when steamers are meeting head to head, or nearly so; or, as is explained in the paragraphs following, when in the daytime each vessel sees the masts of the other in a line, or nearly in a line, with her own; or at night when each vessel is in a position to see both the side lights of the other.

If steamers are meeting on opposite courses so far on the starboard of each other as not to come within the above definition of a meeting end on, or nearly so, as is stated in more detail in the Inland Rules, they are to pass starboard to starboard.

The manner of passing is not in any sense optional, nor does the rule permit of any deviation from its express requirements. On the contrary, its terms are positive and mandatory.

*Manner of Passing Not Optional. Rule Mandatory.*

The positions of the steamers in relation to each other when meeting is the determining factor as to how they must pass, and such passing must be conducted in accordance with the requirements of the rule.

The court in *The Transfer No. 10,* 137 Fed. 666, 667, said:

> "The evidence satisfies me in this case that when these two vessels saw each other they were end on, or nearly so. The rule does not permit two vessels to pass starboard to starboard if they are not exactly end on; the rule is 'end on, or nearly so.' The general rule is to pass to the right. That is the

foundation of all the rules of the road. It is only in exceptional cases where you pass to the left. The cases where you are entitled to pass starboard to starboard are when two vessels are approaching each other, on lines each of which is so far to starboard of the other as to justify the exception to the general rule. I think in this case the vessels were about end on, and in any event the *Mary J.* was not on a course sufficiently to the left of the other's course to justify her in sounding two whistles and endeavoring to pass starboard to starboard. But whether she was or not, she, in fact, sounded one whistle, and, if the transports believed that it would be dangerous to acquiesce in that whistle, they should have sounded alarms. That is the rule. If they were not going to acquiesce in her course, they should have sounded alarms, . . ."

"He [the officer on watch] says: '. . . she was about a point on our starboard bow. I blew two blasts and starboarded for her.' Why did he do that? It was contrary to art. 18 . . . Now, I think that the *Aberdonian* was to blame, first of all for starboarding instead of porting under art. 18."

*The Aberdonian* (Admiralty), 11 Asp. M.C. (N.S.) 393, 394.

**Both Vessels Must Act Seasonably. Failure of One Will Not Excuse the Other.**

Neither vessel is justified in relying upon the other to do all that is necessary to be done. Both vessels are required to act seasonably and to adopt the required precaution and neither will be excused upon the ground that she expected the other to act.

"Steamships meeting end on, or nearly end on, should seasonably adopt the required precaution; and neither can be excused from responsibility, in case of omission, merely upon the ground that it was the duty of the other to have adopted the corresponding precaution at the same time, if it appears that the party setting up that excuse enjoyed equal facility to obey the requirement with the other party, and might have prevented the disaster. Imperative obligation is imposed upon each to comply with the rule of navigation; nor will the neglect of one excuse the other in a case where each might have prevented the disaster, as the law requires both to adopt every necessary precaution, if practicable, to prevent the collision, and will not tolerate any attempt of either, in such an emergency, to apportion the required precaution to avoid the impending danger, in case where both or either might secure perfect safety to both ships and all intrusted with their control and management."

*The America,* 92 U.S. 432, 433.

Prompt<br>
Interchange of<br>
Passing Signals<br>
Required.

The International Rules require the passing to be made as prescribed and helm signals to be given to indicate any change made in the vessel's course.

The Inland Rules require the passing to be made as prescribed and signals to be given indicating the side on which the passing is to be made.

Under the Pilot Rules the signal signifies the intention to change the course of the vessel, as indicated.

Under both rules such signals must be given promptly. (See Article 28.)

Vessels proceeding in opposite directions, on courses which, without change, will pass clear of each other without risk of collision, do not come within the rule, except that when in inland waters Pilot Rule III prescribes that such signals shall be given and answered by steamers when passing or meeting at a distance within half a mile of each other. (See, however, p. 213.)

Danger at<br>
Night—Steam-<br>
ers Approaching<br>
on a Fine<br>
Angle—Diffi-<br>
culty in Dis-<br>
tinguishing<br>
Passing and<br>
Crossing<br>
Vessels.

As the side lights, even in conjunction with the mast-head lights, do not indicate with sufficient exactness the precise course of a steamer,* it is not always readily apparent, when steamers are approaching on a fine angle at night, whether they are crossing or meeting. The difficulty lies in the possibility that they may be approaching in such a situation that the green light only may be open to one vessel, while both colored lights of the latter may be open to the other.

Such a situation is fraught with serious danger, for a steamer, seeing only the green light of the other vessel

---

* The use of range lights permitted by the rules and referred to on pp. 19–20 would go far to relieving this difficulty.

nearly ahead, may hold her course and speed on the assumption that they are crossing vessels, or, as passing vessels, may alter her course to port, while the steamer which sees both lights, nearly ahead, may alter her course to starboard on the assumption that they are passing vessels. This was pointed out at the International Conference:

> "You know that there are situations in which vessels may be in doubt whether they are crossing vessels or whether they are meeting nearly end on. The distance gradually widens, of course, where both lights are seen. Within this arc a vessel may find herself meeting another vessel when it can not be known whether the other vessel is seeing both of her lights or not. A vessel sees, a little on her starboard bow, the green light of another vessel, and the green light only a very few points—or only half a point, more or less, perhaps—on her starboard bow. She takes this vessel to be a vessel which does not see both of her lights, and therefore, in order to pass quite clear of her, she starboards a little. The other vessel, finding herself within this arc, sees both of the lights of the approaching vessel and thinks that the vessel is seeing both of her lights also, and that they are meeting vessels, and she ports her helm. This is a very frequent cause of collision, as is known to every one here."
>
> *Prot. of Proc.,* p. 562.

Also,

> "In this diagram you will find there are two ships, marked A and B, which are both steamers. . . . A sees only B's green side light and holds her course; B sees both side lights of A and steers to starboard. In this way imminent risk of collision is brought on. . . . B sees the red and green light of A nearly ahead, . . . and therefore she has to turn to starboard. But A sees the green light of B on her starboard bow nearly a point and a half, and under the provisions of Article 15 [now Art. 21] she is to keep her course. [Or if a passing and not a crossing steamer she has to turn to port.] I think you will remember that in cases of collisions the case is not infrequent where the ship says: 'I proceeded, keeping my course, and saw the green light on my starboard bow; all at once I saw that the ship was turning across my bow and I saw both lights.' That is the case which happens very often, and I believe that a part of the collisions

which have been brought about may be explained in this way."

*Prot. of Proc.,* pp. 1163, 1164.

In all such cases extraordinary care should be exercised by both vessels. It is most important that each should know not only what lights the approaching vessel is showing, but also what lights she can see. The vessel having the other on her starboard bow, if nearly end on, should be the first to act, and should port promptly and immediately signal that she is doing so, and this whether she sees both side lights or the green light only of the other steamer. Action should not be unduly delayed as the other vessel may be in doubt and may otherwise starboard to a green light as a meeting steamer (under Art. 18), or hold her course and speed as the holding-on vessel under the crossing rule (Art. 21). The duty of the vessel having the other on her starboard bow is the same under both conditions; if meeting, she should pass port to port; if crossing, her obligation is to keep out of the way and not cross ahead of the holding-on vessel.

For vessels meeting in narrow channels end on or nearly end on, see Article 25.

## ARTICLE XIX

### TWO STEAM VESSELS CROSSING

| *International Rules* | *Inland Rules* |
|---|---|
| *Article 19.* When two steam-vessels are crossing, so as to involve risk of collision, the vessel which has the other on her own starboard side shall keep out of the way of the other. | *Article 19.* Identical with International Rules. |

This article does not apply except where two steamers are crossing "so as to involve risk of collision."

**Starboard Hand Rule.** Mention has already been made under Article 18 of certain situations in which at night steamers approaching on a fine angle may find it difficult to determine whether they are "meeting" under Article 18, or "crossing" under Article 19. In such cases, misunderstandings should be avoided by the steamer which would be the giving-way vessel, if the situation were a crossing one, promptly indicating by signal her intended course before the risk of collision becomes imminent. The steamer which would be the "holding-on" vessel, if the situation proved a crossing one, cannot, under the International Rules, properly give any signal (except the detonating signal under Art. 12), as under Article 21 she is required to hold her course and speed, for which no signal is provided.

Where steamers are crossing, and because of their respective positions it is deemed desirable, as a matter of precaution by the "giving-way" steamer, that she alter her course, such action will be considered by the courts as sufficient to show that the risk of collision existed, and to impose upon the "giving-way" vessel the obligation of keeping clear. *The Carroll,* 8 Wall. 302, 305; *The Ashton,* 10 Asp. M.C. (N.S.) 88.

Navigation in narrow and tortuous channels and winding rivers is usually controlled by the narrow channel rule (Article 25), but in some instances Article 19 will also apply.

When, in such waters, steamers are crossing so as to involve risk of collision, Article 19 will govern, and the burdened or giving-way steamer must keep out of the way of the other. *The Leverington,* 6 Asp. M.C. (N.S.) 7; *The Pekin,* 8 Asp. M.C. (N.S.) 367.

As to whether steamers navigating narrow and tortuous channels are "crossing steamers" so as to involve the risk of collision, must, however, be determined by their presumable courses, having regard to the sinuosities of the channel. Of such situations, the United States Supreme Court said in the case of *The Victory & The Plymothian,* 168 U.S. 410, at p. 418:

> "Indeed the rule applicable when two vessels 'are crossing so as to involve risk of collision,' that 'the vessel which has the other on her own starboard side shall keep out of the way,' is ordinarily inapplicable to vessels coming around bends in channels, which may at times bring one vessel on the starboard of the other. It has often been held as a general rule of navigation that vessels approaching each other in narrow channels, or where their courses diverge as much as one and one-half or two points, are bound to keep to port and pass to the right, whatever the occasional effect of the sinuosities of the channel . . . "

The court quoted with approval the following from *The Pekin* [1897], App. Cas. 532, at p. 536:

> "The crossing referred to in article 22 [now Art. 19] is 'crossing so as to involve the risk of collision,' and it is obvious that, while two vessels in certain positions and at certain distances in regard to each other in the open sea may be crossing so as to involve risk of collision, it would be completely mistaken to take the same view of two vessels in the same positions and distances in the reaches of a winding river. The reason, of course, is that the vessels must follow, and must be known to intend to follow, the curves of the river bank, but vessels may no doubt be crossing vessels within article 22 [now Art. 19] in a river. It depends on their pre-

*Crossing Rule —Narrow Channels.*

*Presumable Course.*

sumable courses. If at any time two vessels, not end on, are seen, keeping the courses to be expected with regard to them respectively, to be likely to arrive at the same point at or nearly at the same moment, they are vessels crossing so as to involve risk of collision; but they are not so crossing if the course which is reasonably to be attributed to either vessel would keep her clear of the other. The question, therefore, always turns on the reasonable inference to be drawn as to a vessel's future course from her position at a particular moment, and this greatly depends on the nature of the locality where she is at that moment."

Both Article 19 (crossing rule) and Article 25 (narrow channel rule) may be operative at the entrances to narrow channels.

**Entering and Leaving Narrow Channels.** Steamers entering or leaving narrow channels must, when it is safe and practicable, keep to that side of the fairway, or mid channel, which lies on the starboard side of such vessel, as required by Article 25. Where two steamers are crossing at such entrance so as to involve risk of collision, the vessel having the other on her own starboard side must keep out of the way of the other, as required by Article 19.

Article 19 also applies in a narrow channel at the junction of two narrow channels. *The Leverington* (Ct. of App.), 6 Asp. M.C. (N.S.) 7.

The principle of presumable courses applicable in narrow channels has no application in open waters. The usual track of steamers in such waters, or in rounding points, buoys, lightships, etc., will not be accepted as any excuse for a failure to observe the "crossing rules" as covered by Articles 19, 21, 22 and 23. *The Franconia* (Ct. of App.), 3 Asp. M.C. (N.S.) 295; *The Ashton*, 10 Asp. M.C. (N.S.) 88; *The Kingston*, 173 Fed. 992.

When two vessels are approaching and have reached a position to make the crossing rules operative, no subsequent changes in their position will alter their relative status of "holding-on" vessel and "giving-way" vessel.

See Articles 22 and 23, under which the duty of the burdened vessel is discussed.

## ARTICLE XX
## STEAM VESSEL SHALL KEEP OUT OF THE WAY OF SAILING VESSEL

*International Rules*

*Article 20.* When a steam-vessel and a sailing-vessel are proceeding in such directions as to involve risk of collision, the steam-vessel shall keep out of the way of the sailing-vessel.

*Inland Rules*

Identical with International Rules.
Identical with **Rule VIII** of Pilot Rules.

Under the Preliminary Definitions,

"Every steam vessel which is under sail and not under steam is to be considered a sailing-vessel, and every vessel under steam, whether under sail or not, is to be considered a steam-vessel.

"The words 'steam-vessel' shall include any vessel propelled by machinery."

Signals indicating a steam vessel proceeding under sail only are provided for by Article 14, viz.:

"A steam-vessel proceeding under sail only but having her funnel up, shall carry in day-time, forward, where it can best be seen, one black ball or shape two feet in diameter."

Article 20 is operative in all situations except when the sailing vessel is an overtaking vessel. In such cases, the sailing vessel must, under Article 24, keep out of the way.

Although the obligation of the steamer only is prescribed by this article (the duty of the sailing vessel being covered under Art. 21), a short reference may be made to the duty of the sailing vessel.

An unfortunate and erroneous impression seems to exist amongst many navigators that sailing vessels are a preferred class and are accorded by the rules of the road special privileges. That is not so. No vessels are ac- **Duty of Sailing Vessel.**

corded special privileges by the rules.   All are equal in the eyes of the law, and each is held to a strict accountability for the performance of the duty or duties imposed upon her by the rules.

Because of the inability of a sailing vessel to stop her headway, reverse, or maneuver with the same facility as a steamer, the rules (which have been framed for practical navigation) do not require of her the impossible, but, nevertheless, have prescribed for her navigation certain positive obligations and duties with which she can comply.   A failure on the part of the sailing vessel to observe these requirements is at her peril, for it will be visited with the same consequences and penalties as the failure of a steamer to obey the rules provided for her navigation.   (See Art. 21.)

Under the conditions described in Article 20, the steamer must keep out of the way of the sailing vessel and the sailing vessel must, under Article 21, hold her course and speed.

The United States Supreme Court has said in respect to the obligations of each:

> "One of these rules requires the steamer to keep out of the way of the sailing vessel; but to enable her to do this effectively, the law imposes the corresponding obligation on the sailing vessel to keep her course.   If, therefore, the steamer adopts proper measures of precaution to avoid the collision, which would have been effective if the schooner had not changed her course, she is not chargeable for the consequences of the collision."
>
> *The Potomac,* 8 Wall. 590, 592.

> "The rule is for a sailing-vessel meeting a steamer to keep her course, while the steamer takes the necessary measures to avoid collision.   In *Crockett v. Newton* we said that 'though this rule should not be observed when circumstances are such that it is apparent its observance must occasion a collision, while a departure from it will prevent one, yet it must be a strong case which puts the sailing-vessel in the wrong for obeying the rule,' 18 How. 581, 583; and in *New York & Liverpool U. S. Mail Steamship Co. v. Rumball,* that

'under the rule that a steamer must keep out of the way, she must of necessity determine for herself and upon her own responsibility, independently of the sailing-vessel, whether it is safer to go to the right or left or to stop; and in order that she may not be deprived of the means of determining the matter wisely, and that she may not be defeated or baffled in the attempt to perform her duty in the emergency, it is required, in the admiralty jurisprudence of the United States, that the sailing-vessel shall keep her course, and allow the steamer to pass either on the right or left, or to adopt such measures of precaution as she may deem best suited to enable her to perform her duty and fulfil the requirement of the law to keep out of the way.' "

*The Adriatic,* 107 U. S. 512, 518.

" 'It is the duty of a steamer to keep out of the way of a sailing vessel when they are approaching in such directions as to involve a risk of collision. The correlative obligation rests upon the sailing vessel to keep her course [under new rules also her speed] and the steamer may be managed upon the assumption that she will do so.' (*The Free State,* 91 U. S. 200.)"

*The Britannia,* 153 U. S. 130.

The obligation upon the steamer to keep out of the way of the way of the sailing vessel is absolute. Failure to do so will not be excused unless the steps taken were amply sufficient to avert even the danger of collision, and unless such efforts were made unsuccessful solely by an improper change of course by the sailing vessel, or by inevitable accident.

**Duty of Steamer to Keep Out of the Way of Sailing Vessel.**

"These rules were established in the interest of commerce— for the protection of life and property, and must be observed. They require, where a steamship and sailing vessel are approaching from opposite directions, or on intersecting lines, that the steamship, from the moment the sailing vessel is seen, shall watch with the highest diligence her course and movements, so as to be able to adopt such timely measures of precaution as will necessarily prevent the two boats coming in contact. This the *Carroll,* on this occasion, failed to do. Porting the helm a point, when the light of the schooner was first observed, and then waiting until the collision was imminent before doing anything further, does not satisfy the requirements of the law. The safe-guards against danger, in order to be effectual, must be season-ably employed, and in this case they were not used until the danger was threatening."

*The Carroll,* 8 Wall. 302, 306.

"Meeting a sailing vessel proceeding in such a direction as to involve risk, it was her [the steamer's] duty to keep out of the way, and nothing but inevitable accident, or the conduct and movements of the ship can repel the presumption that she was negligent, arising from the fact of collision. But this duty of the steamer implies a correlative obligation of the ship to keep her course, and do nothing to mislead."

*The Scotia,* 14 Wall. 170, 181.

For further discussion of the duty of the steamer, see Articles 22 and 23.

## ARTICLE XXI
## COURSE AND SPEED

### International Rules

*Article 21.* Where, by any of these rules, one of two vessels is to keep out of the way, the other shall keep her course and speed.

Note—*When, in consequence of thick weather or other causes, such vessel finds herself so close that collision cannot be avoided by the action of the giving-way vessel alone, she also shall take such action as will best aid to avert collision.* (See arts. twenty-seven and twenty-nine.)

The International Rules do not contain any sound signals to be given by a privileged vessel to indicate that she will keep her course and speed. (See Art. 28.)

### Inland Rules

*Article 21.* Where, by any of these rules, one of the two vessels is to keep out of the way, the other shall keep her course and speed.

#### PILOT RULE VII

When two steam vessels are approaching each other at right angles or obliquely so as to involve risk of collision, other than when one steam vessel is overtaking another, the steam vessel which has the other on her own port side shall hold her course and speed . . .

If from any cause the conditions covered by this situation are such as to prevent immediate compliance with each other's signals, the misunderstanding or objection shall be at once made apparent by blowing the danger signal, and both steam vessels shall be stopped and backed if necessary, until signals for passing with safety are made and understood.

The last half of this Pilot Rule is invalid, at least so far as it may be invoked against the holding-on vessel to require her to do otherwise than hold her course and speed as prescribed by the statutory rule.

See pp. 134, 216, 217; also *The Transfer No. 15,* 145 Fed. 503, 504; *The John H. Starin,* 162 Fed. 146, 147; *The Haida,* 191 Fed. 623.

**Duty of Preferred Vessel to Hold Course and Speed.**

The definite and precise duty to keep her course and speed is imposed upon the holding-on vessel. Failure to observe this rule is as much a fault as is the failure of the giving-way vessel to keep clear.

The only circumstances under which a holding-on vessel is excused for failure to keep her course and speed are those mentioned in the note appended to the rule, and in Articles 27 and 29, as follows:

### Article 27

"In obeying and construing these rules due regard shall be had to all dangers of navigation and collision, and to any special circumstances which may render a departure from the above rules necessary in order to avoid immediate danger."

### Article 29

"Nothing in these rules shall exonerate any vessel  .  .  . or master or crew thereof, from the consequences of any neg-

The respective duties of the privileged and burdened vessels were discussed at considerable length at the International Conference. As it is not practicable to segregate the discussion as applicable to each rule, the following excerpts in connection with Articles 17, 19, 20, 21, 22, 23, 24 and 26 are here shown without special reference to the text:

Article 21—privileged or holding-on vessel shall keep her course and speed.

Articles 17, 19, 20, 24 and 26—Burdened vessel shall keep out of the way.

Article 22—Burdened vessel shall avoid crossing ahead of the other.

Article 23—Burdened vessel shall, if necessary, slacken her speed or stop or reverse.

Mr. Hall (Great Britain): "  .  .  . So far as we can get at the

lect . . . of any precaution which may be required by the ordinary practice of seamen, or by the special circumstances of the case."

These exceptions do not relieve the holding-on vessel from the obligation of strict compliance with the rule, nor do they permit of any privileges, but, on the contrary, they throw upon her the added responsibility and duty of determining if and when it is necessary in order to avoid immediate danger to depart from the rule. When she does so, she takes upon herself the obligation of showing both that her departure from the rule was necessary at the time it took place in order to avoid immediate danger, and also that the course adopted by her was reasonably calculated to avoid that danger.

Any change of course or speed will be most carefully scrutinized by the courts and unless immediately necessary at the time made, either to assist the burdened vessel in averting the collision, when it is certain she cannot by her own actions do so, or to avoid an impending danger, will not be excused.

*Deviation Permitted Only when Necessary to Avoid Danger.*

That the holding-on vessel shall keep her course and speed does not relieve her, however, from the obligations of good seamanship and the exercise of ordinary precautions. The following decisions make this clear:

preponderance of opinion of sailors, it is that it is safer for a vessel which keeps her course to keep also her speed, and for this reason, the vessel which has to keep out of the way ought to know what the other vessel is doing. . . . I think I may say that there is almost a unanimous consensus of opinion among nautical men that it would really do a great deal towards avoiding collisions, because the steamer which has to keep out of the way of the other vessel would know exactly what is safe for her to attempt to do. . . .

"In Article 22 [present Art. 21] we propose to offer as follows:

" 'Where, by any of these rules, one of two ships has to keep out of the way of the other, she shall keep her course and speed.'

"Then, of course, if the Conference decide to adopt that proposition, it will be necessary to alter Article 18 [present Art. 23], the article now under discussion, in order to have it in conformity with such cases. . . .

"Owing to the wording of the rule as it stands at present it has been argued seriously that as the words 'if necessary' only appear at the end of the article, that the rule itself says, 'Every steam-ship approaching another ship so as to involve risk of collision shall slacken her speed,' it has been argued that the meaning of these words, there being no con-

"  .   .   .   the privileged vessel has no right to keep her course with her eyes shut.  The rule requiring a lookout is imposed alike upon the burdened and privileged vessel.  The duty of the privileged vessel is to hold her course; the duty of the burdened vessel to keep off that course.  But the privileged vessel is to hold her course, constantly observing the burdened vessel, in order to notice if the latter fails in her duty.  When the failure of the burdened vessel becomes apparent, the privileged vessel must change her course as prudence commands.  If she thereafter keeps her course by reason of failure to observe the fault of the burdened vessel, she is at fault.  Want of watchfulness on the part of the privileged vessel does not altogether excuse the burdened vessel, but it is none the less a fault."

*The Devonian,* 110 Fed. 588.

"The master of a preferred steamer cannot, by blindly adhering to his course, atone for the neglect of other precautions."

*The New York,* 175 U. S. 187, 206.

Departure from the rule as an accommodation or courtesy to the other vessel is no excuse.

"Signaling upon some theory of 'courtesy' instead of in conformity to rule, had much to do with the confusion which brought both vessels into trouble  .   .   ."

*The George S. Shultz,* 84 Fed. 508, 510.

"It will thus be seen that the *Pocomoke's* master, by what he in his evidence termed a matter of courtesy, was proceeding in utter violation of all rules and regulations, in that he allowed the outgoing *Portsmouth* ferryboat, over which he had the right of way, to go across and ahead of his vessel, and

---

trolling words, 'if necessary,' as they are at the end of the sentence, is an injunction to the vessel to at once slacken her speed under all conditions.  It is obvious that the legislature would never intend that, because there are many cases where it is necessary for a vessel to keep on her speed as the only possible means of avoiding a collision.  So that we propose to put in the words 'if necessary' after each of the three evolutions which are laid down; that she shall slacken her speed, if necessary, or stop, if necessary, or reverse, if necessary.  These words are only inserted to meet the difficulties which have arisen from the construction of that rule."    *Prot. of Proc.,* pp. 105, 106.

Dr. Sieveking: "  .   .   .   This is certainly a very serious question.  I think I fully understand the reasons which have induced the learned delegate from Great Britain to propose this amendment to 'keep her

he in turn did the same thing with the incoming *Berkeley* ferryboat, as he claimed, none of which he should have done."

*The Pocomoke,* 150 Fed. 193, 195.

The course and speed required under Article 21 are the course and speed which are to be presumed from the circumstances of the nautical maneuver in which the holding-on vessel is engaged, and of which the giving-way vessel has knowledge, or should have knowledge, from what can be seen.   It does not necessarily mean the actual compass course she is holding at the time sighted, nor the same rate of speed that she was making at that time.

*Course and Speed not Necessarily Actual Compass Course and Uniform Speed.*

> "In my judgment 'course and speed' in art. 21 mean course and speed in following the nautical manœuvre in which, to the knowledge of the other vessel, the vessel is at the time engaged. . . . The 'course' certainly does not mean the actual compass direction of the heading of the vessel at the time the other is sighted. . . . A vessel bound to keep her course and speed may be obliged to reduce her speed to avoid some danger of navigation, and the question must be in each case 'Is the manœuvre in which the vessel is engaged an ordinary and proper manœuvre in the course of navigation which will require an alteration of course and speed; ought the other vessel to be aware of the manœuvre which is being attempted to be carried out?' "
>
> *The Roanoke,* 11 Asp. M.C. (N.S.) 253, 257.

A signal for a pilot at a pilot station, with a pilot boat maneuvering into position ahead, is sufficient to convey knowledge of the other vessel's maneuver.

---

speed.'   It has been explained here, and it has been said that it is safer for a vessel which is to keep out of the way to know that the other vessel is to keep her speed, so that she need not be afraid that if she intends to pass behind her this intention could be frustrated by the other vessel slacking her speed.  This is very true.  But then the question arises whether this advantage to the vessel which is to keep out of the way is sufficient to outweigh the disadvantage which the amendment will bring along with it for the other vessel which is to keep her way.

"Now, all of us who have dealt with these cases know that a vessel, which according to the rules is to keep her way, is very often in a painful situation.  She has to stand on.  She has to wait quietly to see what the other vessel will do.  That has been decided by our courts, certainly, and, so far as I know, by the courts of Great Britain and the

*The Ada; The Sappho,* 2 Asp. M.C. (N.S.) 4; *Owners of the Albano v. Allan Line Steamship Company,* 10 Asp. M.C. (N.S.) 365; *The Roanoke,* 11 Asp. M.C. (N.S.) 253.

In the case of the *Owners of the Albano,* that vessel was approaching a pilot station and the *Parisian* (the giving-way vessel) was in the act of picking up a pilot and had a speed of one knot per hour. The *Albano* (the holding-on vessel) was proceeding at the rate of nine knots. The *Albano* held her course and speed in accordance with Article 21 until shortly before the collision, in the expectation that the *Parisian* would stop to let her pass. At the time of the collision, the *Albano* had been going astern about two minutes. The *Parisian* was held solely at fault for failure to keep out of the way by stopping.

In the case of *The Roanoke,* both vessels were approaching the pilot station signaling for a pilot. In the usual course the *Roanoke* slowed and stopped her engines to take the pilot on board. The *Windsor* (the giving-way vessel), expecting that the *Roanoke* would pass ahead, kept her course and, because of the *Roanoke's* reduction in speed, crossed the bow of that vessel. Before the collision, the engines of the *Roanoke* were reversed full speed and three short blasts were sounded, but she struck the *Windsor* on the starboard quarter. The *Roanoke* was exonerated and the *Windsor* found solely at fault.

In the case of *The Albano,* the holding-on vessel was

---

United States. She has to stand on, as it were, until the moment arrives when she has come to the neighborhood of despair. Only then she is allowed to become active and to manœuvre herself. So, in very many cases, the master of the vessel which has to keep her course, finds himself in a very painful situation. He is waiting for the other vessel to change her course, and she is keeping on. . . .

"Now what I want to say is this: If this is the meaning of the rule, then the vessel which is to keep out of the way ought to change her course and do the necessary manœuvres to keep out of the way before there is any risk of a collision, and at a time when the vessels are so far distant from each other that there is no risk."

*Prot. of Proc.,* pp. 108, 109.

Mr. Goodrich (United States): " . . . The object of these rules, as I understand them, is to put upon one of two approaching vessels the

exonerated for maintaining her course and speed, whereas, in *The Roanoke,* the holding-on vessel was held blameless although she slowed and stopped her engines to take on board a pilot.    The explanation of these apparently contradictory decisions is that, as the *Roanoke* was signaling for a pilot, the giving-way vessel should have acted with that circumstance in view, and kept out of the way.

Shoal water, a river bank, or an ice floe close ahead of a sailing vessel are presumptive indications that she is about to tack.    The winding channel of a river presumes a knowledge that a vessel intends to follow the channel.

Speculation as to whether a vessel intends to alter her course at a promontory or lightship with open water on one side is not knowledge within the meaning of the word as here used.    The holding-on vessel in such circumstances that, but for the presence of the giving-way vessel, she would have altered her course in the ordinary course of navigation at such place is not entitled to signal, under Article 28, "I am directing my course to port," for she is not thereby taking any course authorized or required by these rules.    She is bound to keep her course and speed until risk of collision is over and the giving-way vessel must keep out of the way by stopping if she has no room to port.

A change of course and speed may be rendered necessary by the presence of a third vessel.    For instance, an overtaken vessel may have to alter her course for a cross-

burden of avoiding a collision; and there is hardly a situation in which vessels approach each other which is not provided for in these rules.    In all of them the burden is put upon one of the two vessels to keep out of the way of the other.    Now, it seems to me that this suggestion of an amendment by the learned delegate from Great Britain is a very proper thing, because it does add another element to the knowledge of the burdened ship by which she can judge quickly and surely of the position, course, and speed of the other vessel, and so take measures proper to the situation to avoid a collision. . . .

"Now, if you take this rule in connection with Article 23 [present Article 27] which says: 'In obeying and construing these rules, due regard should be had to the dangers of navigation and to any special circumstances which may render a departure from the above rules necessary in order to avoid immediate danger,' I think there will be no dif-

ing vessel; or an overtaken steamer may have to alter her course because of meeting another steamer end on; or a steamer being crossed by another steamer from port to starboard may have to starboard for a third vessel. In all such cases the giving-way vessel has knowledge, or should have knowledge, of the presumable course and speed of the holding-on vessel and must govern her actions accordingly.

In the case of *The Banshee,* 6 Asp. M.C. (N.S.) 221, the *Kildane,* the overtaken steamer, ported and put her engines half speed to avoid a smack. At the time, the *Banshee,* the overtaking vessel, was 800 yards astern. The *Banshee* was held at fault, for with reasonable care she could have kept out of the way. Approved in *The New York,* 175 U. S. 187.

**Deviation from "Course and Speed" not Permitted until and only to Extent Necessary to Avoid Impending Danger.**

The holding-on vessel is not permitted, however, to deviate from her course and speed until it is actually necessary, nor to any greater extent than is necessary to avoid the impending danger.

In the case of *The Illinois,* 103 U. S. 298, 299, 300, the court said:

> "Had the schooner kept her course for a minute or two longer, there is scarcely a doubt that the steamer would have got by in safety. It was clearly a fault, therefore, for her to change her course, unless there was a necessity for it. Mere convenience was not enough. . . . In the present case, it is not found expressly that the ice was so close under the port bow of the schooner as to make it dangerous for her to keep on as she was going until the steamer got by."

ficulty, because, although you provide in the article under consideration that the vessel shall keep her course and her speed, circumstances may arise, as in the case which I have just recited, which would justify the sailing ship or the ship which was bound to keep her course in disobeying the article we are considering. Of course, that is a very delicate matter for a ship to do, one which is bound to keep her course; because if she varies her course or disobeys the rules she takes the burden of proof upon herself to justify this alteration under the twenty-third article. This, in the trial of law cases, as delegate Hall well knows, is a very serious matter. But the rule has been made under the theory that, so far as it can be done, the burden of avoiding collision shall be put upon one of two vessels in any situation in which they might find themselves, and that that vessel shall be given as many elements of knowledge as to the course, speed, and direction and movements of the other vessel as it is

In the case of *The Saragossa*, 7 Asp. M.C. (N. S.) 289, the *Ambient* was overtaking the *Saragossa*. The *Saragossa* starboarded to pass astern of a sailing vessel and the *Ambient*, which had been coming up on her starboard quarter, also starboarded for the same vessel. Then the *Saragossa* hard-a-ported for a smack, which had opened up her red light nearly ahead of her. In doing so she struck the *Ambient* on the port side amidships, causing her to sink. The court said:

> "If she were obliged to port to avoid immediate danger to the smack, I think she would be excused from deviating from her course, but the learned judge has found that she was not obliged to deviate at all, and secondly that if she was she was not entitled to deviate as much as she did. Then I cannot help thinking that, if she is not excused for deviating at all, or deviated more than was necessary to avoid danger, she broke the rule."

At times those in charge of the navigation of the holding-on vessel (preferred or privileged vessel) have anxious and painful moments because of inability to understand the actions of the burdened or giving-way vessel, and of not knowing whether she will perform her duty of keeping out of the way. In such cases it is always safer to follow the rule and to rely upon the burdened vessel doing her duty, for not until it is at least reasonably certain that the latter is failing to do so, and cannot by her own efforts avert a collision, is the holding-on vessel

*Where Burdened Vessel Fails to Signal and Act Promptly— Duty of Preferred Vessel in Difficult Situation.*

possible to give her. If that is the correct theory under which these rules are to be made, all the elements of knowledge which we can add are of very essential service." *Prot. of Proc.*, pp. 110, 111.

Mr. Hall (Great Britain): " . . . He referred, in the first place, to the painful position in which the vessel is placed that has to keep her course, because she does not know what the other vessel is going to do. She does not know whether that vessel is going to try to cross ahead of her or is going under her stern; and she naturally feels very considerable fear that if she keeps on her speed she may be negativing what will be attempted by the other vessel, viz., to get across her bow. We had already thought of that in connection with this case, and not only in connection with this case, but in connection with the general steering and sailing rules as they exist at the present time. When the proper time comes we intend to propose a new rule, which I can not help thinking

permitted to change her course or speed. The United States Supreme Court has said:

> "That her primary duty is to keep her course is beyond all controversy." [As the rule has been amended since, she is under an equal duty to keep her speed.]
>
> "The cases of *The Britannia,* 153 U. S. 130, and *The Northfield,* 154 U. S. 629, must be regarded, however, as settling the law that the preferred steamer will not be held in fault for maintaining her course and speed, so long as it is possible for the other to avoid her by porting, at least in the absence of some distinct indication that she is about to fail in her duty. If the master of the preferred steamer were at liberty to speculate upon the possibility, or even of the probability, of the approaching steamer failing to do her duty and keep out of his way, the certainty that the former will hold his course, upon which the latter has a right to rely, and which it is the very object of the rule to insure, would give place to doubts on the part of the master of the obligated steamer as to whether he would do so or not, and produce a timidity and feebleness of action on the part of both, which would bring about more collisions than it would prevent. . . . "
>
> *The Delaware,* 161 U. S. 459, 468.

See also, *The Chicago,* 125 Fed. 712; *The Cygnus,* 142 Fed. 85.

Generally speaking, in the case of steamers, a giving-way vessel must be very close if she cannot by her own action avoid collision.

In the case of *The Umbria,* 153 Fed. 851, that steamer (the privileged vessel) was held at fault for change of course and speed. It does not appear from the decision

---

will commend itself to the common sense of the delegates, and that is a rule laying down that, so far as the circumstances of the case will admit, the vessel that has to keep out of the way shall avoid crossing the bows of another vessel. Of course, there may be some cases in which it is necessary to cross the bows of a vessel that has to be avoided, but generally it is desirable to have it laid down as a proposition or rule that, so far as the circumstances of the case admit, the vessel which has to keep out of the way of another vessel shall avoid crossing the bows of that vessel.

"There are two other matters, one of which has already been pointed out by the learned delegate from the United States, and that is with regard to the position in which the vessel is placed that has to keep her course. It is provided already by Article 23 [present Art. 27], as the delegate from the United States pointed out, that under the general rule the vessel would be justified in also taking steps to avoid a collision if

that the disobedience of the rule caused or contributed to the collision. On the contrary, the court found that the master of the colliding vessel heard the *Umbria's* signals, but paid no attention to them. In fact, nothing was done by the *Matthews* (the colliding vessel) until the scow was almost in the jaws of collision, when her engines were ordered slow ahead. The court said in respect to the *Umbria,* at p. 853:

> "We are not called upon to decide what the *Umbria* should have done or speculate as to the result if she had obeyed the rule. It is enough that she disobeyed it at a time when for aught that appeared the *Matthews* was intending to follow it."

The privileged vessel has the right to rely on the performance by the burdened vessel of her duty to keep out of the way, and, so long as it is possible for the burdened vessel to avert a collision through her own efforts, it is the duty of the privileged vessel to maintain her course and speed. A clear indication that the burdened vessel is failing in her duty will alone justify the privileged vessel changing her course and speed to avert collision. *As Between Steamers.*

*The Chicago,* 125 Fed. 712; *The Deveaux Powell,* 165 Fed. 634; *The Haida,* 191 Fed. 623 (Affd. 196 Fed. 1005).

The privileged vessel is entitled to presume that the burdened vessel will still conform to the rules of naviga-

the circumstances of the case were such that it was proper for the officer in charge of her as a practical seaman to take such steps. But we have thought it desirable, perhaps, to dot the 'i' and cross the 't' upon this matter, and to have a further rule, making it clear to seamen that they would be justified, although the rule prescribed for them is that they are to keep their course and speed—that they would be justified in a case in which they found that the other vessel which ought to keep out of the way was standing on and apparently not taking steps in sufficient time to prevent a collision—that then they would be bound to act also in order to avoid a collision. Originally, as has been pointed out, the duty is cast upon one vessel to keep out of the way of the other vessel, and the other vessel is to keep on and give all the information she can. She is to keep on her speed, as we propose, but if she sees as the vessels narrow together, that the other vessel is not taking any steps or has got so near that even if she does take steps, her individual action alone will not prevent a collision, then the

tion, even if the latter's request for the right of way is
denied by the privileged vessel.

> *The Chicago,* 125 Fed. 712; *The Cygnus,* 142 Fed. 85;
> *L. Boyers Sons Co. v. United States,* 195 Fed. 490.

**Effect of Pilot or Inspectors' Rules.**

The Pilot or Inspectors' Rules imposing conditions inconsistent with the provisions of the statutory rules are
invalid.

It was said in *The Haida,* 191 Fed. 623, at p. 626:

> "  . . . (art. 19), which gives the privilege to the
> vessel having the other on her port hand, and (art. 21)
> which requires her to keep her course and speed, do not admit
> of the imposition upon that privilege by the pilot rules of a
> condition that she answer a signal."

So, in *The Transfer No. 15,* 145 Fed. 503, at p. 504:

> "  . . . when under the steering and sailing rules a
> vessel has the right to make a particular maneuver, she can-
> not be deprived of such right by any rule of the inspector
> forbidding her to sound a signal which would indicate her
> intention to make that particular maneuver.  The power of
> the inspector to make rules is restricted to such as are 'not
> inconsistent with the provisions of [the] Act of June 7, 1897,
> c. 4, 30 Stat. 96 [U. S. Comp. St. 1901, p. 2875].' "  . . .

Privileged vessels were held free from fault for holding their course and speed in the following cases:

> *The Cygnus,* 142 Fed. 85; *The Transfer No. 15,* 145 Fed.
> 503; *The Montauk,* 180 Fed. 697; *L. Boyers Sons Co. v.
> U. S.* 195 Fed. 490; *The Haida,* 196 Fed. 1005; *The Putney
> Bridge,* 219 Fed. 1014.

---

other ship should try to prevent a collision.  She certainly would not be
justified in keeping on her course and speed when she saw that a collision
would ensue unless she took steps as well as the other vessel to prevent
it.  Therefore, it is to meet this point that we have drafted a new rule,
which I shall move shall follow the rule now under discussion, and which
I may, perhaps, read now:
"  'When, in consequence of thick weather, or other causes, two ships
find themselves so close together as to make it doubtful whether by the
action of one ship alone collision can be avoided, the ship which by the
above article is directed to keep her course and speed shall also take
such action as will best aid to avoid collision.'
*Prot. of Proc.,* pp. 112–113.
"  . . . What we consider is this: That it is most important in mod-

Privileged vessels were held at fault for failing to maintain course and speed in the following cases:

> *The Britannia,* 153 U. S. 130; *The Northfield,* 154 U. S. 629; *The Delaware,* 161 U. S. 459; *The Straits of Dover,* 120 Fed. 900; *The Chicago,* 125 Fed. 712; *The Umbria,* 153 Fed. 851; *The John H. Starin,* 162 Fed. 146; *The Deveaux Powell,* 165 Fed. 635; *The Wm. E. Gladwish,* 206 Fed. 901.

Vessels with signals or lights indicating that they are not under command are bound to keep their course and speed, leaving it to other vessels to keep out of the way.

A sailing vessel is always (except when an overtaking vessel) the privileged vessel as against a steamer, and the duty is imposed upon her to hold her course and speed. This duty is no less onerous upon her than it is upon a privileged steamer. The rule has been laid down by the United States Supreme Court in the following cases, from which pertinent excerpts have been taken:

*As Between Sailing Vessels and Steamers.*

> ". . . which boat was blamable for producing this peril? The schooner was not, because she was obliged to keep her course. She could not choose because the law had chosen for her. It was otherwise with the steamer. She could go to the right or left, and change as often as there was, in the apprehension of her officers, a necessity for change."
> *The Carroll,* 8 Wall. 302, 305.

> "The responsibility of avoiding a collision with a sailing-vessel is put by the Act of Congress and the sailing rules primarily on a steamer. But the sailing-vessel is under just the same responsibility to keep her course, if she can, and not embarrass the steamer, while passing, by any new move-

---

ern times, for these very fast steamers, especially, when one steamer has to get out of the way of the other, that she should know what the other steamer is doing. We also consider it a matter of very great importance, and we are glad to find this same thought has crossed the minds of other delegates to this Conference, that a steamer which has to keep out of the way should, when she can, do so by going under the stern of the other vessel, and not by trying to cross ahead of her bows.

"Sailors will say at once: We think a vessel is to be encouraged to go under the stern of another vessel, and it is only fair to her that she should know that the other vessel is going to keep on. As it stands at present, the holding-on vessel is not bound to keep her speed, and the steamer which has to keep out of the way of her may find herself foiled in her endeavor to do so. Now, to make my meaning clear, suppose two

ment.  A steamer has the right to rely on this as an imperative rule for a sailing-vessel, and govern herself accordingly.  .  .  .  It was clearly a fault, therefore, for her [the sailing-vessel] to change her course unless there was a necessity for it.  Mere convenience was not enough."

> *The Illinois,* 103 U. S. 298, 299.

Also in the case of the *Britannia,* 153 U. S. 130, which arose out of a collision between two steamers, involving the duty of one to keep out of the way and of the other to hold her course and speed, the Supreme Court of the United States, in discussing the obligations of burdened and privileged vessels, said at p. 144:

> " 'It must be remembered that the general rule is, for a sailing vessel meeting a steamer, to keep her course while the steamer takes the necessary measures to avoid a collision.  And though this rule should not be observed when the circumstances are such that it is apparent its observance must occasion a collision, while a departure from it will prevent one, yet it must be a strong case which puts the sailing vessel in the wrong for obeying the rule.'  'But the duty of the steamer [to port her helm and go to starboard] implies a correlative obligation of the ship to keep her course.'  *The Scotia,* 14 Wall. 170, 181.
>
> " 'It is the duty of a steamer to keep out of the way of a sailing vessel when they are approaching in such directions as to involve a risk of collision.  The correlative obligation rests upon the sailing vessel to keep her course and the steamer may be managed upon the assumption that she will do so.'  *The Free State,* 91 U.S. 200.
>
> "It is true that some of the cases just cited were cases wherein the vessel whose duty it was to keep her course was

---

steamers going along like that (indicating), and this one is to keep out of the way of the other.  If he tries to go under the stern of this one, and this one slackens her speed, he runs into the very danger which he wishes to avoid; whereas, if he knows that this vessel, out of the way of which he has to keep, is to keep her course and speed, he knows it is perfectly safe for him to go under the stern of that vessel.  Therefore, we say it is essential that these steamers, at night, should know what the other vessel is going to do.

"The delegates well know that until there has been time enough to watch a vessel carefully or to take the compass bearings, it is very difficult to arrive at the actual speed a vessel is going, but if every sailor knows that the vessel out of the way of which he has to keep will keep her speed as well as her course, then he will know when it is perfectly

a sailing vessel, yet the principle involved is the same in the case of two steamships crossing, where it is the duty of the one who has the other on her starboard bow to keep out of the way of the other, and of the latter to keep on her course. . . ."

It has also been said by the District Court in *The Europa*, 116 Fed. 696, 698:

"Where a sailing vessel and a steamer are proceeding in a direction that may involve collision, the duty of the former is to hold its course, while the latter keeps out of its way. The observance of the rule is no more strictly required of one than of the other. The rule creates a mutual obligation, whereby the sailing vessel is required to hold its course in order that the other may know its position, and not be led into erroneous maneuvers in endeavoring to comply with the requirements of the rule. The rule is imperative, and admits of no option or choice."

And again:

"The duties of these vessels [sailing vessel and steamer] were mutual, and the strict observance of the rule was required no more by one than the other. The rule is imperative, and the vessel departing from it is liable for the damages resulting from such departure. . . . Where a sailing vessel by her unnecessary deviation from her course renders a collision with a steamer unavoidable, the steamer should not be charged with damages."

*The Georg Dumois,* 153 Fed. 833, 837.

Mere apprehension of danger is not sufficient to exonerate a sailing vessel for failing to hold her course, unless it is apparent that a collision is imminent. *The Europa,* 116 Fed. 696.

---

safe to attempt to go under her stern, so as to avoid risk of collision. We have considered this very carefully and have taken the best advice we can obtain from nautical men and experts, and they inform us that this is a desirable course, because it enables the officer in charge of a vessel, upon whom the onus is cast of keeping out of the way, to know what the other ship is going to do, and leaves his hands free and enables him to take the very course which, I think, nearly all sailors think they ought to take, that is to go under the stern of the vessel, when he can, out of the way of which he has to keep.

"I admit that this is a serious change. I do not wish it to be considered a light question. I hope the Conference will consider it very carefully. We have thought, acting upon the best advice which we have had the benefit of receiving, that it is desirable that we should say to

In the following cases the sailing vessel was held at fault for not keeping her course:

*The Blue Jacket,* 144 U. S. 371; *Jacobsen et al. v. Dalles P. & A. Nav. Co.,* 114 Fed. 705; *The Europa,* 116. Fed. 696; *The Georg Dumois,* 153 Fed. 833; *The Edda,* 173 Fed. 436; *The Old Point Comfort,* 187 Fed. 765; *The Kirkwall,* 11 Asp. M.C. (N.S.) 173.

In *The Nacoochee,* 137 U. S. 330, 340, it was contended that the schooner could have avoided the collision by porting her helm, but the United States Supreme Court decided that contention as follows:

"It is contended that the schooner could have avoided the collision by porting her helm when she saw the steamer. But it was the primary duty of the schooner, under Rule 23 [present Rule 21] to keep her course; and, when her master was notified of the approach of the steamer, he told the man at the wheel of the schooner to keep his course, and no change was made in her helm up to the very moment of collision. Even if it was an error of judgment in the schooner to hold her course, it was not a fault, being an act resolved upon *in extremis,* a compliance with the statute, [rule] and a manœuvre produced by the fault of the steamer. . . . "

The foregoing decisions establish the principle that, while there may be circumstances in which a sailing vessel would be justified in departing from the rule, they would have to be extreme to render her liable for holding her course and speed.

---

the vessel that has to keep her course, 'Keep your course and speed, and if you do that, then it will enable the other vessel to take such steps as are necessary and prudent under the circumstances.' "

*Prot. of Proc.,* pp. 522, 523.

Dr. Sieveking: ". . . It is proposed to make it compulsory on the vessel which has to hold on, to also keep her speed. That imposes upon her two duties—not to slacken her speed, and not to increase her speed. It is a principle which I think is firmly established, and which is a sound principle, and which ought not to be abandoned or weakened in any way, that this rule given for the holding-on vessel is to be observed with the utmost stringency. The rule is taken, and it has been taken by the courts always to be a particularly stringent one, and for the very obvious reason that confusion would occur and dangers would be greatly increased if there were not a certainty that the vessel which has to keep out of the way can take it for certain that the other vessel is to act in such and such a way. Therefore, it has often been said that the holding-on

In such cases, however, when they do occur, the sailing vessel must take such action as is necessary to assist in the avoidance of a collision. This was pointed out in the following decision:

> "As a privileged vessel [sailing vessel], she was bound to maintain her course so long as it was possible for the burdened vessel to avoid her, at least in the absence of some distinct indication that the burdened vessel was about to fail in her duty. We are of the opinion that the schooner had notice of the intention of the tug [the burdened vessel] to hold her course, and thus create a situation where disaster was inevitable unless the schooner gave way, at a time when there was ample opportunity to have avoided a collision had she acted promptly and with ordinary skill and prudence. . . . The tug gave no indication of changing her course, and the situation was one calling for the utmost caution on the part of the schooner. . . . The tug, by her own negligence, of course, had brought about a situation where a collision could be avoided only by the prompt intelligent action of the schooner. Can there be a doubt that it was her duty so to act? Was she justified in holding her course with stubborn determination when it was demonstrated that such action could only result in a collision? We think not. The law provides that in obeying and construing the rules of navigation 'due regard shall be had to all dangers of navigation, and to any special circumstances which may render a departure from the above rules necessary in order to avoid immediate danger.' The rules are not to be blindly followed to certain disaster. It behooves every navigator to avoid a collision if he can do so and for manifest error, except in the

---

vessel must comply with this rule to the very last moment of danger, and it is only in the moment of immediate danger that she is allowed to depart from it. So I think it would have to be taken, if the rule that is proposed were adopted, to compel the vessel not *only* to keep her course but also to keep her speed. . . . if the rules are carried out according to the spirit of them, I am sure every one will agree with me in saying that it is necessary for the keeping-out-of-the-way vessel to manœuvre so as to leave the way free for the other vessel in time, not only in time to avoid a collision, but, as far as possible, in time to avoid even the risk of a collision. Close shaving is to be avoided. If that is true, then the keeping-out-of-the-way vessel will have to commence her manœuvres at a great distance. She ought to manœuvre so as to leave a good fair-way for the other vessel. If she intends to go astern, she ought not to go close astern; but in all cases where she can, that is to say, where she sees the other vessel in time, she ought to so far turn from her course as to leave ample room between her and the stern of the other vessel. If that is the case, I think the speed of the other vessel is not such an element of

jaws of collision, he must be held responsible.  He cannot
plead that his was the privileged vessel to relieve him from
consequences which were induced by his own lack of prudence
and common sense."

*The Gladys* (C.C.A.), 144 Fed. 653, 657.

See also, *The Patria*, 107 Fed. 157.

Sailing vessels hearing the signal provided for in Article 15 (e), indicating either a vessel towing or a cable
ship or a vessel not under command or unable to maneuver, are not bound to hold their course.

**As Between Sailing Vessels.**  Identically the same principles are applicable between
sailing vessels in the relation of preferred and burdened
vessels as are effective between steamers.  The privileged vessel is required to keep her course and speed, and
by a departure therefrom takes upon herself the burden
of showing that the change was necessary to avoid otherwise inevitable collision, or other impending danger.

---

calculation so important that it must be laid down as a rule that the
holding-on vessel shall keep her speed."    *Prot. of Proc.,* pp. 523, 524.

Mr. Hall (Great Britain): " . . . May I point this out to him?  The
English law and the American law, as I believe—and I am now speaking
in the presence of a master of admiralty law—is that a man in charge of
a vessel is to blame if he goes on blindly.  When he sees that a collision
will ensue, he is not justified in keeping on when he sees that, under the
peculiar circumstances of the case, it is necessary for him to act as well
in order to avoid a collision.  I have a reference to the American cases as
well as the English cases to that effect.  Therefore I think this gets us out
of that difficulty.  As is pointed out by the learned delegate from the
United States, that is provided for under general Article No. 23" [present
Art. 27].                                            *Prot. of Proc.,* p. 528.

Admiral Molyneux (Great Britain): " . . . There is one point I would
like to bring to the notice of the Conference in answer to the learned
delegate from Germany.  He asks whether this is not putting a very
great burden on the holding-on ship to compel her to keep her speed.
I think that before we can answer that we must consider what is the
position now under the present rule.  The holding-on ship can not tell,
and has no right to ask, or to know, how the other ship is going to act,
or how she is going to get out of her way.  The other ship may be trying
to cross her bow, or go under her stern; but up to the very moment of a
collision there is nothing to guide her.  She has a perfect right to go
across the bow or to go astern, and to do anything she likes, except to
come into collision.  So I doubt if you can make the burden of the holding-on ship worse than it is at present.

"I think that if you make it perfectly clear that one ship *is not* to do a
certain thing and the other ship *is* to do a certain thing, you will at all
events remove a certain amount of doubt.  I think after all that is the
main trouble.  The man on the holding-on ship now must have a very
bad time of it; and I cannot conceive of anything more trying than his

## ARTICLE XXII
### CROSSING AHEAD

*International Rules*

**Article 22.** Every vessel which is directed by these rules to keep out of the way of another vessel shall, if the circumstances of the case admit, avoid crossing ahead of the other.

*Inland Rules*

**Article 22.** Identical with International Rules.

Also identical with Rule IX of the Pilot Rules (except every *steam vessel*).

## ARTICLE XXIII
### STEAM VESSELS SHALL SLACKEN SPEED OR STOP

*International Rules*

**Article 23.** Every steamvessel which is directed by these rules to keep out of the way of another vessel shall, on approaching her, if necessary, slacken her speed or stop or reverse.

*Inland Rules*

**Article 23.** Identical with International Rules.

Article 22 is applicable to both sailing vessels and steamers.

Article 23 refers only to steamers. Both rules cover instructions to the burdened vessel and can with advantage be discussed together.

These articles are operative only as to vessels so approaching as to involve risk of collision. With a col-

position. Under the present rule he is obliged to keep his speed, and he knows that the other ship is not to cross his bow. If he sees that the other ship, in spite of the rule, is blundering across his bow, he knows that he has to deal with a fellow who does not know his business, and knows then that he will probably have to act. But under the existing rule he has got no right to assume that the other man does not know his business.

"Therefore I think that in both ways this rule is a gain. Under the old rule he has no right to assume when the other vessel is trying to cross his bow that the captain does not know his business; but he will know it, if we pass these two rules, because they are both strung on one string. I think that we should bear in mind that so far from putting a burden on the ship, we are taking a very great burden off of her. There is one

lision occurring, however, it would be difficult, if not impossible, to show that no risk of collision existed. A change of course, even though slight and made solely as a precaution, is sufficient indication of a risk of collision. It was so held by the United States Supreme Court in *The Carroll,* 8 Wall. 302, 305:

> "The fact that the vessels did collide, explodes the theory that there was no risk of collision, and besides why did the mate port his helm, if in his judgment there was no risk of it?"

See also, *The Ashton,* 10 Asp. M.C. (N.S.) 88.

When a collision or other impending danger cannot be avoided except by crossing ahead, Article 22 permits of this being done. The rule only requires that crossing ahead shall be avoided, "if the circumstances of the case admit." This exception, however, is not intended to, nor does it modify or weaken the positive requirement of the rule; nor will it excuse any departure from the rule except in a case of great emergency. Crossing ahead of the holding-on vessel is permitted when, and only when, the situation is such that that is the only means of avoiding collision or other impending danger. If the danger can be avoided by any other maneuver not in contravention of the rules, as, for instance, by slackening speed, stopping or reversing (as prescribed by Art. 23), it must be made and the crossing ahead avoided. And it matters not how inconvenient or troublesome such other maneuver may be. The courts have said of these exceptions to the general rule:

> "Exceptions to the general rules of navigation are admitted with reluctance on the part of the courts, and only

---

other point. Under the present rule I think there is no doubt that the holding-on ships should consider that they have the right of way, and the right of way includes not only course but speed. If it is the custom and practice of seamen to keep their speed, I think it is better to put it down in black and white that they are to do so. My experience, at all events, is that they are in the habit of doing so, that we are really not altering the custom very much. We are trying to make it absolute instead of open to doubt, as it was before. And this is another great point in favor of this amendment."                     *Prot. of Proc.,* p. 529.

Admiral Bowden-Smith (Great Britain): " . . . We want to make it

when an adherence to such rules must almost necessarily result in a collision,— . . . ”

The Albert Dumois, 177 U. S. 240, 249.

“The *Jamaica* was the burdened vessel, and was required to keep out of the way of the *Starin*, and to avoid crossing ahead of her if the circumstances of the case admitted. Act June 7, 1897, c. 4, arts. 21, 22, 30 Stat. 101 (U. S. Comp. St. 1901, p. 2883). We are at a loss to see what circumstances there were which did not admit of her executing such manœuvre. Instead of doing so, she persisted in crossing ahead. . . . ”

The John H. Starin, 162 Fed. 146.

On the theory that the attempt of two approaching vessels to avoid each other by both maneuvering at the same time will work confusion and possibly result in collision, the rules prescribe with exactness the duties of one vessel in certain situations, so that, having knowledge of her movements, the other may with confidence take such steps as are necessary to avert threatened collision.

Articles 17, 19, 20, 24 and 26 define the vessels upon which, and the situations from which, devolve the duty of keeping out of the way, and Article 21 imposes upon the other vessel the positive obligation of holding her course and speed.

With knowledge that the privileged vessel is required to hold her course and speed, the burdened vessel is free to maneuver as those in charge of her navigation deem safest. No instructions are given as to how the burdened vessel shall keep out of the way, except that, under Article 23, a steamer shall, if necessary, slacken her speed

*Duty of the Burdened Vessel.*

---

perfectly plain that the giving-way ship, in avoiding the holding-on ship, may do anything she pleases except one thing, and that is, that when there is risk of collision she is not to try to cross her bow. I am particularly anxious that my colleague should understand what I mean by that. We do not say that she is to go under her stern. As a sailor I would not agree to the words saying that she is to go under the stern of the holding-on ship. If a sailing ship, you can go off the wind; or if a steamer, when the danger is broad on the bow, more than four points, the safest way is to put her helm to starboard and stop her engines and reverse. So I do not like the expression ‘going under the stern.’ What we wish you to do is to give to the ship which is to keep out of the way

or stop or reverse. One restriction only is imposed upon her, namely, that she shall not cross ahead of the holding-on vessel unless that maneuver presents the only means of avoiding collision or other impending danger (Art. 22). Save for the foregoing, the method by which the keeping out of the way shall be accomplished is left entirely to the judgment and good seamanship of those in charge of the navigation of the burdened vessel, who are held strictly responsible for the result. A failure will not be excused unless the steps taken were amply sufficient and would have been successful but for an improper act (change of course or speed) by the holding-on vessel.

If it is thought desirable as a matter of precaution by the giving-way vessel to change her course, it must be altered to pass astern and not ahead of the holding-on vessel. The courts impose absolute responsibility for the success of the maneuver:

> "The burdened vessel is to 'keep out of the way.' How it shall do so is not prescribed. It may, of course, turn to starboard sufficiently to allow the privileged vessel to pass, and then proceed under the stern of that vessel. This is the path of safety. It may 'keep out of the way' by crossing the bows of the privileged vessel, but, in undertaking this maneuver, it is chargeable with the knowledge that the other vessel is by express rule required to keep her course. Unless, then, the burdened vessel has time and space thus to cross in safety without the help of the privileged vessel, prudent navigation would forbid her making such attempt. If she make the attempt, and thereby brings about collision, she is in fault for not keeping out of the way of the privileged vessel. The inspectors' rules give her the opportunity of agreeing with the privileged vessel that this usually risky maneuver shall be at-

---

anything she pleases except, when there is risk of collision, the right to try to cross the bow of the other vessel. I wish particularly to emphasize the words 'risk of collision,' because it is only when the risk of collision applies that these rules apply."                                     *Prot. of Proc.*, pp. 531, 532.

Captain Saldanha de Gama (Brazil): " . . . As a seaman, and as an old seaman, as I pretend to be for my age, I desire to state that I will have to come to the support of the proposition of the honorable delegate from Great Britain. Before I begin to make a few explanations to the Conference, I must say that I feel very sorry to see seamen at difference amongst themselves, like lawyers. I believe that the amendment proposed

tempted, and that the privileged vessel will co-operate to that end. Such agreement would constitute a special circumstance, within the meaning of rule 24 [now Art. 29]. This agreement is effected when the burdened vessel's signal indicating an intention to cross in front of the privileged vessel is accepted by a corresponding signal from the privileged vessel. But the burdened vessel which without such agreement undertakes to navigate as if she had the privilege, and the other the burden, assumes all responsibility for the consequences resulting from such failure to conform to regulations. All this has been explained in the opinions of the courts over and over again."

*The George S. Shultz,* 84 Fed. 508, 510.

" . . . prudent seamanship ordinarily requires that the obligated [burdened] vessel shall take a course, which, if the preferred [holding-on] vessel perform her own duty, will certainly avoid a collision, viz., port and go astern. If, upon the other hand, she elects to starboard and cross the bows of the other vessel, she incurs the manifest danger of not passing the point of intersection before the preferred vessel strikes her, and is justly considered as assuming the responsibility for the success of her manœuvres."

*The New York,* 175 U. S. 187, 202.

"Under these rules the *Modoc* was the burdened vessel. It was her duty to keep out of the way of the *Camano* and to pass under her stern. The *Modoc* contends that she gave two whistles, indicating that she would cross the bow of the *Camano,* thus leaving her on the starboard side of the *Modoc.* Rule 9 [Pilot Rule identical with Art. 22] authorizes such a manœuvre only when it can be executed without involving risk of collision. The *Modoc,* by this manœuvre, took the risk of collision."

*The Modoc,* 216 Fed. 445, 447.

---

by the honorable delegate from Great Britain is so strong that it will meet all objections. As a complement to the strict rule contained in the second part of the amendment, No. 59, amendment No. 61 says:

" 'When, in consequence of thick weather, or other causes, two ships find themselves so close together as to make it doubtful whether by the action of one ship alone collision can be avoided, the ship which by the above article is directed to keep her course and speed shall also take such action as will best aid to avoid collision.'

"These two amendments provide that a ship which is to keep out of the way of another ship shall avoid crossing the bow, and also provide that in case a collision can not be avoided by the action of one ship alone,

**The Burdened Vessel must Act Promptly and Avoid Close Shaving.**

Not only must the action of the burdened vessel be timely, but the intended maneuvers must, so far as possible, be promptly indicated to the holding-on vessel by the appropriate sound signals.

It was said at the International Conference:

" . . . If the rules are carried out according to the spirit of them, I am sure every one will agree with me in saying that it is necessary for the keeping-out-of-the-way vessel to manœuvre so as to leave the way free for the other vessel in time, not only in time to avoid a collision, but, as far as possible, in time to avoid even the risk of a collision. Close shaving is to be avoided. If that is true, then the keeping-out-of-the-way vessel will have to commence her manœuvres at a great distance. She ought to manœuvre so as to leave a good fair-way for the other vessel. If she intends to go astern, she ought not to go close astern; but in all cases where she can, that is to say, where she sees the other vessel in time, she ought to so far turn from her course as to leave ample room between her and the stern of the other vessel . . . "

*Prot. of Proc.,* p. 524.

Any undue delay on the part of the burdened vessel in taking action, or in communicating her intentions to the holding-on vessel, is not only unfair to the latter (which may be in the uncomfortable and anxious position of not knowing whether she has been seen or whether the giving-way vessel is going to perform her duty of keeping out of the way), but is a violation of the spirit of the rules, for which the burdened vessel will be held responsible if collision ensue.

---

then the other ship is to act. The amendment proposed by my gallant friend, the delegate from Chili, makes it more imperative; but it is directed to the same purpose as the amendment of the learned delegate from Great Britain. It is my experience and my knowledge that most of the cases of collision on the sea are in consequence of both ships endeavoring to manœuvre, and his amendment is to reach that point. It provides that no ship shall cross the bow of any ship in motion where there is risk of collision; but if extraordinary circumstances require that it be done, then the ship crossing the bow of the other shall be responsible

"The safeguards against danger, in order to be effectual, must be seasonably employed, and in this case they were not used until the danger was threatening."

*The Carroll,* 8 Wall. 302, 306.

The burdened vessel was held at fault for failure to keep out of the way, for attempting to cross ahead, or for failure to slacken speed, stop or reverse, in the following cases:

*The Delaware,* 161 U. S. 459; *The Britannia,* 153 U. S. 130; *The Republic,* 102 Fed. 997; *The Straits of Dover,* 120 Fed. 900; *The Chicago,* 125 Fed. 712; *The Cygnus,* 142 Fed. 85; *The Pocomoke,* 150 Fed. 193; *The Umbria,* 153 Fed. 851; *The John H. Starin,* 162 Fed. 146; *The Deveaux Powell,* 165 Fed. 634; *The Montauk,* 180 Fed. 697; *The Thielbek,* 241 Fed. 209.

The master of a steamer approaching a sailing vessel whose course is varying with the wind, should bear in mind that the direction of the wind as it appears to the steamer under way is not always the true direction of the wind.

*As Between Steamer and Sailing Vessel.*

The inability of a sailing vessel to maneuver with the same facility as a steamer imposes upon those in charge of the latter the duty of exercising more than ordinary precaution in any maneuvers undertaken to avoid the sailing vessel.

While identically the same guiding principles already stated as applicable between burdened and holding-on steamers are operative, in practical navigation when a sailing vessel is involved, even more precautions are, perhaps, necessary to keep out of the way and avoid collision. Certainly the courts hold a steamer to a strict observance of the rule and require her to avoid even the risk

for the consequences. Now, most of the cases of collision on the sea come in consequence of both ships endeavoring to manœuvre at the same time."

*Prot. of Proc.,* pp. 535, 536.

Mr. Hall (Great Britain): " . . . It has been stated, I think, by several of the delegates, that it is better that the vessel which has to keep out of the way should avoid crossing the bows of the other vessel. Of course you can not lay down a hard and fast rule. She may be compelled by the exigencies of the case to adopt such a manœuvre under some circum-

of collision by giving the sailing vessel a berth wide enough to allow ample margin for all contingencies of navigation.    This is shown by the following decisions:

> "   .   .   .   the collision was the result solely of the negligence of the pilot   .   .   .   in failing to properly and seasonably observe the customary rules and regulations   .   .   . It was the duty of the navigator   .   .   .   not only to have avoided the collision   .   .   .   but to have avoided the risk of collision, and that there was such risk of collision is apparent from the result which followed."
>
> *Donald v. Guy et al.* 135 Fed. 429, 430, 431.

> "   .   .   .   while the *Bayport* [steamer] had the right to navigate upon the theory that there would be no change in the *Jackson's* [sailing vessel] course, she should not have proceeded in such close proximity thereto as to endanger or run risk of collision, by reason of a sudden and unanticipated movement on the part of the approaching vessel, particularly where, as in this case, there was ample room for the vessels to pass each other in safety.    The obligation to avoid risk of collision was imposed upon the *Bayport*   .   .   .   To avoid the risk of collision, as well as the collision, was the obligation imposed upon her as the burdened vessel."
>
> *The Job H. Jackson,* 144 Fed. 896, 898.

> "It was the duty of the steamer to keep out of the way of the sailing vessel.   .   .   .   This rule required the steamer to do more than merely to so shape its course as to pass the schooner without striking it.    Its duty was to give the schooner a berth wide enough to allow a sufficient margin for safety, taking into account the contingencies of navigation   .   .   .   [The steamer,] under the circumstances presented, failed to give the schooner the wide berth demanded, allowing insufficient margin of safety to meet the contingencies of navigation which should have been anticipated."
>
> *Bonnah et al. v. Lakeside S. S. Co.,* 221 Fed. 40, 41, 43.

Close and diligent observation of the course and movements of the sailing vessel is required of a steamer.

---

stances; but so far as I have heard to-day, there has not been one single opinion advanced by any sailor that it is not desirable for vessels to avoid crossing the bows of other vessels.    Accordingly, we venture to propose this: 'A ship which is required by these rules to keep out of the way of another ship, shall, if the circumstances of the case admit, avoid crossing ahead of the other.'    If we put into the rule, 'if the circumstances of the case admit,' the onus would be on the man who tried to cross the bows of

" . . . the estabished rule is: 'That the steamship, from the moment the sailing vessel is seen, shall watch with the highest diligence her course and movements, so as to be able to adopt such timely measures of precaution as will necessarily prevent the two boats coming in contact.' *The Carroll,* 8 Wall. 302, 306."

*The Oceanic S. S. Co. v. Simpson Lumber Co.,* 186 Fed. 764.

"In such case, when the bright light became visible to the officer in charge of the steamer, it certainly was incumbent upon him, in the exercise of careful seamanship, to give close attention to the light and have his own vessel perfectly in command until it could be determined without doubt just what the approaching vessel was, and its direction."

*Wilder's S. S. Co. et al. v. Low et al.,* 112 Fed. 161, 170.

If in doubt or uncertainty as to the course of the sailing vessel, the steamer must immediately stop until such course has been ascertained.

"The federal courts in early cases declared it to be the duty of a steamer, when the lights of an approaching vessel were fluctuating, or for any reason there appeared to be uncertainty as to her course, to slacken its speed, and, if necessary, stop, neither proceeding nor changing its course until the course of the other vessel has been ascertained."

*Wilder's S. S. Co. et al. v. Low et al.,* 112 Fed. 161, 171.

"If the boats [steamer and bark] were in such position that there was not time to correctly ascertain what course the bark was holding, and to estimate whether the steamer could go to port or should proceed across the bark's bows, then the steamer should have stopped and reversed so as to lessen the danger of the position."

*The Diana,* 181 Fed. 263, 265; (Affd. 194 Fed. 1021.)

A steamer when approaching a sailing vessel must take into account any obvious necessity for a change of tack on

another vessel to show why he adopted that manœuvre and did not adopt the more prudent and safer one."      *Prot. of Proc.,* p. 542.

Mr. Hall (Great Britain): " . . . Every sailor will agree that there must be conditions when it will be necessary that both vessels should act and not merely one of them, in order to avoid a collision. Accordingly, we ought to emphasize that as much as we possibly can, and for that reason we have brought forward this proposition. We want to make it clear to

the part of the latter, such as the proximity of shoal water or other dangers (*The Palatine,* 1 Asp. M.C. (N.S.)
468), but a sailing vessel is not permitted to embarrass a
steamer by tacking when it is merely a matter of convenience, and there is no apparent necessity for an immediate change of course.   *The Illinois,* 103 U.S. 298.

The duty of the giving-way vessel to act promptly and
by proper sound signals, given seasonably to indicate her
intended change of course or other maneuver, is not less-
ened or altered by the fact that the privileged vessel is a
sailing vessel.   *The Triton,* 118 Fed. 329.

**As Between Sailing Vessels.**   Article 17 defines as between sailing vessels the privileged and the burdened vessel.   The obligations of each
to the other are identical with those between steamers.

every sailor that he must not say: 'The rule is that I am to keep my course
and speed, and I shall stick to it under all circumstances.'   When it is
necessary for him to act, as well as the other ship, he ought to do so, and
we have endeavored to impress that duty, if possible, more strongly upon
him."
                                        *Prot. of Proc.,* p. 543.

Admiral Bowden-Smith (Great Britain): " . . . I would be very glad
if the sailors of the Conference would give their minds to this and see if
it is possible to find something which will give the officer on the holding-
on ship no excuse for insisting on his right when it would cause loss of
life and property."
                                        *Prot. of Proc.,* pp. 543, 544.

## ARTICLE XXIV

## OVERTAKING VESSELS

*International Rules*

*Article 24.* Notwithstanding anything contained in these rules every vessel, overtaking any other, shall keep out of the way of the overtaken vessel.

Every vessel coming up with another vessel from any direction more than two points abaft her beam, that is, in such a position, with reference to the vessel which she is overtaking that at night she would be unable to see either of that vessel's side-lights, shall be deemed to be an overtaking vessel; and no subsequent alteration of the bearing between the two vessels shall make the overtaking vessel a crossing vessel within the meaning of these rules, or relieve her of the duty of keeping clear of the overtaken vessel until she is finally past and clear.

As by day the overtaking vessel cannot always know with certainty whether she is forward of or abaft this direction from the other vessel she should, if in doubt, assume that she is an overtaking vessel and keep out of the way.

*Inland Rules*

*Article 24.* Identical with International Rule.

See also

Article XVIII

Rule VIII. When steam-vessels are running in the same direction, and the vessel which is astern shall desire to pass on the right or starboard hand of the vessel ahead, she shall give one short blast of the steam-whistle, as a signal of such desire, and if the vessel ahead answers with one blast, she shall put her helm to port; or if she shall desire to pass on the left or port side of the vessel ahead, she shall give two short blasts of the steam-whistle as a signal of such desire, and if the vessel ahead answers with two blasts, shall put her helm to starboard; or if the vessel ahead does not think it safe for the vessel astern to attempt to pass at that point, she shall immediately signify the same by giving several short and rapid blasts of the steam-whistle, not less than four, and under no circumstances shall the vessel astern attempt to pass the vessel ahead until such time as they have reached a point where it can be safely done, when said vessel ahead shall signify her willingness by blowing the proper signals. The vessel ahead shall in no case attempt to cross the bow or crowd upon the course of the passing vessel.

Article 24 and Article 18, Rule VIII, are identical with Rule VI of Pilot Rules.

The sound signals prescribed by the International Rules in Article 28—viz.:

The sound signals prescribed by the Inland Rules to be given by an overtaking or overtaken vessel are covered by Article 18, Rule VIII, as above—viz.:

One Short Blast
To indicate: "I am directing my course to starboard."

One Short Blast
From the overtaking vessel indicates a desire to pass on the starboard hand of the vessel ahead.

From the overtaken vessel it indicates an assent to such passing.

Two Short Blasts
To indicate: "I am directing my course to port."

Two Short Blasts
From the overtaking vessel indicates a desire to pass on the port hand of the vessel ahead.

From the overtaken vessel it indicates an assent to such passing.

Three Short Blasts

To indicate: "My engines are going full speed astern"

are applicable to overtaking and overtaken vessels, and any change of course by either vessel must be indicated by the appropriate signal.

Several Short Rapid Blasts
(not less than 4)

From the overtaken vessel indicates that a passing is unsafe and a dissent to the proposed passing at that time and place.

A failure to sound immediately a dissent if it is not thought safe to pass at that point constitutes a fault on the part of the overtaken vessel.

The courts so hold.

"I think the conduct [failure to sound dissenting signal] . . . was calculated to mislead the *Mesaba* and to some extent did so; particularly in view of the common but blamable practice of pilots to omit signals which they think unnecessary, though required by the rules; and as failure to answer was in direct violation of the positive requirement of the rules of navigation, the *Martello* must be held in part to blame for the collision."

*The Mesaba,* 111 Fed. 215, 222.

An overtaking vessel may not pass an overtaken vessel against her dissent; nor may the overtaken vessel change her course or crowd upon the course of the overtaking vessel. *The*

*James L. Morgan,* 225 Fed. 34.

Also in the case of *The George W. Elder,* 249 Fed. 956, the court said, pp. 957, 958:

"It was the *Elder's* duty, on hearing the first danger signal, to proceed no further in the attempt to pass. By the rules of navigation the pilot of the *Kern* was made the judge of the necessity for giving the danger signal. Responsibility for the collision must be determined from the situation as it existed from and after the time when that signal was given. The duty was imposed upon the *Elder* 'under no circumstances' to attempt to pass at that point, or until the *Kern* signified her consent. At that time, and for some appreciable time thereafter, it was obviously possible for the *Elder* to keep clear of the *Kern,* as it was her duty to do."

The duty of the overtaken vessel is to keep her course and speed. (See Art. 21.) Any deviation therefrom is excusable only if necessary to avoid danger (see Art. 27), and, even then, must not be made until immediately necessary; nor can it be more than is essential to avoid the danger. *The Saragossa,* 7 Asp. M.C. (N.S.) 289.

It was held in the case of the *Mesaba,* 111 Fed. 215, where, at the time an overtaking vessel signaled her intention to pass the vessel ahead, the latter had already stopped her engines to permit a schooner to cross her bows (a purpose which was obvious to the overtaking vessel), that the resumption of her former course and speed by the overtaken vessel after the temporary purpose of her stopping had been accomplished did not constitute a violation of the rule requiring her to keep her course and speed.

The first paragraph of Article 24 (International Rules) contains the rule; the second and third paragraphs are simply definitions of what shall constitute an overtaking vessel.

When this rule was framed by the International Conference, the British delegate, in proposing it, made the following explanatory comments:

" . . . the question has arisen sometimes as to whether or not a vessel is an overtaking ship, and it has been argued that when vessels are in such a position that their courses are divergent, that they then come within the operation of the crossing rule, and not within the operation of the overtaking rule. I know that it has been attempted to be argued that a vessel is only an overtaking vessel so long as she is aft of the vessel she is overtaking, and that immediately when a vessel is on a crossing course the crossing rules apply, and she is not bound by the article with regard to overtaking vessels. Accordingly, in dealing with these cases, our courts have laid down what an overtaking vessel is; and it appears to be so clear and explicit as to leave no doubt in the mind of any seaman, if he had this definition before him, as to what an overtaking vessel was. We have thought it desirable to impress this upon his mind clearly, so that he could not shield himself on the pretense that they were crossing vessels and not overtaking vessels." *Prot. of Proc.,* pp. 122, 123.

"Mr. President, I explained when I had the honor of introducing this amendment, at the first reading of these rules, the object we had in view in proposing it. There is no doubt whatever that there have been cases in which a vessel which has been overtaking another vessel, has occasionally attempted to excuse herself, from obeying this rule by saying: I was not an overtaking vessel, because I had got in front of your beam, and directly I got in front of your beam we were then crossing vessels; therefore, it was your duty to keep out of my way.   I think that all sailors will agree with this: That if one vessel overtakes another the duty is upon her to comply with the rule, with the spirit as well as the letter of the rule, that she shall keep out of the way of the vessel she is passing, and she is not to excuse herself for not obeying this rule, both in the spirit and in the letter, by being able to say: It was true I was an overtaking vessel, but directly I got in front of your beam I was no longer an overtaking vessel; then it was your duty to keep out of my way.

"I venture to say that we have drawn this rule from the actual words which were used by one of our most eminent judges in order to describe what an overtaking vessel is. Therefore, we have thought it desirable to put any doubt at rest in the mind of the sailor as to what an overtaking vessel is, and to lay it down so that there shall be no mistake whatever about it.   I think that all sailors will agree with the principle which is there laid down.   We want to compel a vessel which overtakes another vessel to do it at her own risk and to make her keep out of the way.   If we do that she will be obliged to take such precaution that a collision will be rendered practically impossible.   I therefore have the honor to move this amendment."

*Prot. of Proc.*, p. 573.

A vessel lying dead in the water is under way, if not at anchor or made fast to the shore or aground, and is an overtaken vessel in respect to any vessel approaching from any direction more than two points abaft her beam. *The George W. Elder,* 249 Fed. 956, 958.

The rule provides that every vessel overtaking another shall keep out of the way of the overtaken vessel.   A sailing vessel, therefore, when overtaking a steam vessel, must, as an overtaking vessel, keep out of the way of the steamer.   *The Charles C. Lister,* 182 Fed. 988.

If, however, after the sailing vessel has passed and cleared the steamer, the wind should drop and the sailing vessel becomes the slower vessel, the steamer must, as an overtaking vessel, in her turn keep clear.

A sailing vessel having been overtaken and passed by a tug and tow may later become an overtaking vessel and obligated as such under Article 24 to keep clear. *The Mary E. Morse,* 179 Fed. 945.

Special care and caution is necessary where one steam vessel is overtaking another in a narrow or winding channel.

The overtaking vessel must be prepared for any changes in course which the overtaken vessel may find necessary in following the channel. She must bear in mind that the overtaken vessel cannot be forced to leave the right side of the channel (see Art. 25), and she must make ample allowance for suction, and not approach so close to the overtaken vessel as to cause her to sheer.

This danger of suction causing a sheer has been recognized and commented upon by the courts in a number of cases, of which the following are illustrative.

**Cases Involving Suction.**

The *Aureole* attempted to pass the *Willkomen* in the Delaware River above Marcus Hook. The *Aureole* claimed that she was passing with 300 feet between the vessels. The *Willkomen* maintained that the distance did not exceed 150 feet; some of the witnesses claimed not over 75 or 100 feet. When the *Aureole* had passed so that her stern was ahead of the bridge of the *Willkomen,* the latter took a rank sheer and struck the *Aureole* a glancing blow upon the starboard quarter about 35 feet from her stern. The court found the *Aureole* solely at fault for attempting to pass too close to the *Willkomen,* "recognizing the existence of the force called suction and its power under favorable circumstances to draw one vessel towards another."

*The Aureole,* 113 Fed. 224.

The *Sif* attempted to pass the *Murcia* in the Delaware River. The *Sif* claimed that she was passing with a distance of from 300 to 400 feet between the two vessels, and the *Murcia* alleged that the distance between the two vessels was from 100 to 150 feet. As the *Sif* gradually drew ahead, the distance between the two vessels decreased until they were not exceeding 50 to 100 feet apart.   When the *Sif* was about half way past the *Murcia,* it was noticed that the bow of the latter was drawing towards the former.   The engines of the *Murcia* were put full speed astern, and the helm aport, albeit the *Murcia* continued to approach the *Sif* more rapidly until she gave a sudden dive in the direction of the *Sif,* striking that vessel on the starboard side at a point 100 feet from her stern.   The court said:

> "The 'dive' or 'plunge' which the *Murcia* finally made into the side of the *Sif* indicates some unusual force as the cause, and the influence of the suction of one vessel over another has been recognized in navigation in a number of cases, especially where the sudden 'plunge or dive' indicates that there is some force other than the motion of the vessel from her propelling force.   That suction has been recognized as a fruitful cause of collision appears from the following cases:   *The Ohio,* 91 Fed. 547, 33 C.C.A. 667; *The Aureole, supra; The Atlantic, supra; The Mesaba* (D.C.) 111 Fed. 215; *The Fontana,* 119 Fed. 853, 56 C.C.A. 365; *The Bremen* (D.C.), 111 Fed. 228; *The City of Brockton, supra; The North Star* (D.C.), 132 Fed. 145; *The U. S. and The Monterey* (D.C.) 171 Fed. 442."
>
> *The Sif,* 181 Fed. 412, 416.

In the case of *The Mesaba,* 111 Fed. 215, the court said at p. 227:

> "From these and other cases, I think there is no doubt that the strength and the lateral extent of suction caused by passing vessels, depends on quite a number of circumstances, of which the most important are the size and speed of the two vessels, and particularly the depth of the water beneath them, as well as the mass and extent of the water on each side. In abundance of water the effect is probably slight; in scanty waters, at its maximum and operative for a considerable distance.   In the present case the circumstances were all favorable to its powerful action, and I think it not improbable that it was one of the operative causes of this collision, though I find no reported decision except in the *City of Brockton* in which the collision has been ascribed to the suction of a vessel passing at a distance of from 100 to 150 feet.   Prudent navigation, however, requires the allowance of a sufficient

margin for the unavoidable incidents of deviation from an exact course, through the influence of wind, of tide and of currents, and the impossibility of absolute steadiness. Where large vessels are navigating side by side at high speed, as in this case, for a distance of over a third of a mile, prudence requires, in my judgment, a separation of at least from 200 to 300 feet, as stated by the witnesses for the *Martello,* to avoid all these contingencies of navigation."

Also, in *The Monterey,* 171 Fed. 442, it was said at p. 449:

"Suction is a force that has existed a long time and been recognized as a danger in close navigation especially in shallow waters. No instances have been given of a collision due to it at this particular place but many have occurred in the Lower Bay and have always resulted from a too close approach. That seems to have been the cause here. The *United States,* the larger vessel, and navigating without much water under her keel, in passing the *Monterey,* approached too close to her, with the result that the *Monterey* lost all power over herself and turned into the *United States,* with the disastrous result of causing damages to the two vessels, said to have been in excess, of $300,000. I cannot see any cause for this collision except the fault of the *United States* in endeavoring to pass the *Monterey* when the vessels were on slightly converging courses in close proximity, due to the *United States* getting over in the waters to which the *Monterey* was primarily entitled."

Again, in *The Queen City,* 189 Fed. 653 at pp. 654, 655:

"All the positive testimony and all the reasonable inferences from the undisputed facts are to the effect that this change of course was due to a sheer, resulting from the *Townsend's* suction, which caught the stern of the *Moore* and pulled it up stream for a moment, so that when this suction let go the *Moore* was headed partly across the channel. The conditions attending the creation and exercise of this force called 'suction' seem to be imperfectly known, but many of the characteristic conditions were here present. The *Townsend* was more than twice as long as the *Moore* and was running ten miles (past the land) as against the *Moore's* seven. The sterns were, at the instant of the sheer, about abreast and quite close together. The draught of the *Townsend*, 8 feet forward and 16 feet aft, whereby the full displacement occurred only at the stern, may have been of some importance. . . . No other cause, except this suction, reasonably accounts for the *Moore's* extraordinary action."

From the foregoing cases it will be apparent that the overtaking vessel must exercise great care to make ample allowance for the force of suction, leaving, especially in shallow waters, a good margin of safety.

The burden of proving that the collision is the fault of the overtaken vessel rests upon the overtaking vessel, as stated in *The Sif, supra,* at p. 415:

> "As it was the duty of the *Sif* to select a place and to keep at a safe distance in attempting to pass and as she was the overtaking ship, it was her duty, in order to exonerate herself, to show that the fault was that of the *Murcia*. This we think she has wholly failed to do."

Article 24 requires the overtaking vessel in a stream to give the vessel ahead such wide berth as the condition of the currents may require. *The Ruth,* 186 Fed. 87.

While the overtaking vessel must keep out of the way of the overtaken vessel, it is the correlative duty of the latter to keep her course and speed, and avoid any maneuver calculated to embarrass the overtaking vessel in passing. *The Charles R. Spencer,* 178 Fed. 862.

## ARTICLE XXV
## NARROW CHANNELS

| *International Rules* | *Inland Rules* |
|---|---|
| *Article 25.* In narrow channels every steam-vessel shall, when it is safe and practicable, keep to that side of the fair-way or mid-channel which lies on the starboard side of such vessel. | *Article 25.* Identical with International Rules. Identical with Rule X of Pilot Rules. |

The courts have defined a narrow channel as a body of water navigated up and down in opposite directions, and do not include harbor waters with piers on each side where the necessities of commerce require navigation in every conceivable direction. *The No. 4,* 161 Fed. 847.

What is a Narrow Channel?

Applying this definition in connection with the bay and harbor of New York, the court said:

". . . the rule [narrow channel] does not apply to the waters of the upper bay or of the lower, considered each as a single body of water, it does apply to the well recognized channels which are familiar to navigators in those bays. To the Swash, the Main Ship, the East, the Bay Ridge and the Red Hook Channels, we have already indicated that the rule applies. We see no reason for differentiating the Main Ship Channel which runs from the mouths of the two rivers, between Governor's Island on the east and Ellis and Liberty Islands on the west, across the Upper Bay to the Narrows. It is a well-known channel, charted and buoyed, and a steam vessel navigating it should follow the rule that requires her 'when it is safe and practicable' to keep to that side of the fairway or mid-channel which lies on her starboard side. The circumstance that there is a great deal of cross-travel in the upper bay itself does not seem a sufficient reason for abrogating the wholesome rule that vessels moving up or down some designated channel therein shall keep to the starboard side of it. Rule 25 is not to be construed as prohibiting vessels from crossing such channel at any convenient angle whenever the exigencies of their own navigation make it necessary or desirable for them to proceed from one to the other side of such channel; but when no such exigency exists they should keep to the proper side of the channel."

The La Bretagne, 179 Fed. 286, 287.

The Upper Bay to 23rd Street, New York, along the shore of which on both sides is a continuous succession of wharves and piers, is not a narrow channel within the meaning of the rule.  *The Islander,* 152 Fed. 385.

The Hudson River above 23rd Street, New York, and within the city limits where there are piers on each side, is not a narrow channel.  *The No. 4,* 161 Fed. 847.

The Hudson River in the vicinity of Yonkers, where there is a single deep and straight channel for a number of miles, is a narrow channel.  *The Benjamin Franklin,* 145 Fed. 13.

The Columbia River in the vicinity of Westport Light is a narrow channel.  *United States v. Port of Portland,* 161 Fed. 193.

A dredged channel in the Chesapeake Bay six hundred feet wide is a narrow channel.  *The Acilia,* 120 Fed. 455.

Gedney Channel, the entrance to New York Harbor, is a narrow channel.  *The Delaware,* 161 U. S. 459.

The entrance to Cherbourg Harbor, the entrance to Falmouth Harbor, the River Scheldt, the Bosphorus, Crosby Channel in the Mersey, and Swin Channel at the entrance to the Thames, have all been held by the courts to be narrow channels.

The Strait of Messina, two miles wide, was, in the case of *The Rhondda,* 5 Asp. M.C. (N.S.) 114, deemed a narrow channel within the meaning of the rule.

**"When it is Safe and Practicable."**  The words "when it is safe and practicable" are intended to cover the reasonable necessities of practical navigation.   A vessel may have to enter or leave a dock situated on her left side of the channel, or she may be obliged to swing in the channel, and in the course of the maneuver, get on the wrong side.   Allowance is made for such reasonable necessities of navigation. If navigation is not safe and practical on the right side of the channel, the necessary deviation therefrom is permitted, subject, however, to the requirement that the vessel return as soon as possible to her right side. It was so held in *The Three Brothers,* 170 Fed. 48, at p. 50:

> ". . . the rule must be construed in the light of common sense. Its purpose is to prevent collisions not to produce them. It is not an inflexible rule to be followed in all cases, and, where it is manifest that a blind adherence will produce disaster, it is not only the right but the duty of the navigator to disregard it. The rule so states explicitly. It must be followed only 'when it is safe and practicable.' "

Any deviation or departure from the rule will not be excused, however, unless an immediate and actual danger exists which cannot be avoided by an otherwise permitted maneuver.

In the case of *The Albert Dumois,* 177 U. S. 240, that vessel, proceeding up the Mississippi River below New Orleans, was on the east side of the river (her right water). The *Argo* was proceeding down the river, also on the east side, and claimed by the *Dumois* to be approaching "end on or nearly end on." The *Dumois* sounded two whistles indicating her intention to sheer out into the river and pass the *Argo* starboard to starboard, her excuse being that on the east bank of the river was a cluster of white lights belonging to a tug and two luggers which were an obstruction to her course. The court said at p. 249:

> "We cannot, however, accept this as a 'special circumstance' within the meaning of Rule 24 [present Article 27] rendering a departure from Rule 18 [present Article 25] necessary 'to avoid immediate danger,' since if there were any danger at all it was not an immediate one, or one which could not have been provided against by easing the engines of the *Dumois* and slackening her speed. Exceptions to the general rules of navigation are admitted with reluctance on the part of the courts, and only when an adherence to such rules must almost necessarily result in a collision—such, for instance, as

a manifestly wrong manœuvre on the part of an approaching vessel. *Belden v. Chase,* 150 U.S. 674, 699; *The Britannia,* 153 U.S. 130; *The Test,* 5 Notes of Cases, 276; *The Superior,* 6 Notes of Cases, 607; *The Khedive,* 5 App. Cases 876; *The Benares,* 9 Prob. Div. 16; Marsden on Collisions, 480. As was said in *The John Buddle,* 5 Notes of Cases, 387: 'All rules are framed for the benefit of ships navigating the seas, and, no doubt, circumstances will arise in which it would be perfect folly to attempt to carry into execution every rule, however wisely framed. It is, at the same time, of the greatest possible importance to adhere as closely as possible to established rules, and never to allow a deviation from them unless the circumstances which are alleged to have rendered such a deviation necessary, are most distinctly approved and established; otherwise, vessels would always be in doubt and doing wrong.' "

When such deviation is necessary, it must not be more than is required for the purpose, and the vessel must return to her own side of the channel as soon as possible.

"Each of these vessels was entitled to presume that the other would act lawfully; would keep to her own side; if temporarily crowded out of her course, would return to it as soon as possible; that she would pursue the customary track of vessels in the channel, regulating her action so as to avoid danger. *The Servia,* 149 U.S. 144; *The City of New York,* 147 U.S. 72; *Belden v. Chase,* 150 U.S. 674."
*The Victory & The Plymothian,* 168 U.S. 410, 426.

" 'I think it is perfectly clear that the collision occurred in a narrow channel, and that it occurred on the north side of that channel, and then, when one finds that the *Prudhoe Castle,* the downcoming vessel, was on her wrong side of the channel at the time of the collision under a starboard helm, it is very difficult to see how the primary blame of this collision should have been other than on the part of that vessel.' "
*The Florence,* 186 Fed. 57, 62, 63.

". . . it must be found that she was, when in collision with the *Georgic,* on the wrong side of the channel, having gone there with deliberation and without necessity, and was therefore at fault. *The Sea King,* 114 Fed. 535, 52 C.C.A. 349; *The No. 4,* 161 Fed. 847, 88 C.C.A. 665."
*The Georgic et al.,* 180 Fed. 863, 869.

See also, *Screw Collier Co. v. Isabella Webster or Kerr* [1910] App. Cas. 165.

A custom or practice of vessels to use the wrong side of a narrow channel under certain tidal conditions because of it being easier to navigate will not operate to excuse a vessel for such violation of the rule.    Presumption of fault follows, as is shown by the following:

> "These rules [Inland Rules] in this case made it the duty of these transports to be on the right-hand side of the center of the stream, and, in point of fact, admittedly they were on the left.    The fact that it may be the custom to do this when there is an ebb tide, and that it may be easier to go up on the New York side than on the other side, and that they thereby can go a little faster, does not alter the fact that any vessel that goes up in that way violates the law and takes the risk, and, if there is any collision, is presumably in fault."
>
> *The Transfer No. 10, 137* Fed. 666.

See also, *The Acilia,* 120 Fed. 455.

Held at fault for being on the wrong side of narrow channel:

> *The Acilia,* 120 Fed. 455; *The Dauntless,* 129 Fed. 715; *The Bee,* 138 Fed. 303; *The Benjamin Franklin,* 145 Fed. 13; *The Gerry,* 161 Fed. 413; *The Little,* 168 Fed. 393; *The Captain Bennett,* 171 Fed. 199; *The P. J. T. Co. No. 7,* 173 Fed. 1016; *The La Bretagne,* 179 Fed. 286; *The Georgic et al.,* 180 Fed. 863; *The Volund,* 181 Fed. 643; *The George F. Randolph,* 200 Fed. 96; *The P. R. R. No. 32—The John J. Hague,* 240 Fed. 118.

**When Approaching Vessel is in the Wrong Water.** Starboarding in a narrow channel to a meeting steamer approaching so as to involve risk of collision is very rarely a correct maneuver.    A vessel in her right water must assume that a vessel approaching on the wrong side of the channel will obey the rules and cross over to her proper side, but if such vessel continues to approach on the wrong side, the safer maneuver for the other vessel is to stop and reverse.

**Vessels Approaching at Sharp Bends.** When two vessels are approaching and will meet at a sharp bend, the vessel having the tide against her should not attempt to round the point until the vessel having the tide with her has passed clear.

*The Galatea,* 92 U.S. 439, 446; *The Transfer No. 12,* 221 Fed. 409; *The Talabot,* 6 Asp. M.C (N.S.) 602.

The rule (Art. 25) has no application to sailing vessels, and steamers must, under Article 20, keep clear of such vessels and be prepared for any necessary changes in their course.

In the case of *The Bulgaria,* 168 Fed. 457, it was claimed by the steamer that the schooner *Judson* which was tacking across Gedney Channel ought to have kept out of the channel, as the *Bulgaria* with her deep draft was confined to a narrow channel and that the only thing she could do was to stop and reverse, as she did.   Also, that in the emergency when it was apparent that it was necessary to do something to prevent the collision the schooner should have put about instead of holding her course.   The court said at p. 460:

> "The schooner was justified in using the channel and the steamer was required to avoid her.  She should have noticed and provided for the schooner's leeway."

**Entering or Leaving a Narrow Channel.**
A steamer intending to enter a narrow channel should so maneuver in approaching the entrance as to leave ample room for outcoming vessels to pass her port to port, and should, if it is practical, approach the channel from the side she must keep after entering it.

A steamer on leaving a narrow channel should pass out keeping to the starboard side until she is well clear of the entrance, and should not change her course to port (if bound in a direction which requires it) until she is well clear of the entrance and of vessels passing in.

At the entrance to narrow channels either Article 19 (Crossing Rule) or Article 25 (Narrow Channel Rule), or both, may be operative and vessels approaching or leaving from their own proper side may save themselves some very anxious and trying moments as to what rule is applicable, by adhering to the practice above suggested.

See Article 19 (Crossing Rule), page 118.

## ARTICLE XXVI

## RIGHT OF WAY OF FISHING VESSELS

*International Rules*

*Article 26.* Sailing vessels under way shall keep out of the way of sailing vessels or boats fishing with nets, or lines, or trawls. This rule shall not give to any vessel or boat engaged in fishing the right of obstructing a fair-way used by vessels other than fishing vessels or boats.

*Inland Rules*

*Article 26.* Identical with International Rules.

This article is but a codification of the unwritten law of the sea prevailing before the present rules were formulated, that a free vessel must keep out of the way of fishing vessels or boats encumbered by having out nets, trawls or lines.   The article makes mention only of the duty of sailing vessels in respect to other sailing vessels or boats fishing.   The same duty, however, is imposed upon free steamers in respect to steam vessels fishing.

"Fair-way," as used in this article, is clearly intended to signify narrow waters through which vessels must pass. It is not applicable to a fair-way in the open sea.

## ARTICLE XXVII

## GENERAL PRUDENTIAL RULE

| *International Rules* | *Inland Rules* |
|---|---|
| *Article 27.* In obeying and construing these rules due regard shall be had to all dangers of navigation and collision, and to any special circumstances which may render a departure from the above rules necessary in order to avoid immediate danger. | *Article 27.* Identical with International Rules. Identical with Pilot Rule XI. |

**Rule for Exceptional Situations.**

This article is entitled the General Prudential Rule. It is obviously a rule for exceptional situations—an emergency rule.* Although the other rules are so com-

---

*The following from the reported discussion of Article 27 at the International Marine Conference is of interest in this connection:

Captain Sampson (United States): " . . . I would add that to my mind it appears that this rule was formulated to show that the rules which had preceded it were not to be followed when a ship was liable to come to grief from following these rules. That is to say, if a ship is beating up in a narrow channel, it, of course, becomes necessary for her to tack ship when she is close to the opposite shore; and if, in doing so, she goes contrary to any of the preceding rules, it is a sufficient excuse that she is avoiding a danger of navigation."
*Prot. of Proc.,* p. 131.

Captain Shackford (United States): " . . . I want to say a word in regard to the construction of Article 23 [present Art. 27] by Captain Sampson. That is the way I have always construed the rule. I have always supposed that it referred entirely to shoals, rocks, wrecks, etc., and I think that this is the opinion among merchant sailors generally."
*Prot. of Proc.,* p. 134.

Mr. Hall (Great Britain): " . . . Every sailor will agree that there must be conditions when it will be necessary that both vessels should act and not merely one of them, in order to avoid a collision. Accordingly, we ought to emphasize that as much as we possibly can, and for that reason we have brought forward this proposition. We want to make it clear to every sailor that he must not say: 'The rule is that I am to keep my course and speed, and I shall stick to it under all circumstances.' When it is necessary for him to act, as well as the other ship, he ought to do so, and we have endeavored to impress that duty, if possible, more strongly upon him."
*Prot. of Proc.,* p. 543.

Admiral Bowden-Smith (Great Britain): " . . . I would be very glad if the sailors of the Conference would give their minds to this and see if it is possible to find something which will give the officer on

plete as to provide for most situations, they cannot in the nature of things contemplate every possible contingency. Outside perils or the improper navigation of other vessels may present exceptional conditions under which strict adherence to the definite rules would plainly invite collision or other disaster, which skill and good seamanship, though involving a departure from the rules, might avert.    In such circumstances this article permits and even requires maneuvers to avoid pressing danger that would otherwise be a breach of the rules.

" 'Cases arise in navigation where a stubborn adherence to a general rule is a culpable fault, for the reason that every navigator ought to know that rules of navigation are ordained not to promote collisions,   .   .   .' "

*The New York,* 175 U. S. 187, 205.

---

the holding-on ship no excuse for insisting on his right when it would cause loss of life and property."          *Prot. of Proc.,* pp. 543, 544.

Mr. Hall (Great Britain):  "  .  . It was pointed out that it was very possible that sailors would not be quite certain whether the existing words 'dangers of navigation' under special circumstances would include danger of collision. We have thought it very advisable to put an end to such doubt as that. We have also been actuated by another motive which the Conference may remember I pointed out before. When we proposed the important change which the Conference has adopted, to prescribe that the holding-on vessel should keep her speed as well as keep her course, we thought it was most desirable, if we could, to impress upon the minds of sailors that they must not hold on too long under this rule, and so that the sailor would not say, 'This rule tells me to keep my speed; therefore I keep my speed up to a collision.' We think it most desirable, if we can do so, by adding these words, to call still further the attention of sailors to that fact and to impress upon them that although they must obey these rules they are not to hold on under them when they see that danger is brought about by such obedience, at a time when it is necessary for both vessels to act.  .  .  .

"Therefore, it was to make it perfectly clear to a sailor that he is not to neglect the ordinary precautions of seamen, and that he is to have due regard to the dangers of collision as well as to the dangers of navigation—that is to say, that he is not merely to act because he sees a danger of navigation like a rock or a current, but he is also to act when he sees that it is really necessary for him to help the other vessel to prevent collision, and he is not entitled to stick to the rule and say: 'I am obeying the rule; I need not do any more.' He must do his best to try and prevent a collision. Certainly that is what every practical seaman will say he ought to do, but men may be found who do not quite understand the rules, and who may say, 'Here is a rule which tells me to do so and so, and I am obeying that rule.' We want to call to their attention the importance of their acting when it is necessary, when there is a special danger to navigation, and we want to instruct them that they must have regard to special circumstances to determine their actions. It is for these reasons that we venture to propose to insert these words."

*Prot. of Proc.,* pp. 628, 629.

Excuses
Departure
from Rules
only when
Necessary to
Avoid
Danger.

This article for exceptional cases is operative only in such cases. It does not excuse a departure from the definite rules, unless and until such departure is imperative, if imminent danger is to be avoided.

> "Exceptions to the general rules of navigation are admitted with reluctance on the part of the courts, and only when an adherence to such rules must almost necessarily result in a collision—such, for instance, as a manifestly wrong maneuver on the part of an approaching vessel."
>
> *The Albert Dumois,* 177 U.S. 240, 249.

And see *The Acilia,* 120 Fed. 455.

> "The obligation imposed to obey these rules is imperative, and those violating them, except under circumstances contemplated by the rules, must bear the consequences if damages ensue. . . . *The Breakwater,* 155 U.S. 252, 15 Sup. Ct. 99, 39 L. Ed. 139; *The Delaware,* 161 U.S. 459, 466, 16 Sup. Ct. 516, 40 L. Ed. 771; *The Luckenbach,* 1 C.C.A. 489, 50 Fed. 129-134; *The Chittagong* [1901], App. Cas. 597."
>
> *The Straits of Dover,* 120 Fed. 900, 903.

> "I am of the opinion that departure from article 18 is justified when such departure is the one chance still left of avoiding danger which otherwise is inevitable."
>
> *The Benares,* 5 Asp. M.C. (N.S.) 171, 174.

The application of the article may be illustrated as follows: An overtaken vessel, required under Article 25 to hold her course and speed, may, when such navigation is necessary to avoid a danger (say a fixed obstruction or another vessel), alter her course or slacken her speed, but she must not do either until it is immediately necessary, and only to the extent required to avoid the danger. Again, a sailing vessel (a holding-on vessel), required under Article 21 to hold her course and speed, may, when necessary to avoid going aground or other danger, tack or otherwise maneuver, but she is not permitted to embarrass the burdened vessel by doing so, unless and until obliged to do so for her own safety.

And so also, a holding-on vessel, required under Article 21 to hold her course and speed, may, in fact must, when it is clearly apparent that the burdened vessel is failing to keep out of the way and cannot by her own efforts avoid a collision, assist the burdened vessel to avoid the collision by any maneuver that sound judgment and good seamanship seems to require.

Even though the emergency be produced by improper navigation on the part of another vessel, a failure to exercise prudence and common sense to avoid a collision will not be excused.

"As a privileged vessel [sailing vessel], she was bound to maintain her course so long as it was possible for the burdened vessel to avoid her, at least in the absence of some distinct indication that the burdened vessel was about to fail in her duty. We are of the opinion that the schooner had notice of the intention of the tug [burdened vessel] to hold her course, and thus create a situation where disaster was inevitable unless the schooner gave way, at a time when there was ample opportunity to have avoided a collision had she acted promptly and with ordinary skill and prudence. . . . The tug gave no indication of changing her course, and the situation was one calling for the utmost caution on the part of the schooner. . . . The tug, by her own negligence, of course, had brought about a situation where a collision could be avoided only by the prompt intelligent action of the schooner. Can there be a doubt that it was her duty so to act? Was she justified in holding her course with stubborn determination when it was demonstrated that such action could only result in a collision? We think not. The law provides that in obeying and construing the rules of navigation 'due regard shall be had to all dangers of navigation, and to any special circumstances which may render a departure from the above rules necessary in order to avoid immediate danger.' The rules are not to be blindly followed to certain disaster. It behooves every navigator to avoid a collision if he can do so, and for manifest error, except in the jaws of collision, he must be held responsible. He cannot plead that his was the privileged vessel to relieve him from consequences which were induced by his own lack of prudence and common sense."

*The Gladys,* 144 Fed. 653, 657, 658.

There is no right of way on which a vessel is entitled to insist when it is obvious that it will result in a collision. *The John H. Starin*, 162 Fed. 146.

This article does not, however, except in those emergency cases where a departure from the rules is *necessary* in order to avoid immediate danger, in any way modify or lessen the obligation to a strict compliance with the other articles. It does not give to the navigating officer any general latitude of judgment as to obeying the other rules; it only permits a departure from the rules to be made when *necessary* in order to avoid immediate (not remote or problematical) danger, and only to the extent required to accomplish that object.

> "The application of rule 27 is restricted by its terms to situations of immediate danger. That rule applies only to exceptional cases. As said by the Supreme Court in *The Oregon*, 158 U.S. 186, 202, 15 Sup. Ct. 804, 39 L. Ed. 943, exceptions to the rules are to be admitted—'with great caution and only when imperatively required by special circumstances of the case. It follows that, under all ordinary circumstances, a vessel discharges her full duty and obligation to another by a faithful and literal observance of these rules.'
>
> "In Marsden's Collisions at Sea (6th Ed.) p. 455, it is said:
>
> " 'But article 27 applies only to cases where "there is immediate danger, perfectly clear"; and the departure from the rules must be no more than is necessary.' "
>
> *Yang-Tsze Ins. Ass'n et al. v. Furness, Withy & Co., Ltd.*, 215 Fed. 859, 861.

The burden of bringing a departure from the rules within the protection of this article rests upon the vessel that has made it.

> "And while, under Rule twenty-four [present Art. 27], in construing and obeying the rules, due regard must be had to all dangers of navigation and to any special circumstances which may exist in any particular case, rendering a departure from them necessary in order to avoid immediate danger, the burden of proof lies on the party alleging that he was justified in such departure. *The Agra*, L.R. 1 P.C. 501; *The General*

*Lee,* Ir. R. 3 Eq. 155. Indeed, in *The Agra,* it was ruled that not only must it be shown that the departure at the time it took place was necessary in order to avoid immediate danger, but also that the course adopted was reasonably calculated to avoid that danger. And it is the settled rule in this court that when a vessel has committed a positive breach of statute, she must show not only that probably her fault did not contribute to the disaster, but that it could not have done so. *The Pennsylvania,* 19 Wall. 125, 136; *Richelieu Nav. Co. v. Boston Ins. Co.,* 136 U.S. 408, 422.

"Obedience to the rules is not a fault, even if a different course would have prevented the collision, and the necessity must be clear and the emergency sudden and alarming before the act of disobedience can be excused. Masters are bound to obey the rules and entitled to rely on the assumption that they will be obeyed, and should not be encouraged to treat the exceptions as subjects of solicitude rather than the rules. *The Oregon,* 18 How. 570."

*Belden v. Chase,* 150 U.S. 674, 699.

An actual and immediate danger of navigation or collision must exist to justify a departure from the rules. The existence of danger not imminent, though perhaps near, will not excuse a departure. Consideration must be given to the possibility that the apparent maneuvers of the burdened vessel will succeed in avoiding the danger. It is only when sound judgment indicates that the burdened vessel will be unable to avoid the danger that a departure from a positive rule will be justified.

"We think there was likewise fault in the action of the *Beaconsfield* in remaining motionless for a minute and half, in full view of the tardy motion of the *Britannia* in getting astern. This is sought to be excused by the fact that her pilot feared certain rocks, or a rocky bottom, which were not far from the place where his vessel was. The actual existence of such rocks or rocky bottom was somewhat in dispute; but, accepting as we do, the statement of the Circuit Court on the subject, we cannot sustain the conduct of the *Beaconsfield.* That statement is that 'a careful collocation of the testimony of those on both steamers and elsewhere, assisted by elaborate plotting on the chart, indicates that the probabilities are that the *Britannia* would have passed astern of the *Beaconsfield* if the latter had kept her headway, even though she straightened out sufficiently to clear the reef her pilot spoke of, but by a very small margin only.'

"Stress is laid in the argument for the *Beaconsfield* on the eleventh finding, that 'at the time the *Beaconsfield* reversed she had approached so near the New York shore that, in view of her draft of water and the condition of the bottom in that locality, there was some risk of her running aground should she continue her way much longer under her port helm.'

"But the exigency, as shown by the other findings, did not require that she should continue her way 'much longer.' Had she advanced 150 feet, the collision would not have taken place."

*The Britannia,* 153 U.S. 130, 139.

See also, *The Illinois,* 103 U. S., 298, 299.

## ARTICLE XXVIII

### SOUND SIGNALS FOR PASSING STEAMERS

*International Rules*

*Article 28.* The words "short blast" used in this article shall mean a blast of about one second's duration.

When vessels are in sight of one another, a steam-vessel under way, in taking any course authorized or required by these rules, shall indicate that course by the following signals or whistle or siren, namely:

One short blast to mean, "I am directing my course to starboard."

Two short blasts to mean, "I am directing my course to port."

Three short blasts to mean, "My engines are going at full speed astern."

### SOUND SIGNALS FOR VESSELS IN SIGHT OF ONE ANOTHER

*Inland Rules*

*Article 28.* When vessels are in sight of one another a steam-vessel under way whose engines are going at full speed astern shall indicate that fact by three short blasts on the whistle.

See also:

*Article 18, Rule I*, prescribing sound signals for steam-vessels approaching each other end on or nearly so.

*Article 24, Overtaking Vessels*, under which appears Article 18, Rule VIII, prescribing sound signals for overtaking and overtaken steam-vessels.

### ARTICLE XVIII
#### Rule IX

The whistle signals provided in the rules under this article, for steam-vessels meeting, passing, or overtaking, are never to be used except when steamers are in sight of each other, and the course and position of each can be determined in the daytime by a sight of the vessel itself, or by night by seeing its signal lights. In fog, mist, falling snow or heavy rain storms, when vessels can not see each other, fog-signals only must be given.

See p. 200.

*Article 18, Rule III,* prescribing signals to be given by steam-vessels denoting a lack of understanding of the course and intention of the approaching vessel.

See p. 196.

*Article 18, Rule V,* prescribing signals to be given by steam-vessels nearing a short bend or curve in the channel and by steam-vessels moving from their docks.

The Inland Rules do not provide any signal to be given by the burdened or giving-way vessel to indicate an intended change of course. This omission is, however, covered in the

**PILOT RULES**

*Signals:*

The whistle *signals* provided in these rules shall be sounded on an efficient whistle or siren sounded by steam or by some substitute for steam.

A *short blast* of the whistle shall mean a blast of about one second's duration.

A *prolonged blast* of the whistle shall mean a blast of from four to six seconds' duration.

*One short blast* of the whistle signifies intention to direct course to own starboard, except when two steam vessels are approaching each other at right angles or obliquely, when it signifies intention of steam vessel which is to starboard of the other to hold course and speed.

*Two short blasts* of the whistle signify intention to direct course to own port.

*Three short blasts* of the whistle shall mean, "My engines are going at full speed astern."

When vessels are in sight of one another a steam vessel under way whose engines are going at full speed astern shall indicate that fact by three short blasts on the whistle.

All sound signals prescribed by the International Rules for steamers passing in sight of each other are contained in this Article. The Inland Rules are differently arranged and excepting only the three-blast signal indicating the engines are going full speed astern, all the sound signals are contained in Article 18. Supplementing the Inland Rules, the Pilot Rules are also operative in the inland waters of the United States. The Pilot Rules have the force of law except when inconsistent with the Inland

Rules, when the latter take precedence. Certain of the Pilot Rules in respect to sound signals have been held by the courts to be invalid. Reference to such Pilot Rules will be found on pp. 134, 179, 213, 217.

The International Rules contain only three whistle signals for vessels in sight of each other, viz., two signals denoting changes of course, and one denoting "My engines are going at full speed astern."

The Inland Rules and the Pilot Rules contain four whistle signals for vessels in sight of each other, viz., two signals for passing; one signal denoting "My engines are going at full speed astern"; and one denoting a lack of understanding as to the course or intention of the approaching vessel, usually known as a danger signal.

The meaning of each of the passing signals depends upon the situation of the vessels with relation to each other when such signal is given. Thus—

*One Short Blast* indicates, "I am directing my course to starboard." It does not necessarily mean, as do the Inland Rules, a port to port passing. When however, steamers are meeting on opposite courses a change of course to starboard is usually for a port to port passing. This, however, is merely an incident of the maneuver. The sig-

*One Short Blast* between steamers on opposite courses indicates a port to port passing, and, under the Pilot Rules, it signifies intention to direct course to own starboard.

If the situation be an overtaking one, one short blast indicates a desire to pass on the starboard side of the overtaken steamer, and under the Pilot Rules

nal indicates only the change of course to starboard.

The International Rules do not permit any whistle signal by the holding-on vessel to indicate her intention to hold her course and speed. The only sound signal provided for such vessel is the detonating signal (under Art. 12) to attract attention.

All the signals provided by the International Rules indicate either a change of course, or that the engines are working at full speed astern. The holding-on vessel being required (under Art. 21) to hold her course and speed, it necessarily follows that she cannot use a signal indicating a maneuver not permitted under the rules.

*Two Short Blasts* indicate only, "I am directing my course to port." As already stated in connection with the *One Blast Signal,*

it signifies intention to direct course to own starboard.

The Inland Rules do not provide any signal for use of steamers meeting on crossing courses, but under the Pilot Rules one short blast from the burdened vessel signifies intention to direct course to own starboard, whereas the same signal of one blast from the privileged vessel signifies intention to hold her course and speed. This signal is permitted the holding-on steamer, but it is not mandatory upon her.

In respect to such signal, the court said in the case of *The Haida,* 191 Fed. 623, at p. 626:

" . . . (Art. 19) which gives the privilege to the vessel having the other on her port hand, and (Art. 21) which requires her to keep her course and speed, do not admit of the imposition upon that privilege by the pilot rules of a condition that she answer a signal."

*Two Short Blasts* between steamers meeting on opposite courses, indicate an intention to pass starboard to starboard, and, unit does not necessarily indicate a starboard to starboard passing.

der the Pilot Rules, it signifies intention to direct course to own port.

Such signal from an overtaking steamer indicates the desire to pass on the port side of the overtaken steamer, and, under the Pilot Rules, it signifies intention to direct course to own port.

As before mentioned, the Inland Rules do not provide any signal for steamers meeting on crossing courses, but under the Pilot Rules, a two-blast signal from the burdened vessel (the steamer having the other on her starboard bow) signifies intention to direct course to own port.

*Three Short Blasts.* Identical with Inland Rules.

*Three Short Blasts* indicate, under both Inland Rules and Pilot Rules, "My engines are going at full speed astern."

The International Rules do not provide this signal.

*Four Short Blasts* signify, under both Inland and Pilot Rules, a failure to understand the course and intention of the other vessel. This is commonly known as the danger signal, and is so designated in the Pilot Rules.

The differences in the meaning of the signals under the International and Inland (including Pilot) Rules as above outlined are important and should be borne in mind. It will be observed, however, that except for the alarm signal (Inland Art. 18, Rule 3) and the one-blast signal in the Pilot Rules (by use of which the privileged vessel is permitted to indicate her intention to hold her course and speed, but which has been held by the court as not being compulsory upon her) the several whistle signals prescribed indicate in the actual navigation of steamers practically the same maneuver, whether used in International or Inland waters.

The purpose of these signals is that by their use each vessel shall give to the other specific and timely information of its own intended maneuvers.

The proper use of the signals is to indicate the taking of a course or other maneuver authorized or required by the rules.

The Signals are to be Given by Steamers Observing the Other Rules.

The rules clearly so provide:

The International Rules plainly say:

" . . . a steam vessel under way in taking any course authorized or required by these rules, shall indicate that course by the following signals."

The Inland Rules and the Pilot Rules prescribe the maneuver to be made in each situation, and the signal to be given when making such maneuver.

It is, therefore, apparent that the use of the signals does not permit or justify a steamer in a disregard of the other rules; nor will it be accepted as excusing her from any breach of the other articles.

"When vessels are meeting head on, or nearly so, they are under the imperative obligation to pass to the right, by the law of congress, unless some special circumstances justify a departure pursuant to rule 24 [now Art. 27]; and neither can be obliged to depart from the statute at the request of the other. So, when two steam-vessels are crossing so as to involve risk of collision, the vessel which has the other on her starboard side must keep out of the way, and the other must keep her course, unless a departure is necessary pursuant to rule 24 [now Art. 27] and the vessel which is required to keep her course cannot be compelled to depart from it at the instance of the other. . . . If a proposition is given proposing a departure by one vessel, and is consented to by the other vessel, undoubtedly the former is justified in assuming that the other understands that a departure is to be attempted and will govern herself accordingly."

*The John King,* 49 Fed. 469, 472, 473.

See also, *The George S. Shultz,* 84 Fed. 508; *The Cygnus,* 142 Fed. 85; *The John H. Starin,* 162 Fed. 146; *The Pawnee,* 168 Fed. 371; *The Montauk,* 180 Fed. 697.

"Where it [Art. 28] does apply is where a vessel, having a course and being on a course, is found varying it or making some alteration of it *authorized or required by the rules.* For example, if vessels are meeting end on and you port your helm in order to comply with the requirements of the rule then applicable; or, to take another case, where a vessel sees another on her starboard bow, and under the circumstances is required to keep out of the way; or, to take yet other cases, where the following vessel has to keep out of the way of the overtaken ship, or where a steamship has to give way to a sailing vessel. In all those cases the course is authorized by the rules, and if in so doing the vessel alters her course by the action of her helm she is required to give notice to the other vessel."

*The Mourne,* 9 Asp. M.C. (N.S.) 155.

Failure to signal a change of course, or failure to change a course in accordance with a signal given, are both breaches of the regulations and constitute faults under the rules.

For a vessel to alter her course without previously informing the other vessel that she is doing so would leave that vessel in doubt as to what she ought herself to do; or, for a vessel to signal that her course is being changed, and then not alter her course accordingly, is actually to mislead. On the other hand, if the courses of the respective vessels are such that they will pass clear and no changes in course are made, and no signals given, each vessel knows exactly what to expect of the other. *The City of Lowell,* 152 Fed. 593.

In the case of *The New Orleans,* 171 Fed. 764, the steamer *Bayport* was held at fault for being on the wrong side of the channel and for blowing two whistles and doing nothing to carry out the intention expressed thereby. The court said:

> "If her signals were justifiable she has still to account for her own failure to act upon them."

Manifestly, the fact that the course taken may be improper, and one not authorized or required by the rules, will not excuse a failure to indicate such course by the proper signal. A steamer failing to give the prescribed signal would be doubly at fault.

In the case of *The Hero* (Court of Appeals), 12 Asp. M.C. (N.S.) 10 [1911] Prob. Div. 128, it was argued that as the steamer had taken a course not authorized or required by the rules, but, on the contrary, a wrong and improper course, she was not required to sound the signal under the strict interpretation of Article 28.

The court said at p. 159:

> "We cannot accede to such a contention. . . . We do not think that the language of art. 28, fairly and reasonably interpreted, involves such a conclusion."

The failure of navigators to give information, by timely signals (as required by the rule), of their intended movements to an approaching vessel is a prolific source of collision.

*Failure or Undue Delay in Giving Signals Creates Collisions.*

It has already been stated that any change of course or other maneuver must be timely to the end that both collision and danger of collision may be averted. *Prompt* information of maneuvers being or to be made is most important, if the purpose of the rules is to be attained.

*Signals Must be Given Promptly.*

> "Timely signals are required, because such signals tend to avert the natural consequences of carelessness, and the lack

of previous timely observation on one side or the other, as well as to enable the boats to come to a common understanding as to the mode of passing."

*The Clara,* 49 Fed. 765, 767.

**The Signals are Mandatory.**

As between vessels approaching so as to involve risk of collision, and in sight of one another, the rule is compulsory and signals must be given.

Until the present rules were adopted the giving of these signals was optional, or at least the necessity of sounding such signals was left to the judgment of the navigators, depending upon the circumstances of the case.

At the Conference the question of whether the giving of the signals should be left permissive, or made compulsory, was the subject of much discussion. It was decided that the rule should be made mandatory, and it was worded accordingly.*

---

* Mr. Goodrich (United States): " . . . it is the intention of the amendment to change the permissive nature of this rule as it is now adopted to a mandatory character, and make it a positive injunction upon all steamers to indicate their course, as far as they can, and thus remove another element of uncertainty in the manœuvres of vessels which have to approach each other at any time."    *Prot. of Proc.,* p. 116.

Mr. Hall (Great Britain): " . . . There is one great advantage in this, and I think that it is a very great advantage, which we ought to consider. Frequently a small sailing vessel may be sailing and a five or ten thousand ton steamer may be coming up astern of her. It takes a long time for a steamer like that to show that she has altered her course, and we have known of cases, in our experience, where sailing vessels have been frightened at not getting any signal from the steamer which is overtaking them, indicating that she is going to take steps for them; and the sailing vessels have altered their course and by that alteration negatived the steps which the steamer was taking without their knowing it. I think it is a matter of very great importance. It would say to the sailing vessel this, 'I see you; I am going to take steps for you.' It would give confidence. At present the man in a sailing vessel, when he sees a steamer which is not bound to give him any whistle, does not know that he is seen. Then, again, these fast steamers come down upon a sailing vessel so quickly that the sailing master may lose his head, get frightened, and alter his course, and put his helm up or down, and so bring about the very collision which it was intended to avoid.

"I think, therefore, in view of the fact that there is really no hardship on steamers, and in view of the counterbalancing advantage it would be to the vessel to whom they are to give the signal, that the proposition of the learned delegate from the United States is one that deserves our cordial support. . . .

"We also move, further, to have a heading to this rule, which does not exist at the present time, so that it shall be impressed upon the minds of the sailors that these are sound-signals for vessels in sight. We pro-

No latitude of judgment is permitted as to the necessity of giving the signal.   It must be given.

"It was suggested in argument that the tug could in no case be held in fault for not blowing a signal, as under no circumstances was such a signal required to be given to a sailing vessel.   Article 28 . . . provides: 'When vessels are in sight of one another a steam-vessel under way, whose engines are going at full speed astern, shall indicate that fact by three short blasts on the whistle.'   *This article made it obligatory* upon the tug, when she put her engines full speed astern, to give warning of that fact by three short blasts."

*The Triton,* 118 Fed. 329, 332.

"She [privileged vessel] should have kept her course and speed, unless in case of imminent danger, and the *Bluefields* [burdened vessel] had the right to assume that she would do so [*The Britannia,* 153 U. S. 130; *The Delaware,* 161 U. S. 459–469; *The Albert Dumois,* 177 U. S. 240–250; *The Mary Powell,* 92 Fed. 408]; and, in case of emergency justifying a departure therefrom should have followed strictly the rules

pose to give it a heading, 'Sound-signal for vessels in sight of one another.' "
*Prot. of Proc.,* pp. 119, 120.

Mr. Goodrich (United States): " . . . I may perhaps say that it is another exemplification of the manifest desire of the Conference that the rules shall be made, so far as they can be made, positive, and to give another element of certainty in regard to the movements of vessels which are approaching each other where risk of collision is involved."
*Prot. of Proc.,* p. 553.

Dr. Sieveking: " . . . It is a very annoying, a very awkward, and a very disagreeable situation to be put in, to have to hold your course and hold your speed, and to be in doubt whether the other vessel is running into you or not, or trying to avoid you.   Such is the only advantage which I can see given by this amendment.   Is that advantage to be compared with the disadvantage that the signals may be misunderstood? . . . She is *allowed* to give a signal now.   Under the present amendment she is to be *ordered* to give a signal, so that is a new duty."
*Prot. of Proc.,* pp. 560, 561.

Mr. Hall (Great Britain): " . . . The learned delegate from Germany has asked, What is the advantage to the holding-on vessel? I venture to say that it is a very great advantage to the holding-on vessel to know that the other vessel is going to act; that she sees her. It comes to this: It says, 'I see you.   I am going to keep out of your way.'   I venture to think that is an advantage, which cannot be easily overestimated, especially for small vessels, when they see a large steamer coming down upon them which would take a very considerable time before she can act under her helm.   I say that it is a very great advantage for a small vessel to know that the large steamer sees her and is taking the proper steps to keep out of her way."
*Prot. of Proc.,* pp. 566, 567.

[sounding the proper signals] governing such maneuver, which she failed to do; and, upon reversing her engines, she should have also complied promptly with the rules [given the proper signal] governing such movement; . . . "

*The Straits of Dover,* 120 Fed. 900, 904.

"And we agree that the *Raven* was also at fault. If her testimony be accepted, she gave no signals whatever from the beginning to the end, and assuming this to be true she cannot be absolved for such an omission. . . . She may have regarded the *Delaware* as 'practically unmanageable', and may have believed that she herself had the choice of sides; but even in that event she was taking the risk of an unexpected movement on the part of the dredge, and that risk she could have avoided, or at least could have minimized, simply by giving the proper passing signal.

"This fault alone is sufficient to charge her with contributing negligence."

*The A. A. Raven* (C.C.A.), 231 Fed. 380, 386.

"Furthermore, the law required the *Fagelund* to give three blasts of her whistle to indicate the reversal of her engines, with which requirement she wholly failed to comply. It is well settled that, where a vessel has committed a positive breach of a statutory duty, she must show, not only that probably her fault did not contribute to the disaster, but that it could not have done so. *The Pennsylvania,* 19 Wall. 125, 136, 22 L. Ed. 148; *The Beaver,* 219 Fed. 134, 135 C.C.A. 32; *The Ellis,* 152 Fed. 981, 82 C.C.A. 112; *Davidson v. American S. B. Co.,* 120 Fed. 250, 56 C.C.A. 86; *The Dauntless* (D.C.), 121 Fed. 420; *The Admiral Schley,* 142 Fed. 64-73, C.C.A. 250; *Hawgood Transit Co. v. Mesaba S.S. Co.,* 166 Fed. 697, 92, C.C.A. 369."

*The Thielbek,* 241 Fed. 209, 216.

In the case of *The Atkins Hughes,* 199 Fed. 938, the steamer *Bayamo,* at anchor in quarantine grounds, had weighed anchor and was moving out astern. She collided with a barge in tow of the *Atkins Hughes.* The court said at pp. 943-4:

"Nor is it possible to absolve the *Bayamo* from fault. Article 28 of the Inland Rules requires that: [quoting article] . . . The steamship should therefore have sounded three whistles, and, not having done so, the burden of proof is on her to show that failure to comply with the statute did not cause or contribute to collision."

See also, *The Deutschland,* 129 Fed. 964, affirmed 137 Fed. 1018; *The Aurelia,* 183 Fed. 341.

Identically the same requirement, perhaps in more positive language, has been laid down by the English courts: **English Decisions.**

> "The rule is perfectly clear. The word *'shall'* is there— 'shall sound his whistle'—and that word *'shall'* must be obeyed; and if officers of the watch for any reason choose to neglect the duty which that rule imposes upon them [namely, to give the proper signal when they change their course] they have only themselves to blame."
> *Fremona v. the Electra, Shipping Gazette, June 25, 1907.*

The *Fremona* was held at fault because the second officer, having made a proper change in the course of the vessel, failed to indicate it by signal.

In the case of *The Anselm,* 10 Asp. M.C. (N.S.) 257 (Admiralty), that steamer, when proceeding up the Para Estuary, Amazon River, sighted the steamer *Cyril* several miles distant coming down. As they approached, the two steamers were meeting end on. The *Anselm* ported slightly when the steamers were about two miles apart, and then, noticing the *Cyril* was starboarding, ported a little more (the proper maneuver under the meeting rule (Art. 18) and also under the narrow channel rule (Art. 25)), but did not sound the one-blast signal, which was not blown until about two minutes after the first porting. The Admiralty Court said at pp. 259, 260:

> "The first question I have to ask myself is,—Did the fourth officer commit a breach of the regulations by not sounding the whistle one short blast when he first ported? I am of opinion that the rule is conclusive on that matter. Counsel for the defendants say there is nothing in the rule to show that you shall sound the whistle at the same time as you commence to direct your course to starboard; but as I read the rule you shall do it as soon as you are directing your course to starboard. My own feeling is that the fourth officer should have sounded that blast when he first ported. He

certainly should have sounded it when he decided to continue directing his course to starboard. . . . three minutes before the collision—that would be a minute after the first signal was given—the chief officer of the *Anselm* determined to reverse his engines, which he did. . . . No signal was sounded when the *Anselm's* engines were reversed, although the rule says that when the engines are reversed three blasts shall be given. That, again, was a distinct breach of the rule, and I think it is my duty to say it is a serious breach. Officers must obey the regulations."

But on the finding of fact that:

"It is perfectly plain that the question of the signalling in this particular case had nothing to do with the collision. It was perfectly clear to the people on each of these ships what the other vessel was doing. . . . the non-obedience to the regulations had no possible effect upon the collision,"

the court absolved the *Anselm* from blame. Upon appeal, however, the Court of Appeal (10 Asp. M.C. 438) reversed the lower court, and held the *Anselm* at fault both for failure to blow the one blast when she first ported and for failure to give the three-blast signal when her engines were reversed, saying at p. 441:

"I think that from the general seamanship point of view there are three matters in which the *Anselm* distinctly is to blame. In the first place, it seems to me that having the *Cyril* upon her port bow, and seeing the *Cyril* starboarding, and she continuing her port helm, it was certainly right for her and necessary for her to indicate what she was doing to the *Cyril* —I might say almost apart from the rules, but I will take it for the purpose of my judgment that in that particular respect she was disobeying the rules. . . . it being her duty, as undoubtedly it was, to port, it is quite impossible to say that the omission of the *Anselm* to signal that she was porting her helm had no effect upon this collision. Then there is the non-signalling that she was reversing. We are advised by our assessors—who have also advised us with regard to the port helm signal—that the non-indicating to this vessel which was rapidly approaching that the *Anselm* was reversing her engines was abstaining from giving her information which might be useful, if only for the purpose of calling her marked attention to what was going on in front of her. That seems to me the essence and pith and marrow of the rule which indicates that these signals are to be given . . . I therefore come to the conclusion that the *Anselm* was to blame in these three respects, and that as regards two of them—namely, neglect to give sound signals when porting and when reversing—it is quite impossible to come to the conclusion that they had no effect upon the collision."

Again, in the case of *The Corinthian*, 11 Asp. M.C. (N.S.) 208 (Admiralty), that steamer and the steamer *Malin Head* were meeting practically end on in the St. Lawrence River. The *Malin Head* ported, sounding a proper signal, and then steadied for a time variously fixed at two minutes or more, but certainly for an appreciable time. Finding that the *Corinthian* was still sheering towards her, she hard-a-ported her helm, but gave no corresponding sound signal to inform the *Corinthian* of what she had done. The Admiralty Court said at p. 212:

> "I am advised in this case by the Elder Brethren, and I agree with them, that in this particular case the non-blowing of the signal when the hard-a-porting took place had no effect because it is distinctly proved by the *Corinthian's* witnesses that they saw the vessel hard-a-porting for a considerable time before the collision. They put it at five minutes, and, if that be so, who can say that the fact that a blast was not blown had any effect upon the knowledge of those who were navigating the *Corinthian*?"

And because of its finding that had the *Malin Head* blown the signal, it would not have conveyed any information which the *Corinthian* did not already have, and that the failure to blow the signal did not, therefore, in any way contribute to the collision, the court excused the *Malin Head* from fault.

The Court of Appeal (11 Asp. M.C. (N.S.) 264) again reversed the lower court solely upon the failure of the *Malin Head* to sound the signal when she altered her helm to hard-a-port the second time, saying at p. 266:

> "We have come to the conclusion that there was a breach by the *Malin Head* because we have accepted to the full the

rule which was laid down by the House of Lords in the case of *The Duke of Buccleuch* (7 Asp. M.C. (N.S.) 68) [1892]. It is there laid down that in order to exonerate from blame under sect. 419 (4) a ship which has failed to give the proper signal prescribed by art. 28, it is necessary to prove that the failure to give the blast could not possibly have effected the collision and that it is not sufficient—and, indeed, is not admissible—for the ship which has been guilty of this failure to give the proper blasts to say that the failure to give the blasts did not in fact effect the collision."

The following excerpts are from some of the more recent English cases:

". . . What was done in this case? There was a movement of the helm ordered upon three different occasions, according to the story of the defendants themselves—'starboard' some distance off; 'starboard' again; and again 'hard-a-starboard.' It may be it is not often that sound signals are given to a vessel which is at anchor, but the pilot who was navigating the *Elysia* in this case thought he was approaching a vessel under way, and certainly these signals ought to have been given."

*The Elysia,* 12 Asp. M.C. (N.S.) 198, 202.

"I have no hesitation in saying that the *Huntsman* was to blame for this collision. There are many reasons for it. First of all, she did not keep out of the way, secondly, when she altered her course by starboarding her helm she blew no blast; and, thirdly, when she reversed her engines, she blew no blast till sometime later."

*The Huntsman* (Admiralty), 11 Asp. M.C. (N.S.) 606, 607.

". . . we are of the opinion that the *Hero's* allegation that the port helm signal was sounded when she ported across the bows of the *Blackwater* has not been established, and that as the absence of that signal may, . . . possibly have contributed to the collision, the *Hero* must be deemed to blame for a breach of art. 28; . . . "

*The Hero,* 12 Asp. M.C. (N.S.) 10, [1911] Prob. Div. 128, 160.

See also, *The Mourne* [1901], Prob. Div. 68; *The Uskmoor* [1902], Prob. Div. 250.

These decisions of both the American and English courts make it clear that, unless the collision is already inevitable, any failure to sound appropriate signals upon making any change of course with respect to another vessel, or upon reversing the engines, is such a breach of the rules as to place upon the vessel violating them the burden of proving not only that the omission was not one of the causes of the collision, but that it could not have been.

The signals must be given in all situations, in restricted or open waters, where two steamers in sight of each other are approaching, and, to avoid collision or the risk of collision, either makes any change of course in respect to the other.  The change of course, though slight and perhaps unnecessary, and made only out of abundance of caution, must be indicated by the proper signal.

**When Signals Are to be Given.**

These signals are not to be used when two vessels are approaching on courses which will carry them clear of each other and *when no change in course is made.*

Under such conditions the giving of the signal is not only unnecessary, but is in direct violation of the rule, which permits its use only when a change in course is made.

The Inland Rules prescribe that the signals be given when vessels are approaching each other in such a manner as to involve risk of collision, either head and head, or nearly so, or if the courses are so far on the starboard of each other as not to be considered as meeting head and head.

Rule III of the Pilot Rules prescribes that signals be given and answered not only when meeting "head and head," or nearly so, but at all times, *when the steamers are in sight of each other,* when passing or meeting within a half mile.

The validity of the half

mile feature of this pilot rule, however, is at least doubtful. The rules of navigation are applicable when vessels are approaching each other in such manner as to involve risk of collision. It is at such time that necessity for caution begins. The distance separating them is not the determining factor.

See p. 213, *The John King,* 49 Fed. 469; *The Aurelia,* 183 Fed. 341.

**When the Signals Are Not to be Given.** Excepting only the signals prescribed under Rules III and V of Article 18 of the Inland Rules, viz.: the four-blast signal (alarm signal), the one long blast signal for use in approaching short bends in narrow channels, and the signal to be given on leaving a slip or wharf, the above signals are to be used only when the vessels are in sight of each other. Vessels not in sight of each other, either because of fog or other conditions, are not authorized to use them, and their use under such conditions is improper. A steamer assuming to navigate in a fog in reliance upon such signals, whether given by herself or heard from others, will be held at fault for any resulting collision.

The rules plainly say: *"When vessels are in sight of one another."* When the present rules were discussed and formulated at the Conference it was determined that the signals should not

The Inland Rule, Article 18, Rule IX, and the Pilot Rule III, state that these whistle signals are never to be used except when steamers are in sight of each other. Article 28 plainly

be used until two vessels were in sight of each other.

The rule that the signals are not to be used except between vessels in sight of one another applies not only to the helm signals, but to the signal of three blasts indicating "my engines are going full speed astern."

During the Conference it was suggested that this three-blast signal should be permitted whether or not vessels were in sight of each other.

Admiral Nares (Great Britain), in advocating the permission to use in a fog the three-blast signal indicating "my engines are going at full speed astern," said:

"Mr. President, the intention of the committee is this: Under Article 19 [present Art. 28] the signal has been made compulsory, provided a vessel does a certain action, provided she starboards, or ports, or goes full speed astern; but while Article 19 [present Art. 28] has been made compulsory, it is not to be allowed except when the other vessel is in sight. The committee want to go beyond that. They

says *"when vessels are in sight of one another."*

" . . . the whistle blown by the *Lowell* [during a fog] near the bridge [Brooklyn Bridge] was a three-blast whistle. Although one of the witnesses testified that it was customary with steamers navigating in a fog as the *Lowell* was to sound such a signal, it was nevertheless a fault to do so, certainly whenever the engines were not in fact going full speed astern."
*The City of Lowell,* 152 Fed. 593, 596.

"Both vessels claimed that they had stopped their engines, and had slowed down to mere steerageway; . . . and were so navigating shortly before the collision in the fog, when suddenly the *North Point* sounded two blasts of her whistle, *a signal which ordinarily would indicate her purpose of passing the* Pennsylvania *starboard to starboard, but which signal had no place during the existence of fog,* as the rules of navigation in terms prescribe that during such weather passing signals shall not be given, and that fog signals only must be given."
*The North Point,* 205 Fed. 958, 962.

will not allow the starboard
or the port signal to be made
to a vessel which is not in
sight, but they see no reason
why the signal 'I am going
full speed astern' should not
be made whether the other
vessel is in sight or not. You
have already, under Article
12 [present Art. 16], told
the vessel to stop her engines.
. . . Suppose the captain
goes full speed astern instead
of merely stopping his way;
why should he not indicate
that action to the other vessel which is not in sight?
. . . "
*Prot. of Proc.,* p. 808.

Other delegates did not
agree with this view.

Captain Malmberg (Swe-
den) : " . . . I should
not like to introduce into
rules like these a manœuvre
to be made by a steamer not
having the other vessel in
sight, as the issue of such a
manœuvre may, in a fog,
bring about a collision. . . . "
p. 808.

Captain Sampson (United
States) : "Mr. President, I
entirely agree with the last
gentleman who has spoken.
I think that some signal as
provided in Article 19 [pres-
ent Art. 28], to indicate
that a vessel is going full
speed astern, is very needful
when two ships meet in a fog
and approach each other to a

point where they become visible. I think that signal
would be a good one; but
that case would be covered
by Article 19 [present Art.
28]. If the vessels are
not in sight of each other it
seems to me that no useful
information can be conveyed
by indicating that the ship is
going full speed astern. That
may be the direction to avoid
a collision or it may be the
direction to produce a collision." pp. 808–809.

Captain Malmberg (Swe-
den): "Mr. President, I
also do not see the necessity
for introducing that signal in
a fog when you do not see a
vessel. If you do see a vessel, Article 19 [present Art.
28] will cover the case."
p. 807.

Mr. Verbrugghe (Bel-
gium): "Mr. President, I
am of the same opinion." p.
807.

The Conference accord-
ingly voted against the proposal to permit the use of
this signal as between vessels not in sight of one another. *Prot. of Proc.*, p.
809.

## ARTICLE XVIII

### Inland Rule

Not in International
Rules.

*Rule V.* Whenever a steam-vessel is nearing a short bend or curve in the channel, where, from the height of the banks or other cause, a steam-vessel approaching from the opposite direction cannot be seen for a distance of half a mile, such steam-vessel, when she shall have arrived within half a mile of such curve or bend, shall give a signal by one long blast of the steam-whistle, which signal shall be answered by a similar blast, given by any approaching steam-vessel that may be within hearing. Should such signal be so answered by a steam-vessel upon the farther side of such bend, then the usual signals for meeting and passing shall immediately be given and answered; but, if the first alarm signal of such vessel be not answered, she is to consider the channel clear and govern herself accordingly.

When steam-vessels are moved from their docks or berths, and other boats are liable to pass from any direction toward them, they shall give the same signal as in the case of vessels meeting at a bend, but im-

mediately after clearing the
berths so as to be fully in
sight they shall be governed
by the steering and sailing
rules.
**Identical with Pilot Rule V.**

The purpose of this rule is obvious.   It is mandatory   Bend Signal
in its requirement that the prescribed signals be given by   Mandatory.
steamers approaching a short bend or curve in the channel where an unobstructed view of the channel cannot
be had for a distance of at least half a mile.

In a discussion of this rule the court has said:

> "This rule, literally construed, is imperative upon every
> steamer 'nearing' such short bend or curve, whatever may be
> her own intention as to future navigation after she shall have
> reached it.   It makes no difference whether she intends to
> curve around the bend, or to anchor off it, or just short of it,
> or to continue on in a straight line beyond it; if, after she has
> reached a point half a mile away from it, she intends to con-
> tinue her movement, so as to bring herself nearer to it, she is
> 'nearing' such bend, and the language of the rule requires her
> to sound the bend-warning whistle.   And it seems to us that
> the spirit of the rule would require such an interpretation,
> even if the language were obscure.   The signal, which gives
> warning that there is a hidden vessel nearing the bend, is
> manifestly designed to notify the other vessel approaching
> from an opposite direction, not only that if her own approach
> is slow she may suddenly find another vessel in her water, but
> also that if her own approach is swift she is likely, on passing
> the bend, to find herself suddenly in close proximity to
> another vessel.   As the district judge says: 'The reasons for
> the inspectors' rule are almost equally applicable to vessels
> going on either side of the Hook;' and in our opinion the
> language of the rule makes the giving of a bend-warning
> signal by boats approaching such bend from either side im-
> perative, no matter what may be their future course after
> reaching the bend.   We conclude, therefore, that the *Water-
> man* was clearly in fault for not giving such signal when
> nearing Horn's Hook, and are satisfied that her failure to do
> so was the proximate and efficient cause of the collision."
> *The Transfer No. 8,* 96 Fed. 253, 255.

Also,

> "Moreover, as the two tugs were approaching each other in a narrow channel, with the bend at Shooter's Island between them, it was the duty of both tugs to sound a long blast of the whistle on approaching the bend. *No. 32* did so. *The Hague* did not, and because she did not she is not free from fault."
>
> *The P. R. R. No. 32—The John J. Hague,* 240 Fed. 118, 120.

**Dock Signal Mandatory.**

Steamers when moving from their docks or berths are required to give the same signal, viz., one long blast. The precise time at which the signal is to be blown is not stated in the rule. Manifestly, however, the purpose and spirit of the rule require it to be blown at such time as to give seasonable notice of the intended movement

**Time to be Given.**

to any approaching or passing vessel. The signal, if given prior to the time it would afford warning to approaching or passing vessels, is not a compliance with the rule (*The Transfer No. 18,* 188 Fed. 210); nor, *per contra,* is it a compliance if the signal is given too late to enable approaching or passing vessels to avoid collision. *The Bangor,* 212 Fed. 706.

Steamers leaving their docks or berths are also subject to Article 29 and must exercise such precautions as the situation requires by the ordinary practice of seamen or by the special circumstances of the case.

It is to be noted that steamers moving from their docks are subject to the steering and sailing rules "immediately after clearing their berths so as to be fully in sight." Until, however, such vessel gets on her definite course, the Special Circumstance Rule (Art. 27) is also applicable, and it is the duty of each vessel to act with prudence, having regard to the particular conditions. Of such situations the courts have said:

> "This is a case of special circumstances under article 27 of the Inland Regulations (Act June 7, 1897, c. 4, § 1, 30 Stat. 102 [Comp. St. § 7901]), which is found in the margin. In *The William A. Jamison,* 241 Fed. 950, 154 C. C. A. 586, this court declared that a vessel coming out of her slip

and maneuvering to get on her course, or one maneuvering to get into her slip, is not navigating upon any course, and the steering and sailing rules do not apply. . . . It was the duty of each of these vessels to act with prudence."

The Transfer No. 17, 254 Fed. 673, 674.

"The starboard hand rule does not apply to a steamer backing [out of her slip] before she gets on her definite course. The special circumstance rule (art. 27, Act of June 7, 1897, 30 Stat. 102, c. 4 [Comp. St. § 7901]) applies to steamers maneuvering to get on their definite courses. *The Servia and Noordland,* 149 U. S. 144, 156; our own decisions in *The John Rugge,* 234 Fed. 861.

The M. Moran—The Coleraine, 254 Fed. 766, 767.

See also, *The Washington—Rochester,* 241 Fed. 953; *The Bouker No. 2,* 254 Fed. 579.

## ARTICLE XVIII

### INLAND RULES

*Rule III.* If, when steam-vessels are approaching each other, either vessel fails to understand the course or intention of the other, from any cause, the vessel so in doubt shall immediately signify the same by giving several short and rapid blasts, not less than four, of the steam-whistle.

## PILOT RULE I

*Rule I.* If, when steam vessels are approaching each other, either vessel fails to understand the course or intention of the other, from any cause, the vessel so in doubt shall immediately signify the same by giving several short and rapid blasts, not less than four, of the steam whistle, the *Danger Signal.*

This signal which is commonly known as the "Alarm" or "Danger Signal" is not prescribed by the International Rules, but is mandatory upon all steamers navigating the rivers, harbors and inland waters of the United States upon which the Inland Rules apply.

The purpose of the signal is to notify or give warning to the approaching vessel that her course and intention are not understood.

**Alarm Signal does not Indicate any Maneuver.** It is not, as some navigators seem to think, a substitute for the three-blast signal. It does not indicate any maneuver either as to change of course, or that the engines are stopped, or that they are working full speed astern.

In the case of *The Musconetcong,* 255 Fed. 675, that steamer (a ferry-boat) was proceeding from its slip in Hoboken to its slip at 23rd Street, New York, directly opposite. The tug *Hercules,* with a scow in tow, was coming down the river east of the middle, between 30th and 33rd Streets. The *Musconetcong* was the privileged vessel. When near the middle of the river, the *Musconetcong* blew a signal of two whistles, intended for the ferry-boat *Paunpeck,* which in regular trips runs opposite and was bound for the Hoboken slip. This signal was answered by the *Hercules* with a signal of two blasts. The *Musconetcong* immediately blew the alarm signal followed by a signal of one whistle to indicate (under the Pilot Rules) her intention to hold her course and speed. The District Court held the *Musconetcong* at fault "for failing to reverse or slacken her speed at once after blowing her alarm signal," but the Circuit Court of Appeals reversed the District Court in this finding, saying:

> "The *Musconetcong* cannot be held at fault for failing to reverse or slacken her speed at once after the exchange of signals. If the *Hercules* had obeyed the signals and the rule, the collision would have been avoided; and the *Musconetcong,* a privileged vessel, was entitled to assume that, although it was proposed to her to give way by the exchange of the two-whistle signals, rejection thereof by her would result in navigation in conformity to the rule. The District Judge found that the *Musconetcong* ran about a minute and 400 or 500 feet before she started to reverse. She was justified in letting some time elapse, in order to ascertain whether the *Hercules* would continue on or would port her helm, and during this lapse of time she conformed to the law in keeping her speed and course, even though the subsequent events proved that stopping and backing would have been better. *The Chicago,* 125 Fed. 712, 60 C. C. A. 480; *The Cygnus,* 142 Fed. 85.
>
> "As pointed out in *The Chicago,* 125 Fed. 712, 60 C. C. A. 480, the privileged vessel should not be too quick in assuming that the burdened vessel is not going to yield to it, although its behavior may be erratic. Here, apparently, the *Hercules* did not change her course or speed until it was too late to avoid the collision. We think the *Musconetcong* was not at fault. . . ."

It was also said by the court in the case of *The James A. Walsh,* 194 Fed. 549, 550, 551:

> "So far as the *Pollock* is concerned, the ground upon which I am asked to hold her in fault is that, after having given danger signals, she did not back. The pilot rule* says:
>
>> 'Whenever the danger signal is given, the engines of both steamers should be stopped and backed until the headway of the steamers has been fully checked.'

---

* The Pilot Rules have now been changed and the paragraph quoted which the court found to be invalid is omitted from the present rule.

"But the statute does not say so.   The statute (art. 19, Inland Navigation Rules) says:

'When two steam vessels are crossing, so as to involve risk of collision, the vessel which has the other on her own starboard side shall keep out of the way of the other.   Where, by any of these rules, one of the two vessels is to keep out of the way, the other shall keep her course and speed.'

"That is the general rule.   But there is this prudential rule:

'In obeying and construing these rules, due regard shall be had to all dangers of navigation and collision, and to any special circumstances which may render a departure from the above rules necessary in order to avoid immediate danger.'

"The only circumstances under the statute which justify a violation of the rule that the privileged vessel shall keep her course and speed are when there are special circumstances which render departure from the rule necessary in order to avoid immediate danger.  .  .  .   I think this rule [Pilot Rule] is invalid, and one which sometimes, if acted on, violates the statute."

**Vessel Sounding Alarm Signal Required to Observe the Rules in Subsequent Navigation.** The giving of the alarm signal does not relieve the vessel from the obligation to conform otherwise to the rules.   In meeting or passing Article 18 remains operative, or if on crossing courses Articles 19 and 21 are controlling, and the burdened vessel must keep out of the way while the privileged vessel must hold her course and speed.   These and the other duties definitely prescribed by the rules are in no wise modified by this signal, except in so far as the situation may make operative the prudential rule (Art. 27) requiring a departure from the rules in order to avoid immediate danger.   Nor does this signal obviate the necessity for the other sound signals being subsequently given to apprise the approaching vessel of any maneuver then being made.   If after the alarm signal is given the engines are reversed full speed, the three-blast signal must be sounded.

"The *Straits of Dover,* in the position stated, was the favored vessel, and under article 21, *supra,* was required to keep her course and speed; and upon failure to understand the course or intention of the *Bluefields,* should have immediately signified the same by giving several short and rapid blasts, not less than four, of her steam whistle (rule 3, art. 18) ; or, upon reversing her engines and putting the same full speed astern, she should have indicated the fact by three short blasts of her whistle (art. 28) so as to warn the *Bluefields* of her movements. The *Straits of Dover* seems clearly to have erred in the three particulars stated."

*The Straits of Dover,* 120 Fed. 900, 904.

The rule requires that the signal *shall be given imme-diately doubt arises* as to the course or intention of the approaching vessel.

**When Signal Is to be Given.**

Reference has been made to the anxious and painful moments sometimes experienced by those in charge of vessels themselves observing the rules, because of an inability to understand the course or intention of an approaching vessel apparently navigating in disregard of the rules. In such cases the danger signal should be given immediately doubt arises. The rule clearly so states, and the courts have so decided.

In the case of *The Acilia,* 120 Fed. 455, that vessel was proceeding up the Brewerton Channel towards Baltimore, approaching the bend which unites the Brewerton Channel with the Fort McHenry Channel. The Brewerton Channel runs W.N.W. and the Fort McHenry Channel N.W. ½ N., so that they make an angle of 2½ points, or about 28 degrees. The *Acilia* being on the wrong side of the channel, her pilot directed that a signal of two short blasts be given to the *Crathorne,* which vessel was coming down the Fort McHenry Channel, approaching the same bend, but the whistle becoming jammed, it continued for several minutes to blow a long drawn-out blast. The *Acilia* was held at fault for being on the wrong side of the channel, and for excessive speed.

The claim was made that the *Crathorne* should under

the circumstances have blown a danger signal, but the court decided against such contention for the reasons given below:

The court said at pp. 459, 460, 461:

"The fault charged against the *Crathorne* amounts, I think, to this: that when the *Acilia's* whistle continued to blow for more than 3 or 4 seconds the pilot of the *Crathorne* should have treated it as a distress signal, or a signal which he could not understand, and should have blown danger signals, and at once have slowed his vessel, or stopped and reversed. Rule 3 provides as follows: 'If, when steam vessels are approaching each other, either vessel fails to understand the course or intention of the other from any cause, the vessel so in doubt shall immediately signify the same by giving several short and rapid blasts, not less than four, of the steam whistle; . . .' Now the difference, as I understood it, between what it is contended the pilot of the *Crathorne* should have done and what, in fact, he did do, is this: It is contended that, as soon as the *Acilia's* whistle continued to blow beyond the proper duration of a passing signal, the *Crathorne* should instantly have stopped and reversed, while what he did do was to delay giving that order until he saw that the *Acilia* was not directing her course up the channel, but was going off to his starboard and crossing his bow; he having, in the meantime, hard aported his helm and gone close to his starboard side of the channel.

"There was no manifest danger of collision, so far as the pilot of the *Crathorne* could judge, until he could see that the *Acilia's* course was directed toward the southerly side of the channel; and this he could not determine with certainty until the *Acilia* had passed the point where, in order to keep in the channel, she had to port. Until in some way warned to the contrary, the pilot of the *Crathorne* was entitled to presume that the other pilot would act lawfully, and keep to his proper side of the channel, and that, even if by reason of some sheer of his ship he did not enter on that course as soon as he might, he would do so as soon as he could bring his vessel's head around. It cannot be said that the pilot of the *Crathorne* failed to understand the course or intention of the *Acilia* before he could make out that she was under a starboard helm, because he had a right to presume, until he received a signal of two blasts, that she was going to obey the statute and keep to her proper side of the channel. Therefore it was not a fault that he did not blow danger signals."

In the case of *The Straits of Dover,* 120 Fed. 900, that vessel was proceeding down the Chesapeake Bay to the Capes. The *Bluefields* was coming up the bay to Baltimore. The collision between the two steamers occurred at night about 3½ miles below Wolf Trap Lighthouse. The *Straits of Dover* was the privileged vessel and the *Bluefields* was found at fault for attempting to cross her bows, and for failure to keep out of the way.

The *Straits of Dover* was also held at fault for failure to give the danger signal.

The court said at p. 904:

> "The navigators of the *Straits of Dover* observed the green light of the *Bluefields* bearing upon her port bow, in such a manner as to make it apparent that the *Bluefields* was crossing the bow of the *Straits of Dover,* and was persisting in this course, and that there was great danger of collision, and in this condition the *Straits of Dover* . . . nor gave to the *Bluefields* the danger signals required to be given. . . ."

The *Straits of Dover* (being the privileged vessel) was held at fault for failure to sound the danger signal because it was, or should have been, apparent to her that the *Bluefields* was persisting in a wrong course involving danger of collision, while in *The Acilia,* supra, the *Crathorne* was exonerated for the same failure, for the reason that any definite indication was lacking that the *Acilia* would not observe the rules.

Also see, *The Robert Dollar,* 160 Fed. 876.

The case of *The Virginian,* 238 Fed. 156, is also instructive. The *Virginian* was proceeding at night from Seattle to Tacoma. A few moments after having been passed by another and faster steamer, she heard an exchange of passing signals between that steamer and another vessel. A few moments later, she heard another whistle from ahead, which she assumed was intended for her, and being unable to make out the approaching vessel

THE RULES OF THE ROAD AT SEA

or see any light upon it, she stopped her engines, but did not sound the alarm signal. The court found that the lights of the other vessel were obscured from the *Virginian* in her position of approach.

The court said, at page 157:

> "At that point of time we think the obligation was imposed upon the *Virginian* 'immediately,' or at the latest as soon as the *Strathalbyn's* second whistle was heard, to signify that it failed to understand the course of the *Strathalbyn,* to give the alarm prescribed by rule 3, and to reverse."

**Sight Not Essential to Make Necessary Giving of Alarm Signal.** The alarm signal must be given even though the vessels may not be in sight of each other. This has been definitely decided by the District Court (*The Virginian,* 217 Fed. 604, 615):

> "Under these rules, it is the contention of the *Virginian* that she was excused from giving the danger signal required by rule 3, article 18, because she could neither see the *Strathalbyn* or her lights, and that, under such conditions, rule 9 forbids the giving of any whistle signal; that, by her silence, the *Virginian* signalled that the *Strathalbyn* and her lights could not be seen.
>
> "By rule 3, the danger signal is required when 'from any cause' either approaching vessel 'fails to understand the *course or intention* of the other.' Rule 9 forbids whistle signals, unless 'the *course and position* of each (vessel) can be determined,' by seeing the vessel in the daytime, or its lights by night. (The italics are the court's.) It is shown that those navigating the *Virginian* knew a vessel was 'approaching' from ahead; that they knew the vessel's 'intention,' from her whistle, was to pass the *Virginian* port to port, but, not being able to either see the 'approaching' vessel or her lights, they could not understand her 'course.' It was, therefore, the duty of the *Virginian* 'immediately,' and certainly not later than the second whistle of the *Strathalbyn,* to give the danger signal, as required by rule 3."

The Appellate Court, in affirming the decision of the District Court, said at 238 Fed. 156, 157:

> "It is contended that this rule [Rule 9 of Art. 18] is paramount and is without exception, and that it makes rule 3 of

article 18 inapplicable to the situation in which the *Virginian* was placed, and that the *Virginian* not being able to see the *Strathalbyn* was not at liberty to give alarm signals as provided in rule 3. We do not so construe the rules."

## PILOT RULE II

**Not in Inland Rules.**

*Rule II.* Steam vessels are forbidden to use what has become technically known among pilots as "cross signals," that is, answering one whistle with two, and answering two whistles with one.

This rule has been referred to by the court as the unfortunate provision of the Inspectors' Rules, which has been "prolific of disaster." (*The Cygnus,* 142 Fed. 85, 87.) The rule cannot be taken literally but must be interpreted as applying only to signals used for the purpose contemplated in the Articles. The purpose for which the Articles intend the signals to be used, has already been stated, viz., to indicate the taking of a course or other maneuver authorized or required by the Inland Rules.

The giving of a cross signal is a violation of this rule and is forbidden where the steamer giving the first signal has indicated a course or maneuver authorized or required by the Inland Rules. **When the Giving of a Cross Signal is Forbidden.**

It is not a violation of the Statutory Rules for a vessel to give a cross signal when the steamer first signaling has indicated a course or maneuver not authorized or required by the Inland Rules, or has proposed a departure from these rules. For steamers approaching so as to involve risk of collision, the Inland Rules definitely prescribe the duty of each. The obligation imposed by these statutory rules is paramount and the inspectors have no **When a Cross Signal is Not a Violation.**

power or authority to change it in any way.   This is made clear by the courts:

"As we understand the rules of the supervising inspectors, they mean to require steamers at all times, when passing or meeting at a distance within a half mile of one another, to give and answer signals by blasts of the steam-whistle to indicate what course they propose to take; and the signal which indicates a purpose to pass to the right of the other is one blast, and that which indicates a purpose to pass to the left of the other is two blasts; and, when the rules say the other steamer shall promptly answer a signal, they mean that the answer shall be one which indicates her proposed course. Rule 1 prescribes that the answering steamer 'shall answer promptly by a similar blast of the steam-whistle.' If this means that she must give a response indicating that she will conform her movements to the proposed course of the other, we think the rule transcends the authority of the inspectors. We do not mean to be understood that the inspectors may not lawfully require a steamer to give a signal to another indicating that she observes her, and proposes to perform her duty properly in passing or meeting; but the inspectors cannot lawfully require the other steamer to assent to a departure from the statute in cases covered by the rules of navigation as enacted by congress, and the inspectors' rules are not to be construed as meaning to do so.   When vessels are meeting head on, or nearly so, they are under an imperative obligation to pass to the right, by the law of congress, unless some special circumstances justify a departure pursuant to rule 24 [now Art. 29]; and neither can be obliged to depart from the statute at the request of the other.   So, when two steamvessels are crossing so as to involve risk of collision, the vessel which has the other on her starboard side must keep out of the way, and the other must keep her course, unless a departure is necessary pursuant to rule 24 [now Art. 29]; and the vessel which is required to keep her course cannot be compelled to depart from it at the instance of the other.   The rules of navigation enacted by congress are obligatory upon vessels approaching each other from the time necessity for caution begins; and from that time, as the vessels advance, so long as the means and opportunity to avoid danger of collision remain.   Until the necessity for precaution begins, obviously, there can be no fault on the part of either vessel,—

rules of the inspectors to the contrary notwithstanding,—of which the other can justly complain."

*The John King,* 49 Fed. 472, 473.

"We do not agree with her counsel in construing pilot rule 2 as allowing the burdened vessel to abrogate article 22, by blowing a signal which indicates an intention to cross ahead, when the circumstances of the case admit of her crossing behind. The latter part of the rule would seem to indicate that it was framed so as not to be in conflict with the articles, and, if it were, the articles, and not the rules, are of superior authority."

*The John H. Starin,* 162 Fed. 146, 147.

"It is suggested that the tug had no business to give a cross-signal, such suggestion being apparently with reference to the inspectors' rule forbidding the use of such signals. That rule (rule III, as amended January 25, 1899) is by its terms restricted to 'vessels approaching each other from opposite directions,' and does not cover vessels on crossing courses, as these were, where under the steering and sailing rules one is burdened and the other privileged. There is nothing which forbids either of such vessels, while still at a safe distance from the other, to propose a modification of some indicated maneuver. Moreover, as we pointed out in *The John King,* 49 Fed. 469, 1 C.C.A. 319, when under the steering and sailing rules a vessel has the right to make a particular maneuver, *she cannot be deprived of such right by any rule of the inspector forbidding her to sound a signal which would indicate her intention to make that particular maneuver.* The power of the inspector to make rules is restricted to such as are 'not inconsistent with the provisions of [the] Act of June 7, 1897, c. 4, 30 Stat. 96 [U.S. Comp. St., 1901, p. 2875],' adopting regulations for preventing collisions upon harbors and inland waters. See section 2 of that act (30 Stat. 102 [U.S. Comp. St., 1901, p. 2884])."

*The Transfer No. 15,* 145 Fed. 503, 504.

See also, *The Montauk,* 180 Fed. 697; *The Haida,* 191 Fed. 623.

It is not to be understood that if the conditions permit either vessel may not propose a departure from the statutory requirements and, if the other consent, govern herself accordingly. That a departure from the Articles is

A Departure from the Rules Permitted if by Mutual Agreement.

permitted if both vessels agree is recognized in the case of *The John King,* 49 Fed. 469, 473:

> "If a proposition is given proposing a departure by one vessel, and is consented to by the other vessel, undoubtedly the former is justified in assuming that the other understands that a departure is to be attempted, and will govern herself accordingly."

See also, *The George S. Shultz,* 84 Fed. 508; *The Cygnus,* 142 Fed. 85.

To justify a departure from the rules, however, the positive assent of the other vessel to such proposal, indicated by an interchange of signals, is always necessary. Any assumption that the other vessel agrees to the departure is dangerous and at the risk of the vessel presuming to act upon such assumption.

> "This agreement [to depart from the Articles] is effected when the burdened vessel's signal indicating an intention to cross in front of the privileged vessel is accepted by a corresponding signal from the privileged vessel. But the burdened vessel which without such agreement undertakes to navigate as if she had the privilege, and the other the burden, assumes all responsibility for the consequences resulting from such failure to conform to regulations. All this has been explained in the opinions of the courts over and over again."
>
> *The George S. Shultz,* 84 Fed. 508, 510.

The burden of proving an agreement to navigate contrary to the rule is on the vessel which has made the departure from the rules.

> "The burden of proving an agreement to navigate contrary to rule is on the burdened vessel which in this case was the *Scranton.* As it was her duty to slow up and allow the *Flannery* to keep her speed and course, if an agreement was made by the *Flannery* and the *Scranton* contrary to the rule, the burden of proving it rested on the *Scranton.* That burden of proof has not been sustained. The *Scranton* claims she blew a signal of two whistles twice, and was answered each time by the *Flannery* with two whistles. But the captain and

mate of the *Flannery* both declared that they did not hear the first signal alleged to have been blown, and that they did not blow the alleged two signals in reply. If they did not blow those two whistles as alleged, then the *Flannery* never assented to the relinquishment of her privilege. She never agreed that the *Scranton* might pass across her bow."

*The Scranton,* 221 Fed. 609, 611.

If the other vessel does not agree to the proposal she may dissent. Such dissent may be indicated by a cross signal, or by a refusal to answer,* or by the danger signal, as the situation may require.

Other Vessel Not Compelled to Agree to a Departure from the Rules.

The belief that seems to exist among navigators "that by giving the first signal they can relieve themselves of the burden which the rules of navigation impose upon them," and can compel the other vessel to agree to a departure from the Articles, is clearly erroneous. Not only is this made apparent in the decisions already quoted, but this erroneus belief was directly referred to by the Circuit Court of Appeals in the case of *The George S. Shultz,* 84 Fed. 508, 510, as follows:

A First Signal Proposing a Departure from the Rules Does Not Convey Any Special Privileges.

". . . the practice is not uncommon among masters of steam vessels in these waters to navigate in utter disregard of any burden imposed upon them by rule 19. In some cases . . . it has apparently been supposed that the master who first signaled was privileged to prescribe how the other vessel must navigate, sailing rules to the contrary notwithstanding. This curious theory seems to have been based on a misreading of one of the inspectors' rules (Pilot Rule II). It was exploded in *The John King,* supra."

Also in the case of *The Cygnus,* 142 Fed. 85, 87:

"Undoubtedly the unfortunate provision in the inspectors' rules about 'not crossing signals,' which—even before its formal enactment in the amendment of 1899 (where it is restricted to vessels meeting end on)—was generally accepted by pilots as what the board required, has within the experience of this court, been prolific of disaster. It operated to induce a belief among some pilots that by giving the first signal they

---

* A privileged vessel is not required to answer or to signal intention to hold her course and speed (*The Haida,* 191 Fed. 623, 626), but is permitted to do so, and should do so, when it may assist in reaching a prompt understanding and avoid risk of collision.

could relieve themselves of the burden which the rules of navigation imposed upon them.   But it is, indeed, surprising to find that, in this harbor, 11 years after the decision in *The John King,* 49 Fed. 469, 1 C.C.A. 319, and four years after the decision in *The George S. Shultz,* 84 Fed. 508, 28 C.C.A. 476, an excursion boat, carrying sometimes thousands of people, is intrusted to the command of a man who does not know that the starboard-hand rule requires him to keep out of the way of the privileged vessel (which is itself to keep course and speed), unless both vessels have by timely interchange of signals affected an agreement to undertake to navigate otherwise than as the rule provides.   The fault of the *Cygnus* was gross, and was undoubtedly the cause of the collision."

## PILOT RULE III

Not in Inland Rules.

*Rule III.* The signals for passing, by the blowing of the whistle, shall be given and answered by pilots, in compliance with these rules, not only when meeting "head and head," or nearly so, but at all times, when the steam vessels are in sight of each other, when passing or meeting at a distance within half a mile of each other, and whether passing to the starboard or port.

Identical with Rule IX of Article 18.

The whistle signals provided in the rules for steam vessels meeting, passing, or overtaking, are never to be used except when steam vessels are in sight of each other, and the course and position of each can be determined in the day time by a sight of the vessel itself, or by night by seeing its signal lights. In fog, mist, falling snow or heavy rainstorms, when vessels cannot so see each other, fog signals only must be given.

The validity of the half mile feature in this rule is at least questionable. Vessels are required to observe the rules and give the proper signals indicating the maneuver being made, as soon as they are approaching one another, so as to involve risk of collision.

In the case of *The John King,* 49 Fed. 469, the court said:

> "As we understand the rules of the supervising inspectors, they mean to require steamers at all times, when passing or meeting at a distance within a half mile of one another, to give and answer signals by blasts of the steam-whistle to indicate what course they propose to take;  .  .  .  The rules of navigation enacted by congress are obligatory upon vessels approaching each other from the time necessity for caution begins; and from that time, as the vessels advance, so long as the means and opportunity to avoid danger of collision remain. Until the necessity for precaution begins, obviously, there can be no fault on the part of either vessel,—rules of the inspectors to the contrary notwithstanding,—of which the other can justly complain."

The half mile feature was discussed also in the case of *The Aurelia,* 183 Fed. 341, at pp. 343, 344:

> "Counsel seeks to avoid the force of this rule by urging that the words 'in sight of,' in article 28 of the act, mean within half a mile of, and that it is only when vessels are within half a mile of one another that a steam vessel under way, whose engines are going at full speed astern, shall indicate that fact by three short blasts of the whistle.
>
> "In support of this view, reference is made to rule 6 [now Rule III] of the pilot rules for Atlantic and Pacific Coast inland waters, adopted by the board of United States inspectors January, 1902, and approved by the Secretary of Commerce and Labor July 6, 1904, which is as follows:
>
> > " 'The signals by the blowing of the whistle, shall be given and answered by pilots, in compliance with these rules, not only when meeting 'head and head' or nearly so, but at all times when passing or meeting at a distance within half a mile of each other, and whether passing to the starboard or port.'
>
> "Section 4405 of the Revised Statutes of the United States (U.S. Comp. St., 1901, p. 3017) authorizes the board of supervising inspectors to 'establish all necessary regulations required to carry out in the most effective manner the provisions of this title, and such regulations, when approved by the Secretary of Commerce and Labor, shall have the force of law.'

"Section 4412 of the same title (52) empowers the board to 'establish such regulations to be observed by all steam vessels in passing each other' as they shall from time to time deem necessary for safety." (U.S. Comp. St., 1901, p. 3020.)

"Regulations established by the board of supervising inspectors undoubtedly have the force of law, but they are only valid and obligatory in so far as they are not inconsistent with statutory regulations. *The Grand Republic* (D.C.), 16 Fed. 424, 427; *United States v. Miller* (D.C.), 26 Fed. 95, 97; *The T. B. Van Houten* (D.C.), 50 Fed. 590; 7 Cyc. 321.

"It is not within the power of the board by its regulations to relax or nullify plain rules which have been enacted by Congress itself to guard against collisions.

"The statute declares the signal must be given under certain conditions when the vessels are in sight of one another. If the board has the power to say that this shall be construed to mean 'within half a mile of one another,' it may with equal authority declare that the signal need be given only when the vessels are within 500 feet of each other. To admit that article 28 must be interpreted by the rules of the board is simply to admit that the board can amend or nullify an act of Congress. Article 28 must be understood as it reads. No other interpretation is permissible."

## PILOT RULE VII

Not in Inland Rules.

*Rule VII.* When two steam vessels are approaching each other at right angles or obliquely so as to involve risk of collision, other than when one steam vessel is overtaking another, the steam vessel which has the other on her own port side shall hold her course and speed; and the steam vessel which has the other on her own starboard side shall keep out of the way of the other by directing her course to starboard so as to cross the stern of the other steam vessel, or, if necessary to do so, slacken her speed or stop or reverse.

If from any cause the conditions covered by this situation are such as to prevent immediate compliance with each other's signals, the misunderstanding or objection shall be at once made apparent by blowing the danger signal, and both steam vessels shall be stopped and backed if necessary, until signals for passing with safety are made and understood.

This rule does not prescribe any duty not already covered in the Inland Rules. It only restates in somewhat different language the requirements of the Inland Rules as contained in Articles 19, 21, 22, 23, 27, Article 18, subdiv. III, and Article 29. The following restatement of the rule, with bracketed references, makes this clear:

"When two steam vessels are approaching each other at right angles or obliquely [crossing] so as to involve risk of collision, other than when one steam vessel is overtaking another [a situation under Art. 24], the steam vessel which has the other on her own port side [the privileged vessel] shall hold her course and speed [Art. 21]; and the steam vessel which has the other on her own starboard side [the burdened vessel] shall keep out of the way of the other [Art. 19] by directing her course to starboard so as to cross the stern of the other steam vessel [Art. 22, avoid crossing ahead], or, if necessary to do so, slacken her speed or stop or reverse [Art. 23].

"If from any cause the conditions covered by this situation are such as to prevent immediate compliance [Art. 27: due regard shall be had to all dangers of navigation and collision and to any special circumstances which may render a departure from the rules necessary in order to avoid immediate danger] with each other's signals, the misunderstanding or objection shall be at once made apparent by blowing the danger signal [Art. 18, subdiv. III] and both steam vessels shall be stopped and backed if necessary [Art. 29] until signals for passing with safety are made and understood."

It will be noted that the provisions of the second paragraph of this rule are taken from Articles 27, 29, and Article 18, subdiv. III, all emergency rules. This part of the rule, therefore, is not operative except in a situation where the conditions prevent immediate compliance with the articles which prescribe definite conduct. That the situation must be one of actual and immediate (not problematical or remote) danger before the privileged vessel is justified in departing from her course and speed has been fully explained under Article 21.

From the foregoing it seems clear that this rule is not intended to change in any way the obligations under the statutory (Inland) rules, but, as said by the court in the case of *The John H. Starin,* 162 Fed. 146, 147, "if it were, the articles, and not the rules, are of superior authority."

"The supervising inspectors have no power to change in any way the rules [articles] made by congress."

*The Pawnee,* 168 Fed. 371, 376.

## ARTICLE XXIX

### PRECAUTION

**NO VESSEL UNDER ANY CIRCUMSTANCES TO NEGLECT PROPER PRECAUTIONS**

*International Rules*

*Inland Rules*

*Article 29.* Nothing in these rules shall exonerate any vessel or the owner or master or crew thereof, from the consequences of any neglect to carry lights or signals, or of any neglect to keep a proper lookout, or of the neglect of any precaution which may be required by the ordinary practice of seamen, or by the special circumstances of the case.

*Article 29.* Identical with International Rule.

This Article and Article 27 are not infrequently referred to by the courts as the Rules of Good Seamanship. Reference to both articles is also made under Article 21.

The difference between the requirements of the two articles is concisely stated in the descriptive headings. Article 27 is the Rule of Prudence permitting a departure from the General Rules when necessary to avoid immediate danger. Article 29 is the Rule of Precaution and calls for the exercise of all the precautions of navigation and of good seamanship, with particular reference to the special circumstances of a situation. This rule is applicable not only to the immediate maneuvers with respect to the approaching vessel, but also to any precautions which good seamanship would have required to be taken at any earlier time.

**Rule of Precaution.**

Articles 1 to 14, inclusive, contain complete instruc- Consequences
tions as to the lights and signals to be carried by the  of Neglect to
                                                         Carry Lights
several classes of vessels in the different situations.  Any  or Signals.
failure or neglect to carry such lights or signals as are prescribed by these articles will render the vessel guilty
thereof liable for resulting collision.

That all moving vessels shall maintain a careful and  Consequences
efficient * lookout is an elementary rule of navigation and  of Neglect to
                                                         Keep a Proper
good seamanship.   When one lookout is not sufficient,  Lookout.
more should be used.

Vessels are held to a strict performance of this duty.
In this connection the court said in the case cited below:

> "For an officer to leave his vessel entirely without a lookout
> especially when another vessel is known to be in the vicinity,
> is culpable negligence, and *approaches very nearly the line of
> reckless navigation.*   The importance of the lookout and the
> high degree of vigilance required of the person occupying that
> position on a vessel, is clearly stated by the U.S. Supreme
> Court in *The Ariadne,* 13 Wall. 475, 478, 20 L. Ed. 542,
> 543, as follows:
>
> > 'The duty of the lookout is of the highest importance.
> > Upon nothing else does the safety of those concerned so
> > much depend.   A moment's negligence on his part may
> > involve the loss of his vessel, with all the property and
> > the lives of all on board.   The same consequence may
> > ensue to the vessel with which his shall collide.   In the
> > performance of this duty the law requires indefatigable
> > care and sleepless vigilance.  .  .  .   It is the duty of
> > all courts charged with the administration of this branch
> > of our jurisprudence to give it the fullest effect whenever
> > the circumstances are such as to call for its application.
> > Every doubt as to the performance of the duty, and the

---

* Extract from report of Committee on Necessary Qualifications for
Officers and Seamen, International Marine Conference:
  "It is the opinion of the committee that *defective visual power and
color-blindness are sources of danger at sea,* the first both by day and
night, because of the inability of the short-sighted to see objects at a sufficient distance.   Color-blindness is a source of danger, more especially
at night, because of the inability of a color-blind person to distinguish
between the red and green side lights.   The inability on the part of an
officer or look-out to distinguish the color of buoys may be a cause of
accident in broad daylight."

*Reports of Committees,* p. 175.

effect of nonperformance, should be resolved against the vessel sought to be inculpated until she vindicates herself by testimony conclusive to the contrary.'

"No deviation from this statement has been made by the supreme court in later cases (*The Oregon*, 158 U.S. 186, 193, 39 L. Ed. 943) and it is therefore as binding to-day as when first made."
  *Wilder's S.S. Co. et al. v. Low et al.*, 112 Fed. 161, 172.

"The fundamental rule of the admiralty is that a vigilant lookout must be kept on all vessels, so that collision may be prevented even with those which are violating the rules . . . There is no obligation in navigation that this court is more disposed to enforce than the duty of keeping a proper lookout."
  *The Delaware, L. & W. R. Co. v. Central R. Co. of New Jersey et al.*, 238 Fed. 560, 562.

See also, *The J. W. Wonson*, 239 Fed. 857.

**Location of Lookout.**
While no specific location on a vessel is prescribed for a lookout, he must be placed at the point best suited for hearing and observing the approach of other vessels. Ordinarily, the lookout should be stationed forward in the "eyes" of the ship. Lookouts must be vigilant and attentive to their duties. The decisions make this imperative.

"Steamers are required to have constant and vigilant lookouts stationed in proper places on the vessel, and charged with the duty for which lookouts are required, and they must be actually employed in the performance of the duty to which they are assigned. They must be persons of suitable experience, properly stationed on the vessel, and actually and vigilantly employed in the performance of that duty. Proper lookouts are competent persons other than the master and helmsman, properly stationed for that purpose, on the forward part of the vessel; and the pilot house in the night time, especially if it is very dark, and the view is obstructed, is not the proper place. Lookouts stationed in positions where the view forward or on the side to which they are assigned, is obstructed, either by the lights, sails, rigging, or spars of the vessel, do not constitute a compliance with the requirement of the law; and in general, elevated positions, such as the hurricane deck, are not so favorable situations as those more usually selected on the forward part of the vessel, nearer the stem. Persons stationed on the forward deck are nearer the water-line, and consequently are less likely to overlook small vessels, deeply laden, and more readily ascertain their exact course and movement."

*The Ottawa,* 3 Wall. 268, 272.

"Lookouts [says the Supreme Court] are valueless unless they are properly stationed, and vigilantly employed in the performance of their duty; and if they are not, and in consequence of their neglect the approaching vessel is not seen in season to prevent a collision, the fault is properly chargeable to the vessel, and will render her liable, unless the other vessel was guilty of violating the rules of navigation."

*The Colorado,* 91 U.S. 692, 699.

"Her officers failed conspicuously to see what they ought to have seen or to hear what they ought to have heard. This, unexplained, is conclusive evidence of a defective lookout."

*The New York,* 175 U.S. 187, 204.

"We cannot too strongly emphasize the imperative duty of swiftly moving, tall steamers to take every possible precaution to avoid collision with low-lying sailing vessels. Amongst those precautions courts experienced in maritime affairs have recognized that of placing the lookout as low and as far forward as possible. It suffices from the cases to which reference might be made (*Chamberlain v. Ward,* 62 U.S. 548; *The Ottawa,* 70 U.S. 268) to refer only to that of *Eastern Dredging Co. v. Winnisimmet Co.,* 162 Fed. 860, 89 C.C.A. 550, which fairly summarizes them as follows:

" 'The Supreme Court has been constantly rigid in holding vessels to maintaining lookouts as far forward and as near the water as possible. Especially where the water is dark, with otherwise a fairly clear night, it is important that the lookout should be as near it as possible, in order that his eye may follow the surface, and thus be in a position to detect anything low down which may be approaching.' "

*The Prinz Oskar,* 219 Fed. 483, 488.

Good seamanship requires that vessels navigating on a dark night or in a fog or thick weather, especially if in waters where other vessels are apt to be met, should take extra precautions in the matter of lookouts. Where the

Extra Lookouts Necessary when Conditions so Require.

conditions so require, more than one lookout must be employed.

It was said by the Supreme Court in the case of *The Oregon,* 158 U.S. 186, 193:

> "Considering the darkness of the night, her rate of speed, which was fifteen miles an hour past the land, the narrowness of the channel, and the probability of meeting other vessels, the greatest watchfulness was required, and we think that prudence demanded at least an additional lookout. The watch was the smallest that would be tolerated under any circumstances, and even were it sufficient for navigation by daylight, it by no means follows that it was sufficient for running a river in a dark night."

In another case the Circuit Court of Appeals stated:

> "The necessity of a stationed lookout (or lookouts, if the exigency arises for more than one) is well recognized in the authorities, and it has been held a fault calling for condemnation when a vessel fails to maintain one equal to the emergencies likely to arise in a dark night or when there is a dense fog."
>
> *The Patria* (C.C.A.), 107 Fed. 157, 159.

If a low-hanging fog calls for a lookout on the bridge or in the crow's nest, the same condition requires that one be stationed also on the forecastlehead. *The Patria,* 107 Fed. 157; *The Vedamore,* 137 Fed. 844.

See also, *The Prinz Oskar,* 219 Fed. 483.

The officer of the deck or the helmsman cannot serve also as lookout. The latter must devote his attention exclusively to keeping a lookout.

*The Pilot Boy,* 115 Fed. 873; *The Fannie Hayden,* 137 Fed. 280; *New York & Oriental S.S. Co. v. New York, N. H. & H. R. Co.,* 143 Fed. 991.

**Preferred Vessel Lookout.** The fact that a vessel has the right of way does not relieve her from the obligation to maintain a proper and efficient lookout, and a failure to have such a lookout will be deemed a contributing fault, where, if such lookout had been maintained, the collision might have been avoided by prudent navigation. *The Devonian,* 110 Fed. 588.

A vessel leaving her anchorage or mooring must maintain an efficient lookout or lookouts, so stationed that the approach of other vessels may be seen.

> "The obligation of maintaining a very careful lookout on leaving anchorage or mooring is elementary, and navigators cannot take refuge in the proposition that they have no vessel in sight, because nothing is seen from a portion of the ship admittedly obscured by another vessel in proximity."
>
> *The Atkins Hughes,* 199 Fed. 938, 943.

A lookout astern is required where any material change in course is made which may affect other vessels in the immediate vicinity. **Lookout Astern.**

> "It is an important fact that the steamer was not observed from the schooner before the course was changed. While a man stationed at the stern as a lookout is not at all times necessary, no vessel should change her course materially without having first made such an observation in all directions as will enable her to know how what she is about to do will affect others in her immediate vicinity."
>
> *The Illinois,* 103 U. S. 298, 299.

A vessel in tow must exercise ordinary skill and diligence, and when navigating frequented waters, should maintain a proper lookout. The tow is liable for any failure to exercise reasonable precautions which would have enabled her to avoid collision, even though the tug may be also negligent. **Vessels in Tow—Lookout.**

> "The failure to have a lookout by a tow may, under some circumstances, be culpable (*The Virginia Ehrman* and *The Agnese,* 97 U.S. 315, 24 L. Ed. 890), and we think the present to be one of the cases in which it should be held to be so. Tows, like other vessels, must exercise ordinary skill and vigilance, and, while being navigated in greatly frequented waters, are bound to use care and precautions commensurate with the increase of risk of collision from the greater number of craft likely to be met. A tow, using in such waters a hawser one-sixth of a mile long, ought to anticipate that contingencies of navigation may require her to rely on her own

precautions for her own safety and the safety of other vessels, and not depend exclusively upon those which may be exercised by the tug."

*The America,* 102 Fed. 767, 768.

"The *Annasona* was also somewhat to blame for the collision in not having the vessel properly manned, and the failure, to some extent, of the officers in charge to perform the duties required of them. Fincks was at the wheel, who was able, so far as appears, to perform that duty; Van Berg was the lookout, but had been stationed aft on the poop deck by the captain, where he was unable to see promptly what course the tug was taking; they were, to some extent, relying on the general course pursued, and assumed all was safe while they followed the ranges, without observing the required vigilance in having a lookout where he could be of most use. McDougal, the second officer of the bark, was young and inexperienced; he was in charge, and the pilot was down on the main deck nearly the entire time. This neglect on the part of the officers of the *Annasona* was violative of the requirements of navigation even when under tow, and there is no doubt but that the failure to follow promptly the tug in its change of course was due, to some extent, to the failure of its lookout and its officers to promptly discover the movements of the tug to sheer to the westward of the anchored steamer."

*The Annasona,* 166 Fed. 801, 804.

The duty to keep a proper lookout is not an obligation created by the statutory rules, but is a precaution required by the ordinary practice of seamanship, the neglect of which will render the vessel liable for the consequences. The requirement not being one imposed by the Statutory Rules, the absence of a proper lookout does not in itself involve fault such as to create liability, if those in charge of the navigation see the other vessel in time to do whatever is necessary to be done. It should, however, be remembered that the maintaining of a proper lookout is a duty to which the courts attach the highest importance and of which the Supreme Court of the United States has said:

"The duty of the lookout is of the highest importance. . . . In the performance of this duty the law requires indefatigable care and sleepless vigilance.  .  .  .  It is the duty of all courts, charged with the administration of this branch of our jurisprudence, to give it the fullest effect whenever the circumstances are such as to call for its application.   Every doubt as to the performance of the duty, and the effect of non-performance, should be resolved against the vessel sought to be inculpated until she vindicates herself by testimony conclusive to the contrary."

*The Ariadne,* 13 Wall. 475, 478.

In one of the later decisions, it was said:

"There is no obligation in navigation that this court is more disposed to enforce than the duty of keeping a proper lookout."

*The Delaware, L. & W. R. Co. v. Central R. Co. of New Jersey et al.,* 238 Fed. 560, 562.

A proper lookout is therefore an obligation not lightly to be disregarded.

**Nothing in these rules shall exonerate any vessel . . . from the consequences . . . of the neglect of any precaution which may be required by the ordinary practice of seamen, or by the special circumstances of the case.**

This portion of the article gives it its name as the Rule of Good Seamanship.  As no duty of good seamanship is more fundamental or important than the obligation to obey the regulations for preventing collision, this article does not excuse any unnecessary departure from the requirements of any other rule.

But at times situations arise where through no fault of her own (sometimes through the fault of an approaching vessel) a ship is placed in such a position as to make it reasonably certain that strict adherence to the rules will inevitably lead to collision.  Then this article becomes operative so as to impose upon such vessel the exercise of good seamanship, which may, in the particular contingency, require the ship to do what would otherwise be a violation of the rules.  (See, however, Art. 21.)

Consequences of the Neglect of Any Precaution Which May be Required by the Ordinary Practice of Seamen, or by the Special Circumstances of the Case.

**Anchorage
Location.**

An improper anchorage is neglect of a precaution required by good seamanship, and a vessel guilty thereof
will be held responsible for the consequences.

In most of our harbors the authorities have designated
certain districts or zones in which vessels are permitted to
anchor.  So, also, anchoring in other designated waters is
specifically forbidden.  Anchorage grounds are generally
located outside the usual lane of traffic.  Masters should,
by inquiry, if necessary, be certain that their vessels are
anchored in permitted waters.  A vessel anchoring in a
forbidden zone will not only in many cases be subject to a
fine, but will also, in the event of a collision occurring, be
held at fault.  The fact that a wrong anchorage was
selected by the pilot will not excuse the offending vessel,
nor (unless she be anchored in such wrong location by the
written permission of the harbor master) will the fact
that the harbor master knows the situation and acqui-
esces therein relieve such offending vessel from liability
for ensuing collision.  *The Amiral Cecille,* 134 Fed. 673.

Section 15 of the Appropriation Act (Act March 3,
1899; U.S. Comp. St., 1901, p. 3543) provides:

> "It shall not be lawful to tie up or anchor vessels or
> other craft in navigable channels in such a manner as to pre-
> vent or obstruct the passage of other vessels or craft. . . . "

**Anchoring in
Navigable
Channels.**

Although this act does not absolutely prohibit a vessel
from anchoring in navigable channels (unless by so doing
she prevents or obstructs the passage of other vessels),
ships so anchoring are required to take all necessary precaution against monopolizing the channel, and will be
held by the courts to a strict accountability for a violation
of this act.

> "Under the decisions above cited, the court thinks that the
> *Hilton* was clearly in fault in the manner and place of her
> anchorage.  While navigators must necessarily be accorded
> much latitude in determining when and where to anchor,
> they must not fail to reasonably respect and observe the rules

governing them, or the rights of others in what they do. In this case, there was a clear omission on the part of the *Hilton* to measure up to the requirements imposed upon her by law in the respect indicated. The ship was a large one, 315 feet long, and so anchored that when she swung her stern came to within 50 or 60 feet of the banks of the deep water channel. There was certainly no necessity for her so monopolizing the channel either because of the lack of other location, a crowded harbor, or of existing weather or other conditions. Moreover, she should, if necessary so to anchor where she did, have used both her stern and bow anchors in order to keep the vessel parallel to or nearly with, instead of across, the channel."

*The Hilton,* 213 Fed. 997, 1000.

"Aside from any consideration of the requirements of the navigation laws and regulations, the position of the *Maia* was well calculated to confuse, mislead, and impede navigation, and no doubt influenced the errors committed by the *Pocohuntas*. It was obvious that the effect of the tide would be to shift the vessel, and her position when discovered by the *Pocohuntas* was one to be reasonably anticipated. . . . The duty imposed on vessels coming to anchor in navigable channels is to see that they do not under any circumstances (accidents excepted) prevent or obstruct the passage of other vessels or craft. Assuming that the *Maia* had the right to anchor where she did, with the reasonable effect of the tide to be anticipated, her stern as well should have been anchored, or other appropriate measures adopted as would have prevented unnecessary encroachment on the fairway. Section 15 of the Navigation Act (Act March 3, 1899, c. 425, 30 Stat. 1152 [U. S. Comp. St., 1901, p. 3543]) above alluded to provides:

" 'That it shall be unlawful to tie up or anchor vessels or other craft in navigable channels in such manner as to prevent or obstruct the passage of other vessels.'

"Vide *The Delaware,* supra; *The Georgia* (D.C., R.I.), 208 Fed. 636; *The John H. Starin,* 122 Fed. 236, 58 C.C.A. 600; *The Bourgogne* (D.C., N.Y.), 76 Fed. 868; *The Ogemaw* (D.C., Wis.), 32 Fed. 919–925.

"Upon the evidence the court is constrained to hold . . . that the improper anchorage of the *Maia* contributed, and the damages sustained will be apportioned equally . . . "

*The Pocohuntas,* 217 Fed. 135, 138.

Vessels coming to anchorage in foggy weather should, so far as it is possible to do so, avoid the channel, or the usual track of other vessels.

In the case of *The Persian,* 181 Fed. 439, the steamer *Hesperides,* which during a fog had anchored substantially on the range between two lightships in the open sea to the northward of the entrance of the channel through Pollock Rip Shoals, in the direct track of vessels navigating up and down the coast in that locality, was held at fault for a collision.   The court said at p. 447:

> "  .  .  .  We are of the opinion therefore that in anchoring, in this dense fog, substantially on the range, and in the direct track of vessels, instead of hauling off to the eastward so as to leave the thoroughfare unobstructed, the *Hesperides* committed a fault of navigation which directly contributed to bring about the collision  .  .  .  this court has twice indicated that when dense fog obscures a waterway through which there is a well-defined track for moving vessels prudence requires vessels then moving therein to continue with extreme caution, availing of such sights and sounds as they can make out till they reach some anchorage to which they can withdraw from the regular track, leaving the thoroughfare unobstructed by their presence."

In *The Georgia,* 208 Fed. 635, the court said at p. 644:

> "While there was doubtless abundant room to pass on either side of the *Seaconnet,* and while in clear weather only a slight change from the usual course of vessels would have been necessary to avoid her, yet the statute, as it seems to me, is not inapplicable merely for this reason, under the conditions then existing  .  .  .
>
> "The evidence as to the other vessels which passed up and down the river while she was at anchor, as well as this collision, shows, I think, that she was so anchored as to obstruct the passage of vessels.   What in clear weather might not be an obstruction, in a practical sense, may, in a thick fog, be considered an obstruction.   An anchored vessel that can be early sighted and readily avoided by a slight change of wheel may not be an obstruction, but when she can with difficulty be sighted, and when she requires other vessels on their usual courses to stop or to maneuver sharply, she may be

considered an obstruction. As a practical matter, even though a channel is of sufficient width to permit the passage of vessels on either side, so that in clear weather an approaching vessel would have abundant time to so alter her course as to easily avoid the anchored vessel, yet the coming of a thick fog introduces a new element of danger. Although the steamer must in a fog reduce her speed, which tends to give her more time for maneuvering, yet even with a reduced speed, but still with the maintenance of a reasonable headway, the moment of discovery may be so delayed as to leave but a short time for maneuvering, and the risk of collision is, of course, thus greatly increased.

"Safety in a fog is not sufficiently provided for by relying solely upon the reduction of speed of the moving vessel. The statute is designed to avoid the unnecessary embarrassment of vessels on the usual courses by requiring vessels coming to anchor to have due regard for the safety of moving vessels under all conditions of weather.

"While it may be reasonable to say that the statute does not absolutely prohibit anchoring in navigable channels or make it a fault to anchor where controlling conditions make it absolutely necessary, yet the question whether a vessel is anchored in such manner as to prevent or obstruct the passage of other vessels must be determined by looking not alone to the chart and to the geography of the situation but also to weather conditions and to the usual course of vessels using the thoroughfare.

"I am of the opinion that the *Seaconnet* was so anchored as to obstruct the passage not only of the *Georgia* but of other vessels, and that, as she was not forced to this anchorage by any sudden and unavoidable emergency, she was guilty of a violation of the statute."

A vessel is not justified in leaving her dock in thick weather if the conditions are such that she cannot avoid anchoring in the channel, where her presence may be a source of embarrassment and danger to the other vessels. *Leaving Dock in Heavy Fog.*

"But, assuming that under the conditions then existing it was necessary to anchor as she did, we must still consider whether the *Seaconnet* was not in fault in voluntarily exposing herself to such conditions; whether the emergency which required anchoring was not one that should have been anticipated and avoided. In leaving her dock the *Seaconnet* was bound to consider not only her own safety and convenience but the safety of other vessels using the route over which she was to pass . . . It must be held, I think, that conditions which existed and the conduct of the *Seaconnet* in anchoring as she did were anticipated when she left the dock. Assuming, however, that a vessel may anchor in an unexpected fog or wherever controlling conditions overtake her, yet if she has full reason to expect such conditions, and unnecessarily goes on to meet them, they cannot then be urged as a sufficient excuse for an improper anchorage. . . . Being of the opinion that the conditions which caused the *Seaconnet* to anchor, if controlling conditions, of which I am in doubt, were neither unexpected nor unforeseen, I am of the opinion that the *Seaconnet* should not have left her dock in thick weather unless prepared to go not only beyond Conimicut Light but far enough to take her safely out of the usual course of a vessel using either passage."

*The Georgia,* 208 Fed. 635, 641.

**Extraordinary Precautions Required.**

Sudden emergencies may at times require a vessel to anchor where she ought not to anchor under normal conditions. In such cases, the vessel being anchored perhaps in a fair-way or other improper berth, extraordinary precautions adequate to such position should be taken for the benefit of approaching vessels. Moreover, the vessel should be removed as soon as conditions permit.

**Safe Berth Necessary in Anchoring.**

In anchoring, a safe berth must be given to other vessels previously at anchor. A safe berth contemplates all the exigencies likely to arise either by reason of the character of the harbor, the holding ground, the condition of the weather and season of the year. Ample room should be given and close calculations avoided.

"A 'safe berth' should not be construed to mean one from which probable accident might not arise, but ample space; that is, taking into consideration all the exigencies likely to arise, either by reason of the character of the harbor, the conditions of the weather, and the season of the year, no danger of collision would arise, and close calculations should not be made, and risks run in giving room; doubts should be solved with a view of securing safety, having in view the possible contingencies that might arise, making it necessary for each vessel to take greater space than was apparently required at the moment; and particularly is this true where ample anchorage space existed, as it did on this occasion."

*The Juniata,* 124 Fed. 861, 863.

Special precautions may be required in extraordinary situations.

In the case of *The Devonian,* 110 Fed. 588, the facts were as follows: the *Devonian* was entering Boston Harbor. The original ship channel which she was approaching and about to enter was normally of considerable width, but, at this time, owing to the presence of dredges and drill scows, provided a passage not more than 300 to 500 feet in width; it was 2,000 to 2,500 feet in length. Just as the *Devonian* entered this narrow passage, those on board of her perceived the schooner *Perry* coming out through the channel from the other end. The engines of the steamer were stopped and a tug in attendance on the steamer was sent ahead to get the schooner out of the way, but did not succeed in doing so. As the vessels approached, the starboard anchor of the steamer was released, and, as it brought her to a stop, the schooner moving slowly through the water and drifting with the tide struck broadside amidships against the steamer's stem. In holding the steamer partly in fault, the court said at pp. 590, 591:

> "A steamer, which is ordinarily bound to avoid a sailing vessel, ought not to enter upon a narrow passage, where it cannot avoid a sailing vessel, and where a sailing vessel very probably cannot avoid it, until it has done its best to ascertain that the passage is and will remain clear. The steamer might have waited below the gas buoy until the tug had gone ahead, and made proper report. . . . Doubtless a steamer is not ordinarily required to be preceded by a tug, even when maneuvering in a crowded harbor, but where such peculiar privileges are claimed as here, there is no injustice in the requirement."

Vessels backing across a channel in the way of other vessels are required to exercise extreme care to notify other vessels of the maneuver.

*[margin note: Extraordinary Situations may Require Special Precautions.]*

"Any vessel backing across a channel, in the way of other vessels navigating it, is bound to exercise extreme care to notify the other vessels of her maneuver."

*The Sicilian Prince,* 128 Fed. 133.

Upon hearing a fog horn of a sailing vessel nearly ahead, a steamer should at once reverse and go full speed astern until her way is stopped, and she should remain stopped until the location and course of the other vessel are definitely ascertained. *Palmer et al. v. Merchants' & Miners' Transp. Co.,* 154 Fed. 683.

When in a fog the whistle of another vessel is found to be narrowing on the bow, the engines should be reversed full speed astern. *The Koning Willem I,* 9 Asp. M.C. (N.S.) 425.

It is not good seamanship for a vessel to be deliberately placed in a position where she is not free to maneuver, and her inability to maneuver immediately before the collision will not under such circumstances relieve her from fault. *The Transfer No. 10,* 137 Fed. 666.

A tug towing a bark on a hawser in a river where there was only six inches of water between the keel of the bark and the bottom of the river was held guilty of negligence and poor seamanship.

"The facts are fully stated in the opinion of the District Judge and need not be repeated here. He found the *Smith* liable for towing the *Fort George,* which drew 22 feet, into water only 22½ feet deep. With but six inches between her keel and the bottom of the river, she refused to answer her helm and collided with the *Vim* which was anchored near the center of the river, engaged in deepening the channel. The tendency of vessels to steer badly, in such circumstances, is well known and the *Smith* was found at fault for proceeding in so dangerous a locality when all danger from bad steering would have been averted had she waited for the rising of the tide. We are in entire accord with this ruling. The tug knew or should have known every danger to be encountered in the navigation of the Delaware river. Her master was required to know the depth of the channel, the rise and fall of the tide, the dredging operations at Deep Water Range, the location of the three dredges there and all the usual dangers to be encountered from Philadelphia to the break-water. It was for the master of the tug to decide whether he could take the barque to her destination in safety; if he could not do so, or if there were risk in the undertaking, he should not have attempted it. If the situation at Deep Water Range made the trip unusually hazardous—and the presence of the three dredges anchored near the center of the river, together with the shallow water existing there, un-questionably had that effect—he should have waited for the flood tide or procured the services of another tug to assist him. Clearly the *Smith* was negligent in permitting the barque to collide with the *Vim,* which was at anchor and helpless . . . There can be no divided responsibility in such cases . . . Some one must be in command. We understand the rule to be, in the absence of an agreement to the contrary, that when the tug supplies the motive power she becomes the dominant mind, and the tow is required to follow directions from the tug."

*The Fort George,* 183 Fed. 731.

At the International Conference it was suggested that an unencumbered steamer should be required to keep out of the way of a steamer having a tow. The discussion on this proposal was as follows:

*Encumbered Vessels vs. Unencumbered Vessels.*

Mr. Goodrich (United States): ". . . I am free to say that under the twenty-third rule [present Art. 29] there may be circumstances under which a big steamer may keep out of the way of a long tow; but these are special circumstances, and are not to be provided for in a general rule."

Mr. Hall (Great Britain): ". . . Under Articles 23 and 24 [present Arts. 27 and 29], if the master of a vessel sees that another vessel is not able to manœuvre, or that she is in a heavy tide-way, and is not able to stop or reverse, or if the tug cannot stop because the tow would crowd down upon her, then these are exceptional circumstances to be governed by Rules 23 and 24 [present Arts. 27 and 29]. Under such circumstances the large vessel would be grossly to blame if she did not keep out of the way of the vessel towing."

*Prot. of Proc.,* pp. 598, 599.

## LIGHTS ON UNITED STATES NAVAL VESSELS AND REVENUE CUTTERS

*International Rules*

*Article 30.* Nothing in these rules shall interfere with the operation of a special rule, duly made by local authority, relative to the navigation of any harbor, river, or inland waters.

*Inland Rules*

*Article 30.* The exhibition of any light on board of a vessel of war of the United States or a revenue cutter may be suspended whenever, in the opinion of the Secretary of the Navy, the commander in chief of a squadron, or the commander of a vessel acting singly, the special character of the service may require it.

## ARTICLE XXXI

### DISTRESS SIGNALS

*International Rules*

*Article 31.* When a vessel is in distress and requires assistance from other vessels or from the shore the following shall be the signals to be used or displayed by her, either together or separately, namely:

In the daytime—
*First.* A gun or other explosive signal fired at intervals of about a minute.
*Second.* The International code signal of distress indicated by N.C.
*Third.* The distance signal, consisting of a square flag, having either above or

*Inland Rules*

*Article 31.* When a vessel is in distress and requires assistance from other vessels or from the shore the following shall be the signals to be used or displayed by her, either together or separately, namely:

In the daytime—
A continuous sounding with any fog-signal apparatus, or firing a gun.

below it a ball or anything resembling a ball.

*Fourth.* A continuous sounding with any fog-signal apparatus.

At night—

*First.* A gun or other explosive signal fired at intervals of about a minute.

*Second.* Flames on the vessel (as from a burning tar barrel, oil barrel, and so forth).

*Third.* Rockets or shells throwing stars of any color or description, fired one at a time, at short intervals.

*Fourth.* A continuous sounding with any fog-signal apparatus.

At night—

*First.* Flames on the vessel as from a burning tar barrel, oil barrel, and so forth.

*Second.* A continuous sounding with any fog-signal apparatus, or firing a gun.

# GENERAL CONSIDERATIONS BEARING
# UPON COLLISION LIABILITIES

**Duty to Stand By in Case of Collision.** For any masters or officers who are so devoid of humanitarian instincts as to fail in their manifest duty to stand by after a collision, until it is seen whether the other vessel needs assistance, laws have been enacted with severe penalties, requiring in case of collision that each vessel shall (unless the safety of the vessel, her crew or passengers, is endangered thereby) stand by the other and render such assistance as may be practicable until such other vessel has no need of further assistance. The master of each vessel is required to give to the other the name of his own vessel, her port of registry, and her port of departure and destination.

The Statutes of the United States provide as follows:

"In every case of collision between two vessels it shall be the duty of the master or person in charge of each vessel, if and so far as he can do so without serious danger to his own vessel, crew, and passengers (if any), to stay by the other vessel until he has ascertained that she has no need of further assistance, and to render to the other vessel, her master, crew, and passengers (if any) such assistance as may be practicable and as may be necessary in order to save them from any danger caused by the collision, and also to give to the master or person in charge of the other vessel the name of his own vessel and her port of registry, or the port or place to which she belongs, and also the name of the ports and places from which and to which she is bound. If he fails so to do, and no reasonable cause for such failure is shown, the collision shall, in the absence of proof to the contrary, be deemed to have been caused by his wrongful act, neglect, or default.

"Every master or person in charge of a United States vessel who fails, without reasonable cause, to render such assistance or give such information as aforesaid shall be deemed guilty of a misdemeanor, and shall be liable to a penalty of one thousand dollars, or imprisonment for a term not exceeding two years; and for the above sum the vessel shall be liable and may be seized and proceeded against by process in any district court of the United States by any person; one-half

236

such sum to be payable to the informer and the other half to the United States."

*U. S. Comp. St.,* Secs. 7979, 7980.

The penalties for failure to comply with the statutory requirements are drastic, in that they (a) raise a presumption of fault against the offending vessel, and (b) impose a fine or imprisonment upon the guilty master or other officer in charge.

The English law on the subject is embodied in the Merchant Shipping Act, 1894, Sec. 422, and is almost identical with the American law, except as regards the penalty, which is as follows:

> "If the master or person in charge fails without reasonable cause to comply with this section, he shall be guilty of misdemeanor, and, if he is a certificated officer, an inquiry into his conduct may be held, and his certificate cancelled or suspended."

The manner in which log books are kept by some masters and officers makes a word of caution on this subject desirable. **Log Book Entries.**

Every vessel is required to keep an official log book (steamers must keep both a deck and engine room log book) in which shall be promptly entered any unusual happenings of the voyage and the circumstances under which they have occurred.

The laws of the United States provide with respect to collision entries:

> ". . . In every case of collision in which it is practicable so to do, the master shall, immediately after the occurrence, cause a statement thereof, and of the circumstances under which same occurred, to be entered in the official log-book . . ."

*U. S. Rev. St.,* Sec. 4290.

> "Every entry hereby required to be made in the official log-book shall be signed by the master and by the mate, or some other one of the crew, and every entry in the official log-book shall be made as soon as possible after the occurrence to which it relates, and, if not made on the same day as the occurrence

to which it relates, shall be made and dated so as to show the date of the occurrence, and of the entry respecting it; and in no case shall any entry therein, in respect of any occurrence happening previously to the arrival of the vessel at her final port, be made more than twenty-four hours after such arrival."

*U. S. Rev. St.,* Sec. 4291.

A fine of twenty-five dollars is imposed upon the master (under U.S. Rev. St., Sec. 4292) for any case in which a log book is not kept in the manner required, or if any entry is not made at the time and in the manner above directed.

The courts look with suspicion upon a failure to keep the log books in the manner prescribed by the statutes, as shown by the following:

".  .  .  The entries in the *Seneca's* log are also significant.  The statute requires that, in every case of collision, the master shall immediately cause a statement thereof, and of the circumstances under which the same occurred, to be entered in the official logbook.  The entry in the *Seneca's* log, in reference to this collision, is as follows:  .  .  .

" 'Collided with bark *Charles Loring* bound north; the bark striking the *Seneca* on port bow about 60 feet from stem above the water line.'

"Such an entry, so meager, so evasive, so destitute of any statement of the real circumstances under which the collision occurred, not only is a clear violation of the duty imposed on the master by the statute, but it affords strong grounds for the inference that the master, when he made it, knew that the *Seneca* was at fault  .  .  ."

*The Seneca,* 159 Fed. 578, 581.

Masters and officers are especially cautioned against making alterations or changes in an entry once made. Should it become necessary to correct an entry because of an error, it must be done without defacing the original entry otherwise than by drawing a line through the erroneous entry and leaving it legible as first written.   Erasures or any attempt to deface, destroy or make illegible what has once been entered in a log book, should never be permitted, and any attempts thereat are frowned upon by the courts as attempts to conceal the truth.

"The records of the logs of the *Sicilian Prince* are unsatisfactory. The meager entry in the chief officer's log has been already quoted. The chief engineer's log and the engineer's scrap log, in its present condition, contain no entries about the collision. The scrap log shows that a leaf has been cut out between the pages containing entries of March 30th and of April 3rd, and no explanation is given why or how this page was removed. The meagerness of the entry in the chief officer's log, the absence of any entry in the engineer's log and the removal of the leaf in the scrap log all seem to me to have been intentional. It is the universal custom of all vessels to keep a log, and the statutes of the United States require them to do so. This requirement is not fulfilled by having a book called a log in which no entries are made, or in which the entries which are made are intentionally meager, vague, and perfunctory, or in which leaves probably containing entries relating to transactions in litigation are removed. The legitimate inference in all such cases is that, if the true facts were entered in the log, they would be unfavorable to the vessel."

*The Sicilian Prince,* 128 Fed. 133, 136.

". . . for some reason that log has been tampered with, and once you find there has been tampering with a log, as I have had occasion to say before in other cases, the court at once looks with suspicion at the whole matter; . . . If you look at the engineer's scrap log, the matter is worse. It is perfectly plain that in these two lines which affect the collision there has been a rubbing out . . . and there is a general appearance of alteration over the whole of that line. Therefore, I approach this case distinctly with a bias against the credibility of evidence given by the *Corinthian*."

*The Corinthian* (Admiralty), 11 Asp. M.C. (N.S.) 208, 211.

**Pilots.** The mistaken idea prevails among many masters and officers that the presence of a pilot on the bridge of a vessel relieves the master of all responsibility in the management and navigation of his ship. Many serious losses have occurred which would have been averted had the master understood and exercised his proper authority.

The American and English laws differ somewhat in respect to compulsory pilotage, but in neither country is the pilot deemed to be in complete command; nor is the master relieved from all responsibility by the presence of a pilot.

The American Law.

The duties of the pilot are never completely those of a master; nor is the authority of the master ever superseded by the pilot. The master remains at all times in full charge of his vessel, and upon him always rests the responsibility for her safety. It cannot be delegated to a pilot. The United States Supreme Court has said:

"Nor are we satisfied with the conduct of the master in leaving the pilot in sole charge of the vessel. While the pilot doubtless supersedes the master for the time being in the command and navigation of the ship, and his orders must be obeyed in all matters connected with her navigation, the master is not wholly absolved from his duties while the pilot is on board, and may advise with him, and even displace him in case he is intoxicated or manifestly incompetent."

*The Oregon,* 158 U. S. 186, 194.

It is the duty of the master to see that lookouts are properly stationed and attentive to their duties, and that proper lights are in their places; to say when the weather conditions are not safe for navigation, when it is too foggy to go at full speed or to proceed at all. In fact, with him the decision and responsibility rest in regard to everything, excepting only the indicating of courses to be steered through the channels, for which the pilot is employed to navigate the vessel. Even in this, if it is apparent that the pilot is careless, incompetent or foolhardy, it is the duty of the master to interfere and, if necessary, to supersede the pilot.

"While on board, the pilot, in the absence of the master, has the exclusive control and direction of the navigation of the vessel; but if the master is present, the power of the pilot does not so far supersede the authority of the master, that the latter may not, in case of obvious and certain disability, or gross ignorance and palpable and imminently dangerous mistake, disobey his orders and interfere for the protection of the ship and the lives of those on board. Divided authority in a ship with reference to the same subject-matter is certainly not to be encouraged, and can never be justified or tolerated, except in cases of urgent and extreme necessity. While standing by and witnessing a self-evident mistake manifestly and imminently endangering the ship, and certain to cause a collision, the master should not remain silent, but might well interpose, so far at least as to point out the error, and suggest the proper corrective."

*Camp et al. v. The Marcellus,* [1 Cliff. 481,] Fed. Cas. No. 2347.

"There seems to be no doubt of the authority of the master in an extreme case to supersede the authority of the pilot, and to take charge of the ship himself, where it is necessary for the safety of the ship or the avoidance of imminent danger. The cases, however, all agree that it must be an extreme case of obvious danger, or incapacity on the part of the pilot, to authorize such interference."

*Homer Ramsdell Transp. Co. v. Compagnie Generale Transatlantique,* 63 Fed. 845, 846.

That licensed pilots are at times grossly incompetent and either do not understand or absolutely ignore the Rules for the Prevention of Collision is shown by the following cases:

"I cannot pronounce this decree without adding some observations with regard to some of the licensed pilots of the Chesapeake Bay. If I am right in my decision of this case, the owners of the German steamship *Acilia* have suffered a loss which it is said may amount to $100,000 by the inexcusable violation of a rule of navigation by one of our own pilots, employed because he is supposed to know the local rules and whose services they were compelled to accept. . . . this loss could not have happened, in broad daylight and with all natural conditions favorable for safety, if the pilot of the *Acilia* had not willfully disobeyed the rule prescribed by an act of Congress for navigating narrow channels. I have been for a long time disturbed by observing how little attention is paid by many of these members of the Pilot Association to the regulations prescribed by Congress and by the United States supervising inspectors under authority of Congress for preventing collisions. They seem often to be arbitrary and opinionated in their notions of navigation and indifferent to the fact it is the owners of these large and valuable steamships and not themselves who have to pay for their neglects. . . .

In my judgment there should be a more rigid supervision of the members of this body, with a view to requiring of its members character, intelligence, temperance, and obedience to the rules of navigation, and of punishing derelictions by suspension and dismissal."

*The Acilia,* 120 Fed. 455, 462.

"It is thus positively asserted by both pilots that each distinctly heard forward of his beam the fog signal of a vessel the position of which was not ascertained. Yet Nichols heard that whistle repeated three times, and Dougherty four or five times, before they respectively stopped the engines of the valuable vessels they had in charge. I think this is a plain violation, by the pilot of each vessel, of article 16 of the Inland Rules. That article is mandatory in that it declares that a steam-vessel in the position above described 'shall, so far as the circumstances of the case admit, stop her engines.' . . .

"In this as in so many other collision cases arising in New York Harbor, the result is reached with mortification, in that I am convinced that the pilots thrust by local law upon vessels of great cost, well manned and equipped, and carrying valuable lives, are guilty, not of errors of judgment only, but of total ignorance of the fundamental statutes affecting their calling. The depositions of all the pilots testifying in this cause have been scanned in vain to find any indication of knowledge by them of such matters as the narrow channel rule, or of even a statutory recommendation to stop the engines promptly on hearing a fog whistle forward of the beam.

"For the reasons indicated, a decree will be entered, permitting limitations and declaring both steamers at fault."

*The Georgic,* 180 Fed. 863, 870, 871.

See also,

*The Mesaba,* 111 Fed. 215; *The Cygnus,* 142 Fed. 85; *The Umbria,* 153 Fed. 851.

In such cases as those above cited the master has not only the right, but it is his manifest duty, to interfere and to insist upon the observance of the rules, failing which it is clear that he should displace the pilot.

Under American law a vessel is liable *in rem* for damage caused by a collision resulting from the fault of a compulsory pilot.

Under English law although a master is not justified in interfering with the navigation of the vessel by a compulsory pilot or in taking the control of the ship out of the hands of the pilot (unless in the case of manifest incompetence), still the master is not relieved from all responsibility. He remains under certain duties and obligations, a failure to perform which will render the vessel liable for any resulting collision.

Among such duties are those of seeing that proper lights and other signals are exhibited; that lookouts are properly stationed and are attentive to their duty; and that all on board render every assistance to the pilot. It is the master's duty to call the attention of the pilot to any misapprehension on the latter's part of the existing conditions. *The Tactician,* 10 Asp. M.C. (N.S.) 534.

Failure on the part of the pilot to observe the regulations in respect to giving either direction or fog signals should not be passed unnoticed. *The Elysia,* 12 Asp. M.C. (N.S.) 198.

The master should call the attention of the pilot to any breach of the collision rules.

> "The officers of the vessel have no right to take the control of the navigation out of the hands of the pilot, yet he is entitled to every assistance which can be rendered him by those on board the ship. Although they may not compel him to do what they think he ought to do, they should call to his attention that there is a breach of international rules, which he and they have both got to obey."
>
> *The Ape,* 12 Asp. M.C. (N.S.) 487.

Under the English law a vessel is relieved from liability for damages caused by collision while in charge of a compulsory pilot, provided that the master, officers and crew have fully performed their respective duties.

# APPENDIX

## BOUNDARY LINES OF THE HIGH SEAS

The following lines dividing the high seas from rivers, harbors, and inland waters are hereby designated and defined pursuant to section 2 of the act of Congress of February 19, 1895. Waters inshore of the lines here laid down are "inland waters," and upon them the inland rules and pilot rules made in pursuance thereof apply. Upon the high seas, viz., waters outside of the lines here laid down, the international rules apply. The following lines shall be effective on and after March 1, 1913:

*Inland waters on the Atlantic, Pacific, and Gulf coasts of the United States where the Inland Rules of the Road are to be followed; and inland waters of the United States bordering on the Gulf of Mexico where the Inland Rules of the Road or Pilot Rules for Western Rivers are to be followed.*

(All bearings are in degrees true and points magnetic; distances in nautical miles, and are given approximately.)

**Cutler (Little River) Harbor, Me.**—A line drawn from Long Point 226° (SW. by W. ⅞ W.) to Little River Head.

**Little Machias Bay, Machias Bay, Englishman Bay, Chandler Bay, Moosabec Reach, Pleasant Bay, Narraguagus Bay, and Pigeon Hill Bay, Me.**—A line drawn from Little River Head 232° (WSW. ⅜ W.) to the outer side of Old Man; thence 234° (WSW. ½ W.) to the outer side of Double Shot Islands; thence 244° (W. ⅝ S.) to Libby Islands Lighthouse; thence 231½° (WSW. ¼ W.) to Moose Peak Lighthouse; thence 232½° (WSW. ⅜ W.) to Little Pond Head; from Pond Point, Great Wass Island, 239° (W. by S.) to outer side of Crumple Island; thence 249° (W. ¼ S.) to Petit Manan Lighthouse.

**All Harbors on the Coast of Maine, New Hampshire, and Massachusetts Between Petit Manan Lighthouse, Me., and Cape Ann Lighthouses, Mass.**—A line drawn from Petit Manan Lighthouse 205½° (SW. ¼ S.), 26½ miles, to Mount Desert Lighthouse; thence 250½° (W. ⅛ S.), about 33 miles, to Matinicus Rock Lighthouses; thence 267½° (WNW. ¾ W.), 20 miles, to Monhegan Island Lighthouse; thence 260° (W. ⅝ N.), 19½ miles, to Seguin Lighthouse; thence 233° (WSW. ⅛ W.), 18¼ miles, to Portland Light Vessel; thence 214½° (SW. ⅜ W.), 29½ miles, to Boon Island Lighthouse; thence 210° (SW.), 11 miles, to Anderson Ledge Spindle, off Isles of Shoals Lighthouse; thence 176¼° (S. by W.), 19½ miles, to Cape Ann Lighthouses, Mass.

**Boston Harbor.**—From Eastern Point Lighthouse 215° (SW. ⅜ W.), 15¾ miles, to The Graves Lighthouse; thence 139¼° (SSE. ⅜ E.), 7½ miles, to Minots Ledge Lighthouse.

**All Harbors in Cape Cod Bay, Mass.**—A line drawn from Plymouth (Gurnet) Lighthouses 77½° (E. ⅛ S.), 16¼ miles, to Race Point Lighthouse.

**Nantucket Sound, Vineyard Sound, Buzzards Bay, Narragansett Bay, Block Island Sound, and Easterly Entrance to Long Island Sound.**—A line drawn from Chatham Lighthouses, Mass., 146° (S. by E. ¾ E.), 4⅜ miles, to Pollock Rip Slue Light Vessel; thence 142° (SSE. ⅛ E.), 12¾ miles, to Great Round Shoal Entrance Gas and Whistling Buoy (PS); thence 229° (SW. by W. ⅝ W.), 14½ miles, to Sankaty Head Lighthouse; from Smith Point, Nantucket Island, 261° (W. ⅜ N.), 27 miles, to No Mans Land Gas and Whistling Buoy, 2; thence 359° (N. by E. ⅛ E.), 8⅛ miles, to Gay Head Lighthouse; thence 250° (W. ⅝ S.), 34½ miles, to Block Island Southeast Lighthouse; thence 250½° (W. ⅝ S.), 14¾ miles, to Montauk Point Lighthouse, on the easterly end of Long Island, N. Y.

**New York Harbor.**—A line drawn from Rockaway Point Coast Guard Station 159½° (S. by E.), 6¼ miles, to Ambrose Channel Light Vessel; thence 238½° (WSW. ⅛ W.), 8¼ miles, to Navesink (southerly) Lighthouse.

**Philadelphia Harbor and Delaware Bay.**—A line drawn from Cape May Lighthouse 200° (SSW. ½ W.), 8½ miles, to

Overfalls Light Vessel; thence 246¼° (WSW. ½ W.), 3⅛ miles, to Cape Henlopen Lighthouse.

**Baltimore Harbor and Chesapeake Bay.**—A line drawn from Cape Charles Lighthouse 179½° (S. ½ W.), 10½ miles, to Cape Henry Gas and Whistling Buoy, 2; thence 257° (W. ⅝ S.), 5 miles, to Cape Henry Lighthouse.

**Charleston Harbor.**—A line drawn from Ferris Wheel, on Isle of Palms, 154° (SSE. ¼ E.), 7 miles, to Charleston Light Vessel; thence 259° (W. ⅞ S.), through Charleston Whistling Buoy, 6 C, 7⅝ miles, until Charleston Lighthouse bears 350° (N. ⅞ W.); thence 270° (W.), 2½ miles, to the beach of Folly Island.

**Savannah Harbor and Calibogue Sound.**—A line drawn from Braddock Point, Hilton Head Island, 150½° (SSE. ⅝ E.), 9¾ miles, to Tybee Gas and Whistling Buoy, T (PS); thence 270° (W.), to the beach of Tybee Island.

**St. Simon Sound (Brunswick Harbor) and St. Andrew Sound.**—From hotel on beach of St. Simon Island ¹⁵⁄₁₆ mile 60° (NE. by E. ¼ E.) from St. Simon Lighthouse, 130° (SE. ½ E.), 6⅞ miles, to St. Simon Gas and Whistling Buoy (PS); thence 194° (S. by W. ⅛ W.), 8¾ miles, to St. Andrew Sound Bar Buoy (PS); thence 270° (W.), 4¾ miles, to the shore of Little Cumberland Island.

**St. Johns River, Fla.**—A straight line from the outer end of the northerly jetty to the outer end of the southerly jetty.

**Florida Reefs and Keys.**—A line drawn from the easterly end of the northerly jetty, at the entrance to the dredged channel ½ mile northerly of Norris Cut, 94° (E. ¼ S.), 1⅝ miles, to Florida Reefs North End Whistling Buoy, W (HS); thence 178° (S. ¼ E.), 8 miles, to Biscayne Bay Sea Bell Buoy, 1; thence 182° (S. ⅛ W.), 2⅜ miles, to Fowey Rocks Lighthouse; thence 188° (S. ⅝ W.), 6¾ miles, to Triumph Reef Beacon, O; thence 193° (S. by W.), 4½ miles, to Ajax Reef Beacon, M; thence 194° (S. by W. ⅛ W.), 2 miles, to Pacific Reef Beacon, L; thence 196½° (S. by W. ⅜ W.), 5 miles, to Turtle Harbor Sea Buoy, 2; thence 210° (SSW. ½ W.), 4⅞ miles, to Carysfort Reef Lighthouse; thence 209½° (SSW. ½ W.), 5¾ miles, to Elbow Reef Beacon, J; thence 217½° (SW. ¾ S.), 9¾ miles, to

Molasses Reef Gas Buoy, 2 M; thence 235½° (SW. ¾ W.), 6 miles, to Conch Reef Beacon, E; thence 234½° (SW. ¾ W.), through Crocker Reef Beacon, D, 10⅜ miles, to Alligator Reef Lighthouse; thence 234° (SW. ⅝ W.), 10⅞ miles, to Tennessee Reef Buoy, 4; thence 251° (WSW. ⅛ W.), 10½ miles, to Coffins Patches Beacon, C; thence 247° (SW. by W. ¾ W.), 8¾ miles, to Sombrero Key Lighthouse; thence 253½° (WSW. ⅜ W.), 16¾ miles, to Looe Key Beacon, 6; thence 257½° (WSW. ¾ W.), 6⅜ miles, to American Shoal Lighthouse; thence 253½° (WSW. ⅜ W.), 2⅞ miles, to Maryland Shoal Beacon, S; thence 259° (WSW. ⅞ W.), 5¼ miles, to Eastern Sambo Beacon, A; thence 253° (WSW. ¼ W.), 2¼ miles, to Western Sambo Beacon, R; thence 257° (WSW. ⅝ W.), through Western Sambo Buoy, 2, 5½ miles, to Key West Entrance Gas Buoy (PS); thence 262° (W. ⅞ S.), 4¼ miles, to Sand Key Lighthouse; thence 261° (W. by S.), 2¾ miles, to Western Dry Rocks Beacon, 2; thence 268° (W. ⅜ S.), 3½ miles, through Satan Shoal Buoy (HS) to Vestal Shoal Buoy, 1; thence 274½° (W. ⅛ N.), 5¼ miles, to Coal Bin Rock Buoy, CB (HS); thence 324½° (NW. ⅝ N.), 7¼ miles, to Marquesas Keys left tangent; from northwesterly point Marquesas Keys 59° (NE. by E.), 4⅜ miles, to Bar Buoy, 1, Boca Grande Channel; thence 83° (E. ⅞ N.), 9¾ miles, to Northwest Channel Entrance Bell Buoy, 1, Northwest Channel into Key West; thence 68° (NE. by E. ⅞ E.), 23½ miles, to northerly side of Content Keys; thence 49° (NE. ¼ E.), 29 miles, to East Cape, Cape Sable.

**Charlotte Harbor and Punta Gorda, Fla.**—Eastward of Charlotte Harbor Entrance Gas and Bell Buoy (PS), off Boca Grande, and in Charlotte Harbor, in Pine Island Sound and Matlacha Pass. Pilot Rules for Western Rivers apply in Peace and Miakka Rivers north of a 250° and 70° (WSW. and ENE.) line through Mangrove Point Light; and in Caloosahatchee River northward of the steamboat wharf at Punta Rasa.

**Tampa Bay and Tributaries, Fla.**—From the southerly end of Long Key 245° (SW. by W. ⅝ W.) 9 miles, to Tampa Bay Gas and Whistling Buoy (PS); thence 129° (SE. ¾ E.) 6½ miles, to Bar Bell Buoy (PS), at the entrance to Southwest Channel; thence 103° (E. by S.), 2¾ miles, to the house on the north end of Anna Maria Key. Pilot Rules for Western Rivers apply in Manatee River inside Manatee River Entrance Buoy, 2; in Hillsboro Bay and River inside Hillsboro Bay Light, 2.

**St. George Sound, Apalachicola Bay, Carrabelle and Apalachicola Rivers, and St. Vincent Sound, Fla.**—North of a line from Lighthouse Point 246° (SW. by W. ⅝ W.), 13¼ miles, to southeasterly side of Dog Island; to northward of East Pass Bell Buoy, 1, at the entrance to East Pass, and inside West Pass Bell Buoy (PS) at the seaward entrance to West Pass. Pilot Rules for Western Rivers apply in Carrabelle River inside the entrance to the dredged channel; in Apalachicola River northward of Apalachicola Dredged Channel Entrance Buoy, 2.

**Pensacola Harbor.**—From Caucus Cut Entrance Gas and Whistling Buoy, 1A, 3° (N. ⅛ W.), tangent to easterly side of Fort Pickens, to the shore of Santa Rosa Island, and from the buoy northward in the buoyed channel through Caucus Shoal.

**Mobile Harbor and Bay.**—From Mobile Entrance Gas and Whistling Buoy (PS) 40° (NE. ⅞ N.) to shore of Mobile Point, and from the buoy 320° (NW.) to the shore of Dauphin Island. Pilot Rules for Western Rivers apply in Mobile River above Choctaw Point.

**Sounds, Lakes, and Harbors on the Coasts of Alabama, Mississippi, and Louisiana, Between Mobile Bay Entrance and the Delta of the Mississippi River.**—From Sand Island Lighthouse 259° (WSW. ⅝ W.), 43½ miles to Chandeleur Lighthouse; westward of Chandeleur and Errol Islands, and west of a line drawn from the southwesterly point of Errol Island 182° (S. ¼ E.), 23 miles, to Pass à Loutre Lighthouse. Pilot Rules for Western Rivers apply in Pascagoula River, and in the dredged cut at the entrance to the river, above Pascagoula River Entrance Light, A, marking the entrance to the dredged cut.

**New Orleans Harbor and the Delta of the Mississippi River.**—Inshore of a line drawn from the outermost mud lump showing above low water at the entrance to Pass à Loutre to a similar lump off the entrance to Northeast Pass; thence to a similar lump off the entrance to Southeast Pass; thence to the outermost aid to navigation off the entrance to South Pass; thence to the outermost aid to navigation off the entrance to Southwest Pass; thence northerly, about 19½ miles, to the westerly point of the entrance to Bay Jaque.

**Sabine Pass, Tex.**—Pilot Rules for Western Rivers apply to Sabine Pass northward of Sabine Pass Gas and Whistling Buoy (PS), and in Sabine Lake and its tributaries. Outside of this buoy the International Rules apply.

**Galveston Harbor.**—A line drawn from Galveston North Jetty Light 129° (SE. by E. ¼ E.), 2 miles, to Galveston Bar Gas and Whistling Buoy (PS); thence 276° (W. ⅛ S.), 2¼ miles, to Galveston (S.) Jetty Lighthouse.

**Brazos River, Tex.**—Pilot Rules for Western Rivers apply in the entrance and river inside of Brazos River Entrance Gas and Whistling Buoy (PS). International Rules apply outside the buoy.

**San Diego Harbor.**—A line drawn from southerly tower of Coronado Hotel 208° (S. by W.), 5 miles, to Outside Bar Whistling Buoy, SD (PS); thence 345° (NNW. ¾ W.), 3⅝ miles, to Point Loma Lighthouse.

**San Francisco Harbor.**—A line drawn through Mile Rocks Lighthouse 326° (NW. ⅝ W.) to Bonita Point Lighthouse.

**Columbia River Entrance.**—A line drawn from knuckle of Columbia River south jetty 351° (NNW. ⅞ W.) to Cape Disappointment Lighthouse.

**Juan de Fuca Strait, Washington and Puget Sounds.**—A line drawn from New Dungeness Lighthouse 13½° (N. by W.), 10⅜ miles, to Hein Bank Gas and Bell Buoy (HS); thence 337½° (NW. ¼ W.), 10¾ miles, to Lime Kiln Light, on west side of San Juan Island; from Bellevue Point, San Juan Island, 336½° (NW. ¼ W.) to Kellett Bluff, Henry Island; thence 347° (NW. ⅝ N.) to Turn Point Light; thence 71½° (NE. ⅛ E.), 8¼ miles, to westerly point of Skipjack Island; thence 38½° (N. by E. ¼ E.), 4⅜ miles, to Patos Islands Light; thence 338° (NW. ⅛ W.), 12 miles, to Point Roberts Light.

**General Rule.**—At all buoyed entrances from seaward to bays, sounds, rivers, or other estuaries for which specific lines have not been described, Inland Rules shall apply inshore of a line approximately parallel with the general trend of the shore, drawn through the outermost buoy or other aid to navigation of any system of aids.

# GENERAL INDEX

**Adherence to Collision Rules.** See *Collision Rules.*

**Aground, Vessels.**

    Lights:

        A vessel aground in or near a fairway to carry the regulation anchor lights and the two additional red lights for a vessel "not under command," 31

    Sight signals to be exhibited in daytime, 31

    Fog, etc.:

        To sound the fog-signal of a vessel at anchor, 73

    Should take such additional precautions to apprise approaching vessel of her position as may be required by the situation, 73

**Alarm Signal.** See *Sound Signals.*

**Anchor, A Vessel at.**

    May use a flare-up to call attention to her presence (see Art. XII), 48

    When being towed up to her anchor is at anchor, 53

**Anchorage.**

    A vessel leaving her anchorage or mooring must maintain a proper lookout so stationed that the approach of other vessels may be seen, 223

    Local rules forbidding anchorage in certain zones must be observed, 226

    Local rules providing certain districts or zones where anchoring is permitted must be observed, 226

    Anchoring in navigable channels in such manner as to obstruct the passage of other vessels or craft is forbidden, 226

    Decisions of the courts as to what constitutes obstructing the channel, 226–9

    Vessels anchoring in foggy weather should so far as possible avoid anchoring in the channel or in the usual track of other vessels, 228

    Anchoring on the range between two lightships is not good seamanship, 228

    Good seamanship requires extraordinary precautions adequate to the position in which the vessel may be at anchor, 230

    A safe berth is necessary in anchoring and ample room must be given to other vessels at anchor—close calculations must be avoided, 230

**Anchoring.** See *Speed in Fog.*

**Anchor Lights.** See *Lights.*

**"And then navigate with caution until all danger of collision is over."** See *Speed in Fog.*

**Application of Rules.** See *Collision Rules, The.*

**Burdened Vessel**—continued.

caused by an improper act (change of course or speed) by the holding-on vessel, 144

The Courts hold a steamer to a rigid observance of the rule to keep out of the way of a sailing vessel and require the avoidance of even the risk of collision, 147

**Change of Course in Fog.** See *Speed in Fog.*

**Close-hauled.** See *Sailing Vessel.*

**Close Shaving.** See *Burdened Vessel.*

Close shaving must be avoided, 7

**Collisions.**

Collisions usually caused by misunderstandings or want of understanding between vessels as to the intended movements of the other, 1

**Collision Rules, The.**

Historical development, 1

Are necessary to secure uniformity in navigation and avoid confusion, 1

Object is to promote the safety of lives and property on the high seas and inland waters, 2

Apply at the moment the vessels approach each other so as to involve risk of collision, 108

A timely observance of the rules necessary, 7

Close shaving must be avoided, 7

**Binding Force of the Rules, 3**

Are laws binding upon those in charge of the navigation of vessels, 2–3

Are so definite and complete that very little is left to the judgment or discretion of the navigator, 2

Are in no sense optional but are mandatory laws to be strictly observed, 3

Deviation from the rules not permitted except in emergency where adherence to a rule will surely result in collision or disaster, 6

A correct understanding and implicit obedience to the rules is exacted, 3

Lack of knowledge or failure to obey the rules by those in charge of the navigation of vessels little short of criminal, 3

Penalty for loss of life caused by negligence, misconduct, etc., by those in charge of the navigation of vessels, 3

Deviation from the rules to help out or as a matter of courtesy not permitted, 6

Breach of the rules constitutes such a fault as to throw upon the offending vessel the burden of proving not merely that the

**Encumbered Vessels.**

The duty of unencumbered vessels in respect to encumbered vessels, 233

**End on or Nearly end on.**

Rule is applicable only to steamers in sight of one another, 110

Manner of passing is mandatory, 111

The position of the steamers in relation to each other is the determining factor as to how they shall pass, 111

Both vessels must act seasonably, 112

Neither vessel is justified in relying upon the other to do all that is necessary to be done, 112

Failure of one to act will not excuse the other, 112

Sound signals indicating manner of passing must be given promptly, 113

Danger at night—steamers approaching on a fine angle—difficulty in distinguishing passing and crossing vessels. Situation fraught with danger. Extraordinary care should be exercised, 113

Steamer having the other on her own starboard bow, if nearly end on should be the first to act and should port promptly and signal that she is doing so, 115

**Engines, Reversing of, May be Necessary.** See *Speed in Fog.*

**Equality of Vessels.**

All vessels equal under the rules. Passenger or mail steamers have no special rights over smaller vessels, 8

**Equipment.**

Steam vessel must be equipped with an efficient steam whistle or siren, 65

Absence of any minimum fixed standard of the sound-carrying capacity for steam whistles, sirens and fog horns, 65

Why no definite standard fixed, 66

Inefficient and improper whistles and fog-horns the cause of collisions, 66

Steam whistle and fog-horn—whistle or siren must be located so that sound will not be obstructed, 67

Steam vessels must carry efficient fog-horn sounded by mechanical means, 67

Steam vessels must carry an efficient bell, 67

Sailing vessels must carry an efficient fog-horn sounded by mechanical means, 67

Sailing vessels must carry an efficient bell, 67

Failure to carry a "fog-horn" of the character prescribed constitutes a fault under these rules, 67

Duty of U. S. inspectors to inspect the whistles and fog-horns on vessels and rigidly enforce the requirements as to efficient instruments, 67

## Good Seamanship, The Rule of—continued.

Emphasizes the requirement of the rules in respect to carrying proper lights and signals as prescribed by the Articles, 219

### Lookout:

Requirement to keep a proper lookout, 219

Officer of deck or helmsman as a lookout does not meet the requirement of good seamanship, 222

That the vessel is a privileged vessel does not excuse a failure to maintain a proper and efficient lookout, 222

Lookouts must be stationed forward in the "eyes" of the ship, 220

Extra precautions required in the matter of lookouts on dark nights or in fog or thick weather, 221

Low-hanging fogs calling for a lookout on the bridge or in the crow's nest also require a lookout on the forecastle head, 222

Vessels in tow must also maintain a lookout when the situation is such as to require it, 223

A lookout astern is necessary where any change of course is made which may affect other vessels approaching from astern, 223

A vessel leaving her anchorage or mooring must maintain a proper lookout so stationed that the approach of other vessels may be seen, 223

The duty to keep a proper lookout is not an obligation created by the rules but is a precaution required by the practice of good seamanship, 224

### Anchoring:

Anchorage locations must be in districts or zones where anchoring is permitted, 226

Local rules regarding anchorage locations must be observed, 226

Anchoring in navigable channels in such manner as to obstruct the passage of other vessels or craft is forbidden, 226

Decisions of the courts as to what constitutes obstructing the channel, 226–9

A vessel coming to anchorage in foggy weather should, so far as possible, avoid anchoring in the channel or in the usual track of vessels, 228

Fault to anchor on the range between two lightships, 228

To leave a dock in a heavy fog where the conditions are such that anchoring in the channel is unavoidable is a fault, 229

Requires the taking of extraordinary precautions adequate to the position in which a vessel may be placed, 230

A safe berth is necessary in anchoring and ample room must

**Good Seamanship, The Rule of**—continued.
    be given to other vessels anchored and close calculations
    avoided, 230
    Special precautions are required by special circumstances, 231
    A vessel backing across a channel in the way of other vessels
    is required to exercise extreme care to notify other vessels of
    her maneuver, 231
    The sound of a fog-horn nearly ahead requires a steamer to at
    once reverse and go full speed astern, 232
    The fog-signal of another vessel found to be narrowing on the
    bow requires the engines to be reversed full speed astern, 232
    It is not good seamanship for a vessel to be deliberately placed
    in a position where she is not free to maneuver, 232
    It is not good seamanship to tow a vessel in a river where there
    are only six inches of water between the keel and the bottom
    of the river, 232

**Harbor.**  See *Narrow Channel.*

**"Having careful regard for existing circumstances and
conditions,"** 85.  See *Speed in Fog.*

**Helm Signals.**  See *Sound Signals.*

**"Holding-on" Vessel.**  See *Privileged Vessel.*

**Homicidal Negligence.**
    Penalty for breach of Statutory Rules, 3

**"Hove to."**  See *Fog-signals.*
    Lights provided in Art. IV for disabled vessel, does not apply
    to a sailing vessel in irons or becalmed or hove to and unable
    to maneuver, 31
    Vessels hove to or lying to must show a stern light (either a
    fixed white light or flare-up) to vessels approaching from
    astern, 49

**Inconvenience.**
    No excuse for failure to observe the rules, 142

**Inefficient or Improper Lights.**  See *Lights.*

**Inland Rules.**
    Apply to all vessels when on the inland coast waters of the
    U.S., 2

**Inspectors' Rules.**  See *Pilot Rules.*

**International Conference.**  Excerpts from Protocol of Proceedings.
    Mandatory character of rules, 3
    Timely compliance with rules required.  Close shaving not per-
    mitted, 7
    Side Lights: Range of visibility, 12

**Lights**—continued.

Location: Must be placed in their proper position, 13

Must not be obscured by deck houses, deck cargo, sails, or other cause, 13

Hull includes the forecastle deck, 54

Range of visibility—the minimum prescribed by the rules must be maintained at all times, 11

Importance attached by the rules to a strict observance of the requirements in respect to lights, 15

**Colored running lights:**

International Conference considered increase in range of visibility of side lights desirable but impracticable at time rules were adopted, 12

Background must be kept darkened to make them stand out clearly, 13

Screening: Rays of colored side lights must cross at the proper distance ahead of the ship, 14

Special precautions necessary in screening and watching running lights when they are placed in the rigging, 14

Side lights placed in rigging: Change in sail pressure apt to cause trouble with lights so located, 14

**Steamers:**

"White lights" (masthead lights), 17

Range of visibility required, 10–17

Colored (running side lights), 17

Range of visibility required, 10–18

Range lights: their greater efficiency over the colored side-lights makes their use desirable, 19–20

Permissive for ocean-going steamers, 18–20

Mandatory under Inland Rules for steamers (other than ferry-boats and sea-going steamers), 20

**Towing lights:**

For steam vessels when towing, 21

Location of towing lights, 22

Must be of character and carried in the position prescribed by the rule, 23

Responsibility as between towing vessel and vessel being towed for the carrying of proper lights and otherwise, 24

**Special lights:**

For a vessel which from any accident "is not under command," 29

For a vessel employed in laying or picking up a telegraph cable, 29

The lights provided in Art. IV are not to be used except by a vessel which from an accident is no longer under control, 31

Lights—continued.

The lights provided in Art. IV are not to be used by a sailing vessel because of being becalmed, in irons, or hove to and unable to maneuver, 31

The lights provided in Art. IV are not to be used by a steamer deliberately kept in an unmanageable condition, 31

Location of the lights required by Art. IV, 30

The colored side-lights must also be carried when the vessels are making way through the water (subdiv. c), 30

A vessel aground in or near a fairway required to carry anchor light or lights and the two additional red lights prescribed by Art. IV (subdiv. a), 37, 57

For sailing vessels, 34

For vessels in tow, 34

Difference in text of International Rules and Inland Rules in respect to lights for vessels in tow, 34

Lights for small vessels, 36

Lights for small steam and sail vessels and open boats, 36

Lights for pilot vessels, 38

Lights, etc., of fishing vessels, Art. IX, 40

Overtaken vessel: a vessel being overtaken required to show from her stern a white light or a flare-up light, 47

Inland Rules accept the after range light (required under Inland Rules to be carried by all steam vessels (except ferry-boats and sea-going vessels) ) as a compliance, 47

Character of light (whether a fixed white light or a flare-up light) optional, 48

Fixed white light is the safer light to use, 48

Flare-up light if used must be efficient, 49

Use of flare-up throws upon vessel using it the burden of exhibiting the light at the proper time and as often as may be necessary to afford warning to the overtaking vessel so long as she continues to approach, 48–50

A lookout astern is necessary when a flare-up light is used, 49

Stern light (either fixed white light or flare-up light) must be shown by a vessel hove to, or lying to, to a vessel approaching from astern, 49

Anchor Lights:

Must be placed where not obscured in any direction by the masts, spars, sails or rigging, 53

Must be set at sunset and kept burning brightly until sunrise, 54

Character and condition of lights required, 54

Sails and all gear must be so stowed as not to obstruct the anchor lights, 53

**Lookouts**—continued.

A lookout astern is necessary where any change of course is made which may affect other vessels approaching from astern, 223

A lookout astern is necessary when an overtaken vessel depends upon a flare-up as a stern light instead of a fixed white light, 49

Vessels in tow must also maintain a lookout when the situation is such as to require it, 223

The duty to keep a proper lookout is not an obligation created by the rules but is a precaution required by the practice of good seamanship, 224

**Mail Steamers.**  See *Equality of Vessels.*  See *Speed in Fog.*

**Mandatory Character of Rules.**  See *Collision Rules, The.*

**Maneuvers.**

Must be made seasonably, 112, 146

**Master and Officers.**

Negligence, misconduct or inattention to duty causing death a crime punishable by imprisonment, 3

**Master.**

Responsible to see that proper lights correctly located are carried, 15

The master remains in full charge of the vessel when pilot on bridge, 240

Master may displace pilot if the latter is careless, incompetent or foolhardy, 240

Duty of master in respect to lookouts, lights, and the decision as to proceeding under existing weather conditions, etc., 240

**Master, Discretion or Judgment of.**

The rules are laws binding upon those in charge of the navigation of vessels, 2, 3

The rules are so definite and complete that very little is left to the judgment or discretion of the navigator, 2

No latitude of judgment or discretion is allowed as to necessity of stopping the engines upon first hearing a fog-signal apparently forward of the beam, 88

**Masthead Light.**  See *Lights.*

**Meeting Steamers** (Head and head).  See *End on or Nearly end on.*

**Moderate Speed in Fog.**  See *Speed in Fog.*

**Narrow Channels.**  See *Overtaking Vessel.*

Definition of a narrow channel, 161

Steamer must keep to that side of the channel which lies on her starboard side, 161

**Narrow Channels**—continued.

Crossing Rule at times operative in narrow channels, 117

Definition of "when it is safe and practical," 162

Allowance made for the reasonable necessities of navigation, 162

Deviation permitted to avoid danger but subject to the requirement that the vessel return as soon as possible to her right side, 163

Deviation will not be excused unless immediate and actual danger exists which cannot be avoided by an otherwise permitted maneuver, 163

When a deviation is necessary it must not be more than required for the purpose and vessel must return to her right side of the channel as soon as possible, 164

Custom or practice to use the wrong side of channel under certain tidal conditions because it is easier to navigate will not excuse a vessel for violation of the rule, 165

Vessel in her right water should assume that vessel approaching on the wrong side of channel will cross over to her proper side, but if such vessel continues to approach on the wrong side the safer maneuver is to stop and reverse, 165

Starboarding in a narrow channel to a meeting steamer approaching in the wrong water is not a correct maneuver, 165

As between steamers approaching and meeting at a sharp bend, the vessel having the tide against her should wait until the other has passed clear, 165

The narrow channel rule has no application to sailing vessels and steamers must keep clear, 166

Steamers entering or leaving a narrow channel should if practical do so from their proper side of such channel, 166

**"Not Under Command."**  See *Lights*.   See *Fog-signals*.

When a vessel is "not under command," 32

Duty of a vessel "not under command," 33

**Obedience to the Rules.**  See *Collision Rules, The*.

**Obedience to the Rules Required.**   See *Breach of the Rules*. See *Penalty for Breach of the Rules*.  See *Deviation from the Rules*.

**Obscuration of Lights.**  See *Lights*.

**Overtaken Vessel.**  See *Lights*.   See *Hove to*.

Failure of an overtaken vessel to sound immediately a dissent (if it considers a passing at the time and place unsafe) is a fault (under the Inland Rules), 153

## Privileged Vessel—continued.

Privileged vessel is entitled to presume the burdened vessel will conform to the rules, if the latter's request for right of way is denied, 133

Only a clear indication that burdened vessel is failing in duty will justify the preferred vessel in changing course and speed, 133

Duty of holding course and speed does not relieve privileged vessel from the obligation of good seamanship and the exercise of ordinary precautions, 125

That a vessel is a privileged vessel does not excuse a failure to maintain a proper and efficient lookout, 222

As between sailing vessels, the relation of burdened vessel and privileged vessel applies when meeting end on or nearly so, 108

As between sailing vessels, the relation of burdened vessel and privileged vessel determined by courses of vessels in respect to the prevailing wind, 108

## Prudential Rule, The General.

Is operative only in exceptional cases, 170

Does not, except in those emergency cases where a departure from the rule is *necessary* in order to avoid immediate danger, modify or lessen the obligation to a strict compliance with the other articles, 172

An actual and immediate danger of navigation or collision must exist to justify a departure from the definite rules, 173

Does not excuse or permit a departure from the definite rules unless or until such departure is imperative if imminent danger is to be avoided, 170

Application of the rule illustrated, 170

The burden of bringing a departure from the rules within the protection of this article is upon the vessel which has made it, 172

An emergency produced by improper navigation of another vessel will not excuse a failure to exercise prudence and common sense to avoid collision, 171

There is no right of way on which a vessel is entitled to insist when it is obvious it will result in collision, 172

## Range Lights. See *Lights*.

## Range of Visibility. See *Lights*.

## Responsibility of Master to Carry Proper Lights. See *Lights*.

## Reversing Engines.

Good seamanship requires that the engines be at once reversed at full speed astern if a fog-horn is heard nearly ahead, 232